The Shadow and the Act

The Shadow and the Act

Black Intellectual Practice,
Jazz Improvisation,
and Philosophical Pragmatism

Walton M. Muyumba

THE UNIVERSITY OF CHICAGO PRESS
Chicago & London

WALTON M. MUYUMBA is associate professor of English at
the University of North Texas.

The University of Chicago Press, Chicago 60637
The University of Chicago Press, Ltd., London
© 2009 by The University of Chicago
All rights reserved. Published 2009
Printed in the United States of America

16 15 14 13 12 11 10 09   1 2 3 4 5

ISBN-13: 978-0-226-55423-5 (cloth)
ISBN-13: 978-0-226-55424-2 (paper)
ISBN-10: 0-226-55423-6 (cloth)
ISBN-10: 0-226-55424-4 (paper)

Library of Congress Cataloging-in-Publication Data

Muyumba, Walton M.
    The shadow and the act : black intellectual practice, jazz
improvisation, and philosophical pragmatism / Walton M.
Muyumba.
        p.   cm.
Includes bibliographical references and index.
ISBN-13: 978-0-226-55423-5 (cloth : alk. paper)
ISBN-13: 978-0-226-55424-2 (pbk. : alk. paper)
ISBN-10: 0-226-55423-6 (cloth : alk. paper)
ISBN-10: 0-226-55424-4 (pbk. : alk. paper)
    1. American literature—African American authors—
History and criticism.   2. Ellison, Ralph—Criticism and
interpretation.   3. Baldwin, James, 1924–1987—Criticism
and interpretation.   4. Baraka, Imamu Amiri, 1934—
Criticism and interpretation.   5. Jazz in literature.
6. Jazz—History and criticism.   7. Improvisation (Music)
I. Title.
PS153.N5M89 2009
810.9'3578—dc22

2008048657

For Francois Muyumba — my father and my first professor
(December 29, 1939 – February 10, 2006)

Contents

Preface

In *The Shadow and the Act* I examine the relationship between jazz and pragmatism. Specifically, I am interested in critiquing the ways that African American artist/intellectuals like Ralph Ellison, James Baldwin, and LeRoi Jones/Amiri Baraka used their writing about jazz to communicate pragmatist analyses of American culture and for explaining the political and social benefits of integrating African American cultural practices into the mainstream of American life.

While African American intellectual histories typically include my three subjects, their differences are often read as a source for posing the writers in opposition rather than linking them together intellectually. In contrast to this tendency, *The Shadow and the Act* argues that Ellison, Baldwin, and Jones/Baraka represent a literary intellectual trio aligned in their explorations of the contingencies of race, masculinity, and "Americanness" in mid-twentieth-century America and in their uses of jazz as the prime metaphor in creative efforts and philosophical theorizations.

The title of this work purposefully invokes the title of Ellison's famous essay collection *Shadow and Act* (1964). My titular improvisation signifies the pastiche quality of this study and it evokes the literary intellectual's movement between the social observation and cultural chronicling done in the shadows and his action or performance done in the harsh light of the public to manifest political or moral changes in American life. In their works Ellison, Jones/Baraka, and Baldwin describe jazz improvisation as an American aesthetic honed on the whetstone of African American experiences and ingenuity. In their cultural criticism they present improvisation as a pragmatic metaphor for creating more discourse about individual identities and freedoms and for shifting the American social mainstream toward a more inclusive form of democracy.

The Shadow and the Act situates jazz improvisation within African American intellectual practice, among the theories of creative writing in postwar America, and within postmodern and poststructural philosophical thought. More specifically, I address the ways that African American intellectuals like Ellison, Baldwin, and Jones/Baraka interlaced their private philosophical changes and their publicly stated political desires during the civil rights movement. One argument for this grouping is that it helps explain why African American intellectual work sits at the center of American culture. The way these three writers envision American society and American democracy actually forces us to reimagine traditional narratives of African American intellectual history and American literary history because they display various ways of addressing race, history, identity, and political, material realities without positing essentialisms about blackness or American identity.

This study is an improvised composition that rises out of extended riffs on jazz studies, literary criticism, African American cultural theories, and American pragmatism. I have organized the rest of the book as a jazz suite with each chapter acting as a movement of the whole work. I want the shape to emphasize the contrapuntal play of the creative and critical works under consideration here. As well, this formal arrangement encourages discourse about jazz and pragmatism. The study situates Ellison, Baldwin, and Jones/Baraka as a jazz trio so as to reveal how individual works in their oeuvres might be read as a series of calls and responses to each other. Writing in the midst of the civil rights movement, the writers turned to jazz and jazz improvisation to generate substantive critical concepts for American democracy, African American identity, and black masculinity.

As I describe in "Vamping 'til Ready: An Introduction," I have also chosen to concentrate on Ellison, Baldwin, and Jones/Baraka in order to participate in the ongoing discourse that positions black writers within the lineage of American pragmatism. The first half of the vamp is devoted to providing a useful conceptualization of pragmatist philosophy. Then I connect that definition with the work that critics such as Ross Posnock, Michael Magee, Nancy Fraser, and Eddie Glaude, Jr., have done to position writers and philosophers such as W. E. B. Du Bois, Alain Locke, and Zora Neale Hurston as significant participants in the history of pragmatism. I want, however, to intrude on this conversation to correct, for example, Posnock's notion that writers like Baldwin, Jones/Baraka, and Ellison are pragmatists because they eschew race and racialist thinking.

I argue that Ellison, Baldwin, and Jones/Baraka practice pragmatism with a *difference,* using "secondary" racial consciousnesses and "thin" notions of racial identity along with their assertions of race-free identification. Baldwin, Jones/Baraka, and Ellison use jazz improvisation to communicate the unique powers of African American cultural experience and to examine ways of producing an American society and American identities that exemplify the nation's democratic ideals. This idea, which all three writers consider independently, suggests that African American aesthetics are built around a crucial political vision. Modeling their critical attitudes after jazz stylists and innovators, Ellison, Jones/Baraka, and Baldwin practice versions of pragmatist interrogation that draw attention to African American history and the material realities of being racialized in the American context. In other words, they work out a revised and improvised pragmatist tradition that postpones definitions of the tradition that ignore African Americans and their experiences. The second part of the vamp is devoted to illustrating the relationship between enthomusicological definitions of improvisation and improvisation as cultural and philosophical theory. Ellison, Baldwin, and Jones/Baraka use jazz to enlarge our understanding of how African American identities are developed, how concepts of truth about American life and black experiences are transmitted, and how new claims of American citizenship were framed in the civil rights era.

Vamping 'til Ready

Pragmatism and Jazz Improvisation

The life of man is a self-evolving circle, which, from a ring impercep-
tibly small, rushes on all sides outwards to new and larger circles,
and that without end. The extent to which this generation of circles,
wheel without wheel, will go, depends on the force or truth of the
individual soul. **Ralph Waldo Emerson, "Circles"**

[T]he fully orchestrated blues statement . . . [is] a highly pragmatic
and indeed a fundamental device for confrontation, improvisation,
and existential affirmation: a strategy for acknowledging the fact that
life is a lowdown dirty shame and for improvising or riffing on the exi-
gencies of the predicament. **Albert Murray, *The Blue Devils of Nada***

I

In Cornel West's analysis of pragmatism's genealogy, *The
American Evasion of Philosophy* (1989), he contends that Ralph
Waldo Emerson's evasion of European metaphysics offers an intellectual alternative to, rather than a denial of or replacement
of, modern philosophy. Emerson's refusal to engage philosophy's
"quest for certainty and its hope for professional, i.e., scientific,
respectability" or "its search for foundations" marks the elemental
genesis of American pragmatism.[1] When Emerson explains in his
essay "Circles" that the onus of an individual's existential growth
lies with the "force or truth of the individual soul" he is also naming the initiation of a philosophical attitude that understands truth

1

and morality as the products of concentric circles of historical realities, social practices, and experientially tested beliefs. Tracing this attitude from its Emersonian prehistory we find William James polishing pragmatism into its modernist refinement, explaining that truth happens to an idea, that truth, shaped by our experiences and interactions with the social sphere, is willed into belief.

James' pragmatism is a methodology, a way of tracking the practical consequences of our beliefs. Inspired by British empiricists like John Locke and David Hume, James argues that pragmatism turns away from foundational principles of metaphysics toward action and toward power. The pragmatist, in rejecting any claims of certainty, examines language, studying the practical worth of individual words and ideas as a way of investigating how realities might be changed. James believes that we should eschew the notion that beliefs are true or right only if they mirror "reality." Foregoing correspondence with reality, we can get to work, using our thoughts and theories as tools for improving our circumstances rather than using them to answer philosophical enigmas. In this turn away from classical philosophical problems like the search for truth, we will realize that what is true is "whatever proves itself to be good in the way of belief, and good, too, for definite, assignable reasons."[2]

James's concern for the utility of philosophy and his definitions of pragmatist process were influenced in part by the early work of John Dewey. But the professional regard was mutually beneficial: pragmatism came of age through Dewey's revision of Jamesian insight. Dewey believed that professional philosophers were misdirected in their close analyses of the relationship between the mind and the world. But Dewey came to pragmatism by way of Hegel and Darwin—joining historicist and scientific inclinations in order to develop a notion of philosophical "instrumentalism": that ideas and beliefs are tools for coping with social realities. Dewey's pragmatism is built from the hypothesis that "thinking" and "acting" are separate names for the same process: navigating lived experience while acknowledging the contingency of all things.

Taking up Deweyan pragmatism means surely accepting tenets such as antifoundational philosophizing and contextual analysis. But Dewey's approach also includes conceptions of experimentalism in problem solving and constructing solidarity for political achievement. The good pragmatist "turns away" from the abstractions of the philosophical tradition toward concrete social difficulties, toward an "understanding of beliefs, choices and actions as historically conditioned," producing problem-solving social and cultural analysis from an awareness that "all facts are fallible and, as such occasionally afford us the opportunity for revision." The good pragmatist experiments intellectually, using her training and work "to offer some insight into specific conditions of value and into specific consequences of ideas."[3] This attitude is useful for thinking through social and political difficulties while also providing personal psychological therapy and social hope for improving the American democratic experiment.

Richard Rorty presents pragmatism as philosophical therapy because he believes that it helps us massage out of Western democratic, bourgeois life our social hopes for greater human freedom. Rorty finds the Deweyan outlook tailored especially for political liberalism. In the liberal democratic context, Rorty argues, Dewey's experimentalism provides "rationale for nonideological, compromising, reformist muddling-through." Dewey's philosophy urges us to create discourse and consensus about "what we should do next" to make the society better.[4] Rorty frames these claims by discussing the priority of democracy to philosophy. That is, the pragmatist philosopher of liberal democracy develops theories of the human self that comport with the "institutions he or she admires" (Rorty 178).

Ultimately, Rorty argues, Deweyan pragmatists

> urge us to think of ourselves as part of a pageant of historical progress which will gradually encompass all of the human race, and are willing to argue that the vocabulary which twentieth-century Western social democrats use is the best vocabulary the race has come up with so far. . . . But pragmatists are quite sure that their vocabulary will be superseded—and, from their point of view, the sooner the better. (Rorty 219)

Frankly, this is a powerful idea: postmodern bourgeois liberals cloaked as pragmatists have created an ethnocentric vocabulary for building conversations about democracy, for creating more human freedom and equality. Because pragmatists reject epistemological certainties, they are often inclined to also reject racism, racial thinking, ethnocentrism, and colonialism. Pragmatism also seems to encourage relationships between political change or reconstruction and artistic innovation, especially in terms of creating more freedom and better democratic states.[5]

I've built this brief introduction to pragmatism in order to situate my discussion of African American intellectuals practicing in the pragmatist tradition. It is well documented that the key pragmatist thinkers turned away from addressing American racial conundrums directly in their philosophical works. While James and Dewey present pragmatism as a method inclined toward consequences, human affairs, morals, antiessentialism, and anti-imperialism, neither established a practice of questioning power relations, American political culture, or identity in terms of the political imbalances born from racial segregation or the abuse of Negro human rights.

In his study *Color and Culture: Black Writers and the Making of the Modern Intellectual* Ross Posnock brilliantly reimagines the pragmatist tradition by placing African American writing at its center. Posnock argues that *black intellectual* is a useful term for naming the internal conflicts and ambivalences that African American writers combat in their efforts to create art, determine their personal identities, and forward the political hopes of the mass of black Americans. Describing this complex agon is central to Posnock's placement of major twentieth-century African American writers from W. E. B. Du Bois to Adrienne Kennedy in the cosmopolitan, pragmatist tradition.

The complexity of black intellectual work, Posnock argues, stems from the writer's simultaneous attempt to describe the churnings of African American life while trying to jettison racial identity because it occludes universalist identities. This conflict between the artist's desire to champion the race and the intellectual's skepticism of identity logic animates Posnock's work. He claims, for instance, that students of Jamesian pragmatism like W. E. B. Du Bois and Alain Locke, holding Negro identity at bay, revised pragmatism in order to develop an anarchic cultural pluralism meant to anchor their activism on behalf of equality for African Americans.[6] In mid-twentieth-century African American intellectual practice this leads to James Baldwin, in the midst of the civil rights movement (CRM), offering pragmatist critiques of American culture driven by his desire to replace blackness with American cosmopolitan nationalism.[7]

While Posnock's narrative of African American pragmatists is extremely compelling, it rings false on several tolls:

1) As I argue throughout *The Shadow and the Act* writers like Baldwin, LeRoi Jones/Amiri Baraka, and Ralph Ellison were attempting to define African Americanness not escape it. In fact, as these writers disseminated various definitions of blackness, their stands against racial essentialism exposed the crippled condition of American identity when it was based on conceptions of whiteness and white superiority. In other words, their close readings of how blackness functioned provided them with the tools for creating identities.

2) Though influenced by James and Dewey, Jones/Baraka, Baldwin, and Ellison developed what we recognize as pragmatist attitudes from their close examinations of African American culture and experience. They argued that the very tools for escaping race were available in African American aesthetic experimentalism. That is, the very traits attributed to classical pragmatism—the rejection of foundationalism, the critique of belief and truth, and experimentalism—are always already at work in African American culture and aesthetic practices.

3) The best way to chart African American intellectuals' pragmatist inclinations (and it is surprising that Posnock does not) is to examine their use, theoretical and metaphorical, of blues idiom musical forms like jazz. Ellison, Baldwin, and Jones/Baraka each argued that achieving cosmopolitan nationalism would require knowledge of African American aesthetics, especially jazz improvisation.

One cannot think of pragmatism's concentration on language and narrative, Michael Magee argues, without considering the role that ethnic and racialized Americans have had in the formation of the American vernacular. In Ellison's radical interpretation of the founding documents of American democracy, he, like Ralph Emerson, reads both the Declaration of Independence and the Constitution as forms and texts that rhetorically imagined and created the sociopolitical arrangement from the cultural fabric. Ellison compared the arguments and hopes enumerated in the documents to the actual workings of the social context, continually "returning to the social text where symbolic systems involving race had obvious theoretical importance."[8]

This reading of Ellison underscores what several critics and philosophers argue about the relationship between African American intellectual practice and pragmatism: as a way of addressing the challenges and complexities of contemporary African American life, pragmatism offers a philosophical approach attuned to the tragic elements of the human experience, encourages action in problem solving, and is ultimately melioristic. In order to untangle this claim I'd like to return to the early decades of the twentieth century and review a few important analytical points that W. E. B. Du Bois and Alain Locke produced on race, Negro identity and culture, and American politics.[9]

It was the beginning of the twentieth century when Du Bois established his claim of Negro "double consciousness" and his dictum about "the color line." In Du Bois's reading of the separation between Negroes and white Americans he points to the inexorable relationship between the definitions of blackness and whiteness; the color line both produces and maintains a social order and political hierarchy based upon a concept of white superiority. Du Bois's assessment of the seemingly antithetical relationship of blackness and Americanness—double consciousness—is also an elaboration of the philosophical conflict between absolutism (racial fidelity) and radical empiricism (the evidence of individual experience), "two warring ideals in one dark body."[10] Pragmatism helps Du Bois pave a route away from this dilemma and conflict toward specific goals and concrete solutions.

In Du Bois's works we find a keen awareness of the tight-fisted trap that racialized identities work on black bodies. However, Du Bois's Jamesian turn away from "abstraction and insufficiency, from verbal solutions, from bad a priori reasons, from fixed principles, closed systems, and pretended absolutes and origins" was not a swift rejection of racial identity.[11] He understood that the philosophical and political conundrum of "blackness" was at the center of modern democratic politics and American modernism.

Engaging African Americans' specific sociopolitical hopes for first-class American citizenship, and thus acceptance as human beings, Du Bois understood that the problems of the color line and racial thinking were larger than the contest for Negro citizenship, as such. His analysis of Negro life for what James calls *last things, fruits, consequences, facts,* suggested that the major impediment to achieving the ideals of American democracy had always been American society's legal and murderous resistance to black humanity (James, 510). In face of this challenge Du Bois argued for "the conservation of races." That is, Negroes should create "race solidarity" in order to maintain social and political group identity "until . . . the ideal of human brotherhood has become a practical possibility."[12] This theory of protective racial unity—one that neither insists on an essentialist notion of Negro identity nor promotes individual experience at the expense of political hope—is actually a framed advocacy for pragmatist solidarity.

Du Bois's notion of political solidarity and racial affiliation reconstructs pragmatism following Dewey's sense that the pragmatist helps "men solve problems in the concrete by supplying them hypotheses to be used and tested in projects of reform."[13] Du Bois's descriptions of race conservation, double-consciousness, and the color line are hypotheses for understanding and overcoming the racial dilemmas embedded in American social and political circumstances. But understanding and overcoming can only arrive, Du Bois would argue, when Americans confront the social problems begat by Reconstruction's end in the South, the negation of equality arising from Jim Crow legal systems (in the South and urban North), and the human rights problems emergent in policing black bodies by means of lynching. Without willing address of the history of Negro dehumanization, thus the address of democracy withheld, Americans, black and white, cannot fulfill the social hope for more freedoms.

Du Bois's call for racial solidarity is a symbolic political act that requires first an "inquiry into human affairs and hence morals" in American life and second, a recognition of Negro humanity that white Americans refuse to acknowledge (Dewey 1957, xxiii). Thus, in terms of promoting liberal social hopes, Du Bois's notion is a necessary but temporary step toward a meaningful citizenship. Though pragmatism as therapy is a "hopeful, melioristic, experimental frame of mind," Du Bois could only activate that therapeutic mode once he charted a position outside of the battle between absolute "blackness" and radical individual "experience."[14]

Du Bois saw the stream of consciousness stereo-optically—experience is both public and private. Not only does the interaction between the self and the world produce truth, but in the case of the African American, the self must contend with the realities generated to emphasize her humanity and the realities generated by a social experience that often dehumanizes her. In his capacity as public intellectual, Du Bois often argued that outside of academic sociological research, the most persuasive means for Negroes to achieve full citizenship was through advancement in the musical and literary arts. By reevaluating the Negro past, taking its form, color, and reality, black artists can find a truth and romance useful for "propaganda."

Du Bois's contextualization of propaganda defamiliarizes the term, freeing it "from its usual degrading instrumentalism" while promoting it as "the practice of the art of living" (Posnock 1999, 142). In his critique of African American arts practices we can find Du Bois weaving pragmatic romanticism into cultural criticism.[15] Du Bois explains that, "until the art of the black folk compells [sic] recognition they will not be rated as human. And when through art they compell recognition then let the world discover if it will that their art is as new as it is old and as old as new."[16] Though Du Bois has often been chastised for his unabashed claims that African American cultural works, aesthetically shaped propaganda, ought to be used as a means to political ends, the critical advocacy that he and Alain Locke engineered for African American arts, literature especially, was fueled by an Emersonian-inflected vision.

In "The American Scholar," Emerson describes American culture as a specific tradition separate from, but on equal footing with, European and classical cultures. His claim initiated an effort that has dominated the attention of American writers for the last two centuries: to identify an America not yet arrived. This Emersonian charge is also what he named in his journals as the hope for an American renaissance. But rebirth does not suggest that American culture will lose its relation to European or classical cultures. In fact, Emerson offers a model for thinking of American culture as developing out of its relationship to the others. In taking the "least part" of other cultural systems, Emerson argues that American scholars and poets will realize that "one design unites and animates the farthest pinnacle and the lowest trench" (Emerson

1960, 69, 78). Emerson's concept is both cultural and political: while naming and defining a culture that identifies them, Americans will also be affirming their position in the production and continuation of human history. With this in mind, perhaps we can read Emerson's conception of cultural rebirth (or emergence) as the generative notion animating Du Bois's project of naming an African American cultural agenda. We can also read it at play in Locke's theory of political solidarity during the New Negro movement/Harlem Renaissance.[17]

Locke's critical race theory rejects race as a biological category, promoting instead a sense of race born from social particulars and the hope for political change. Examining narratives of blackness operating in the American mainstream during the opening decades of the twentieth century, Locke illustrates that racial constructs are used to cast Negroes as intellectual and cultural inferiors while holding them in the economic underclass. In his essay "Race Progress and Race Adjustments," Locke notes the use of racial constructs in imperial political agendas, highlighting the disenfranchisement of black citizens and the difficulty of asserting Negro humanity in early twentieth-century American society. One tool for grappling with these twinned problems, Locke argues, is a conceptualization of Negro political solidarity framed by "secondary race consciousness."

Secondary race consciousness is a revised notion of racial identity, one that redeems blackness, for instance, from brutish stereotypes. Locke believed that this form of racial solidarity would resolve rather than exacerbate the problems of American racial antagonism. Locke explains that "the only kind of race that is left to believe in and to be applied to modern problems is what we call the idea of social race, defining it more narrowly as a conception of civilization type or civilization kind."[18] Rather than reifying foundational concepts of race, Locke reads race as a social construct that poses concrete political, economic, and psychological difficulties. Secondary racial awareness is a matter of self-defense and self-respect, a way of identifying the political attitudes and cultural attributes that African Americans have developed collectively to assert their civil, political, and human rights.

Locke's formulation is a kind of cultural nationalism "aimed at overcoming a form of racial domination that he understood as ulti-

mately economic and political. Its roots lie in a sophisticated pragmatist understanding of race conjoined with an anti-imperialist
political analysis."[19] Rather than collecting Negroes around biological fictions, Locke promoted social and cultural perspectives that
embraced the hope for full citizenship. His vision of secondary
racial identity asks Negroes to develop self-conscious relationships
to their distinctive social culture, which is a blend of African American and non-Negro American elements. This means "giving expression to African-American traditions in public cultural forms, such
as literature, music, and painting, where they can be recognized by
the larger society" (Fraser 1998, 170).

Locke's cultural citizenship encourages Negro political and social solidarity because it affirms Negro humanity even while white
America degrades it. This solidarity is valuable before winning "respect from Anglo-America" and after winning it because secondary awareness maintains a collective political voice (Locke 1925,
170–71). Once their cultural power is acknowledged Negroes will
earn revaluation, "which must precede or accompany any consid-
erable further betterment of race relationships."[20]

However, for certain pragmatist and neopragmatist cultural critics like Walter Benn Michaels, "ethnic" or "cultural" identity is a
flawed concept because it leads logically to what it claims to de-
bunk, "race." Michaels contends that critics should get rid of modernist conceptions of cultural identity because they rely insidiously
on essentialist racial identities. He argues that cultural identity and
cultural pluralism are markers for "understanding identity as the
privileged object of social contest."[21] But that contest ultimately
reveals identity and culture as interchangeable equivalents.

This equivalency is dubious, Michaels explains, because the
modernist idea of cultural pluralism is an oxymoron: "its commitment to culture is contradicted by its commitment to pluralism. For
on the one hand, the pluralist claim that our practices are justified
only because they are better for us requires us to be able to say who
we are independent of those practices and so requires us to produce
our racial identity" (Michaels, 139). Ultimately, what's wrong with
cultural identity is "not that it developed out of racial identity" but
that, "without recourse to the racial identity that (in its current
manifestations) it repudiates, it makes no sense" (Michaels, 142).

Richard Rorty also believes that it makes no sense to discuss racial identity—blackness, whiteness, whatever. Concerning the politics of racial difference, Rorty suggests that the status quo assumptions of white cultural superiority are defensible against the narratives of cultural studies:

> It seems to me the politics of difference grows out of the notion that there is something called the White Anglo-Saxon Male Heterosexist culture which was (a) a pretty lousy culture, and (b) has insisted that everyone become a member of it. I find this an unrecognizable description. It wasn't a bad culture at all. It had quite a lot of room for all kinds of religious and ethnic identities, associations, parades, things like that. The sense that there was this vast pressure for homogenization seems to me a real Leftist myth. (Nystrom and Puckett, 23–24)

Rorty has always argued that our conversations ought to focus on the narration of stories about folks who give up on group affiliation or group difference in favor of "Emersonian type stories" that emphasize the development and glorification of individual difference. But on this point, Rorty seems to give up on irony and history as he explains that "the problem for stigmatized groups is not to get their 'culture' accepted, but to get the stigmatizers to stop thinking that lack of a penis, black skin, or whatever, is a shameful thing. . . . These groups don't need recognition of their 'cultures'; they just need not to be pushed around."[22]

Here, it seems, Rorty evades the American history of politically, socially, and economically oppressed groups, like African Americans, who have had to use both political *and* cultural means to limit stigmatization in their effort to move toward fuller roles as citizens. And, as Locke asserts, destigmatization of African Americans is preceded and accompanied by the acknowledgment of their cultural power. But, as Michaels's argument shows us, there is still the problem of "race" at cultural identity's core. Michaels, like Rorty, doesn't provide a way of considering identity once we are free of cultural identity or essentialist racial identities. Neither Michaels nor Rorty presents serious philosophical positions or theoretical concepts to either replace cultural identity or provide us the vocabulary for narrating the functions that blackness or whiteness have in framing American social arrangements. So, once we reject "race" and "cultural identity," refusing to interrogate how race functions, how do we grapple with the material consequences of America's racial history or the political and cultural products it has spawned without discussing racial (or ethnic) experiences? How do we discuss the complex task of constructing identities in our (sometimes violently) racist society?

Tommie Shelby has imagined a construct for addressing questions similar to the ones I raise above. Merging concepts like Locke's "secondary racial awareness" and Du Bois's "race conservation," Shelby argues that even in the twenty-first century a "thin" notion of African American identity is still useful for constructing black political solidarity because large swaths of black America continue to suffer from institutionalized oppression.

Rather than turning to cultural nationalism or racial essentialism built on "thick" conceptions of blackness, Shelby suggests that developing a narrative of "thin" black identity is part of a "pragmatic" or "practical" political and social bonding, a contingent strategy in the battle against anti-black racism.[23] Though he is not using "pragmatic" to connect himself to the James-Dewey philosophical lineage, like the pragmatists Shelby is suspicious of "race" and African American "collective identity." However, Shelby also argues that the necessary tools for truly achieving an America that is a "multiracial 'nation' . . . committed to social equality, democratic citizenship for all, self-government, and the cultivation of a vigorous citizenry" are functioning within the narratives of African American survival and striving.[24]

In their attempts to describe the political reasoning behind their formulations of black group solidarity, Du Bois, Locke, and Shelby are also providing sketches of the intellectual's relationship to what Mark Anthony Neal calls "the Black Public Sphere."[25] Though it began as clandestine gatherings during African American slavery, the Black Public Sphere emerged as a way of maintaining cultural continuity as Negroes were migrating en masse out of the rural South into the urban industrial centers of the South and North. The great migration of African Americans into working-class infrastructures in cities such as Buffalo, New York, Pittsburgh, Atlanta, New Orleans, Memphis, Oklahoma City, Denver, Kansas City, Chicago, Detroit, and Cleveland mixed southern Negro cultural rituals, American urban culture, and modern art in a potent new aesthetic matrix—the blues idiom. Urban blues and jazz performers helped

to make visible African Americans' invisible plight while simultaneously communicating what black folk had "contributed not only
materially in labor and in social patience but spiritually as well"
(Locke 1925, 15).

While the racist nation-state did not crumble by cultural means
alone, double consciousness and secondary race awareness are ultimately radical political theories because they draw our attention to
the physical (social, economic, legal), psychological, and spiritual
realities of African Americanness. Those realities were (and often
still are) named and narrated within the comfort of the institutions
(such as black churches, civic organizations, barbershops, beauty
parlors, and jazz clubs) that constitute African American social-
communal spaces. While all those institutions helped to maintain
the values and traditions of African American culture, and were
often designed to accentuate the tenets of American democracy,
Neal notes that the most crucial of Negro public forums was the
"jook joint," the public dance hall.

The public dance ritualized resistance to the social restrictions
placed on African American physical expression. Interestingly, resistance cut against both other black institutions and the white
American mainstream, Neal explains, because the jook "was per-
ceived as transgressive in its very nature and the antithesis of the
black church when compared to more bourgeois sensibilities" (Neal
1999, 6). Cutting both ways, the aesthetic and political ramifications of public blues idiom musical rituals make the abstractions of
secondary racial awareness or thin African American identity into
material, physical realities while also leveling powerful critiques
against the American mainstream.

During the postwar/CRM era, as I will illustrate in the following movements, African American artist/intellectuals like Ellison,
Baldwin, and Jones/Baraka engaged blues idiom cultural practices
in order to 1) develop their own pragmatist vocabularies (extending the cultural and political lineage of Emerson and Locke) for
bonding separate but related public spheres, Negro and American,
and creating discourses to redescribe American citizenry, 2) develop literary aesthetics that could appropriately name and narrate
routes toward antiessentialist individuality while also improvising
visions of a new American social and political mainstream, and
3) develop sophisticated critical tools for navigating the play be-

tween their private existential selves and their thin African American political identities.

II

Many African American thinkers and writers have engaged pragmatist ideals by engaging blues idiom aesthetics. The blues swings poetically, expressing the pendulum of lived experience in all its exuberance and all its low-down dirty shamefulness. As a musical idiom the blues is pluralistic, it is made up of, for example, Negro spirituals, European folk songs and ballads, work chants and field hollers, and popular tunes. The blues "constitutes an amalgam that seems always to have been in motion in America—always becoming, shaping, transforming, displacing the peculiar experiences of Africans in the New World."[26] The contingent elements of the blues are like spores of mercury rolling, connecting, reforming, and blending into potent new expressive forms.

In his address of these contingencies, Albert Murray offers the best assessment of how the blues operates idiomatically:

> [S]winging the blues is generated, as anyone familiar with Negro dance halls knows, not by obscuring or denying the existence of the ugly dimensions of human nature, circumstance, and conduct, but rather through the full, sharp, and inescapable awareness of them. . . . Thus does man the player become man the stylizer and by the same token the humanizer of chaos; and thus does play become ritual, ceremony, and art; and thus also does the dance-beat improvisation of experience in the blues idiom become survival technique, esthetic equipment for living, and a central element in the dynamics of U.S. Negro life style. (Murray 1970, 57–58)

Murray's description of the blues is an extension of Kenneth Burke's conception that we, humans, develop rituals in order to arm ourselves in the management of life's risks and complexities. The blues idiom then, as the metaphorical umbrella covering African American arts—music, literature, visual arts, and dance—is what Burke would call "equipment for living."[27] The blues idiom provides tools for making or sustaining rituals—artful *doing* meant to comfort us therapeutically with lyrical expressions of the beautiful elements *and* dark tragic realities of the lived experience.

Conceptions of idiomatic vernacular practices are central to pragmatist methods. In Murray's language we can hear the "manifestation of republican desires" that undergirded James's understanding of the pragmatic method. When Murray talks about the stylization of chaos into ritual and art, he is accepting that the world grows "not integrally but piecemeal by the contributions of its several parts"; blues idiom ritual practices illustrate that social arrangements grow from genuine cooperative work. When James argues that language tolerates multiple expressive and dialectical options he is being both descriptive and prescriptive: he's "not just telling us what [language] is but what *it should be*." (Magee 2004, 14). In other words, we might better understand vernacular expressive practices, like blues idiom practices, as language systems that help us narrate and perform our personal, social, and political desires.

Ellison, Baldwin, and Jones/Baraka all argued during the CRM (especially the momentous decade 1955–65) that the blues is American culture's central artistic idiom and that blues expressions can have the power of symbolic action.[28] Expanding Murray's claim that the blues is equipment for living, Ralph Ellison's philopolitical definition melds the blues, pragmatism, African American vernacular theory, and literary criticism into a deft critical statement:

> The blues is an impulse to keep the painful details and episodes of a brutal experience alive in one's aching consciousness, to finger its jagged grain, and to transcend it, not by the consolation of philosophy but by squeezing from it a near tragic, near comic lyricism. As a form, the blues is an autobiographical chronicle of personal catastrophe expressed lyrically.[29]

Blues idiom expression squeezes truth from lived experience, acknowledging the interwoven relation of tragedy and comedy. Blues lyricism arises from the willingness to swim against the current of one's own stream of consciousness and make song from the bruising recollections and realizations. Like Murray's reading of blues utility, Ellison's blues attitude is a revision of Burke's analysis of the dialectic relationship between the ridiculous and the sublime, "discomfort" and "comfort." The threat of discomfort, Burke explains, is built into the idea of comfort. Poetry, Burke argues, is produced for the purpose of comfort, but it must also protect us from the threat of discomfort. In our urgent desire for beauty, the sublime, we often overlook the presence of the ugly, the ridiculous, within the beautiful. While Ellison rejects the *consolation* of philosophy as protection from discomfort, his "near tragic, near comic" formulation is an acceptance of Burke's insistence that we generate a dialectical comprehension of the relationship between "discomfort" and "comfort."

Though the blues is an autobiographical form, Ellison's definition also suggests that its lyrical expressions must meet an audience. With concern to identity, blues idiom expression accentuates our tragicomic desires for connection to both our essential selves and our need for ethnocentric unity. We understand, however, that we will find an essential or absolute self because our identities are complex, elusive, jagged, multiple, and fragmented. The "swing" of blues tragicomedy inspires improvisation within communal circumstances. It don't mean a thing if ain't got that swing: an audience who can respond to, critique, or encourage more lyrical expressions. In this sense blues idiom discourse helps in the search for what Dewey calls "the great community." The collective action of ritual circumstances is not enough to frame community. Dewey insists that our social arrangements only become communities when we accept an interlocking, mutually defining relationship between the community and the individual.

> For beings who observe and think, and whose ideas are absorbed by impulses and become sentiments and interests, 'we' is as inevitable as 'I.' But 'we' and 'our' exist only when the consequences of combined action are perceived and become an object of desire and effort, just as 'I' and 'mine' appear on the scene only when a distinctive share in mutual action is consciously asserted or claimed. Human associations may be ever so organic in origin and firm in operation, but they develop into societies in a human sense only as their consequences, being known, are esteemed and sought for.[30]

The blues idiom soloist not only performs the story of her experience, she raises the experience beyond metaphysical subjectivity by connecting it with the audience's own layered experiences. In hearing some element of their own experiences performed the audience recognizes the soloist's humanity. The performance is a model for dealing with the blues as such and for improvising the swing between the individual and the group, present and past, experimentation and tradition, truth and change.

The Murray and Ellison definitions of the blues idiom bring us back to the Du Boisian/Lockean/Shelbyan ideas about "thin" racial identification. The aesthetic practice best suited for negotiating the relationship between the antifoundational, abstract self and the socially necessary black identity is improvisation. As we shall see in the movements devoted to each of the main subjects in *The Shadow and the Act,* the African American literary tradition deals "with the tensions between one's objective/intersubjective acceptance by the white world and one's subjective phenomenological awareness of one's role-playing."[31] The play between public selves and private selves is a tight balance between "the self as socially constituted and the self as internally socially resistant" (Mills 1998, 13). Though swing signifies the movements among these various positions, improvisation is the name for the experimental process of narrating these dialectic relations.

According to Murray, improvisation is the imperative of American creative art. He argues that it is both a product of and response to the American cultural milieu: artists must be not only proficient, masterful in their mediums, but also compositionally innovative. Experimentation and innovation instigate progress — invention that shifts the paradigm of a whole artistic practice. Thus, Murray continues, the great innovation of twentieth-century art was the introduction and refinement of jazz improvisation into a specific aesthetic.

Jazz improvisation, Paul Berliner argues, is not simply a technical routine that musicians use to create music for recording sessions or live performances. Jazz as a way of life requires that musicians give themselves over to the demands of the profession, particularly the world of musical imagination. Jazz musicians must immerse themselves totally in jazz's language in order to "attain fluency as improvisers and enjoy continued artistic growth. Self-directed studies of jazz history, analyses of works by master improvisers, rigorous private practice routines, and interaction with other players in numerous bands continually sharpen abilities and replenish the artist's store of knowledge."[32] Linguistic immersion forces musicians to regard not only the sources of jazz, which are an amalgam of African, European, and African American musical systems primarily, but the roots of their own personal desires and expressive needs.

Jazz musicians create and extend musical "conversations" among themselves while in performance, largely by building improvised solos that "tell stories." The ability to "say something" through one's play relies on a tight network of understanding jazz history and musicological theories, rigorously shaped personal aesthetic, and a willingness to interrogate personal identity through performance. This is where jazz and black pragmatists merge: jazz performance and musicians provide various models for African American intellectuals to think through the making of racialized, gendered, and American identities. Jazz helps us construct histories, create discourses, and build communities.

Studying how musicians communicate in jazz performance is a way of developing a more cultural music theory and a more musical cultural theory. When saying something about jazz during performance, musicians communicate theories about musical performance, the nature of identity, political concerns, and race by improvising sonic interactions, interactively shaping social networks and communities that accompany musical participation, and developing culturally variable meanings and ideologies that inform the interpretation of jazz in American society.[33] African American music emphasizes the contingent relationship of artistic expression, ethnic identity, and political/cultural critique.

Like Ingrid Berliner, Monson argues that jazz asks listeners to regard the "multidimensional cultural and musical knowledge" that musicians draw upon as the unique signs of identity rather than the "liquidation of cultural identity." Monson explains that "the harmonic and melodic expertise of the soloist, which is essential to competent jazz improvisation, must be expressed against the rhythmic flow generated by the musically sociable rhythm section" (70). The rhythmic communication among bassists, drummers, and pianists, for instance, also involves harmonic and melodic expertise as a way of establishing the groove and creating feeling.

More to the point, "The aesthetic and value system by which all these heterogeneous musical and cultural elements are integrated and evaluated," Monson writes, "form the analytical level at which one can begin to speak of cultural identities" (Monson 131). Instead of eliminating cultural identities, the polymusicality of many jazz musicians highlights the importance of cultural identity within the cosmopolitan group. This version of musical cultural identity is not predicated on race but on the experimental development of selves through experience. Jazz improvisation is an African American vernacular language that aids musical and philosophical inquiry: in jazz communities narrating selfhood is always an improvised performance.

Jazz improvisation is the elongation of two old musical concepts: on one hand, the African and African American traditions of spontaneous but disciplined creation in vocal or instrumental music and the Western musical idea "obbligato." While ethnomusicologists like Portia Maultsby and Berliner have charted the routes of relation between African musical methods and African American musical styles, I want to focus on obbligato because the term will be useful for understanding how blues idiom expression functions.[34] Obbligato is an instruction presented to the musician in the lead notes of a piece of sheet music. The term usually refers to a particular instrument (i.e. violino obbligato) and literally means *"part that must not be omitted;* the opposite is *ad libitum."*[35] Michael Jarrett later writes that "through misunderstanding or carelessness, [obbligato] has come to mean a mere accompanying *part that may be omitted if necessary.* As a result, one must decide in each individual case whether obbligato means 'obbligato' or 'ad libitum'" (Jarrett 1998, 61). The decision that the musician makes is between the written part and the chance to improvise an accompaniment to the charted melody.

Improvisation evolves out of obbligato but in jazz it is more than embellishment; jazz improvisation makes the "optional" obligatory. "The improviser can't play only what's required," Jarrett writes, because "[he or she is] bound to contribute a certain excess" (Jarrett 1998, 64). And in that excess the line between scripted composition and improvised composition is worried; any and all distinctions between the composition and the improvisation become "socially constructed and ultimately incomplete" (Jarrett 1998, 64). The improvised composition presents both the musician's and culture's fluctuations; improvisation is a way of articulating the agon among the individual artist, the musical setting, the composition itself, and the larger social matrix that shapes the aesthetic.

Improvisation, however, is also about revising or *othering* all those parts of aesthetic statement. The construction of an improvised solo is designed to articulate the music's openness to renewal and revision while also enabling the public expression of the self as performative—both are othered in the play. When musicians improvise they are detailing some elements of their individual and/or ensemble musical educations and jazz performances, as well as creating spontaneous, new compositions. And as we shall discover in the coming movements, improvisation is a useful name for the process of self-identification.

But improvisation is also a great name for the kind of critical experimentation that Ellison, Baldwin, and Jones/Baraka all engaged in the process of developing their cultural critiques of American life during the postwar/CRM era. Worrying the line between scripted American culture and improvised culture's rising in the wake of sociopolitical changes, these artist/intellectuals used jazz to connect their conceptions of Negro humanity with their narratives about the realization of American democracy.

As scholars such as Penny M. Von Eschen, Ingrid Monson, and Iain Anderson have all detailed recently, at the beginning of the Cold War American democratic theories were disseminated to the world with the aid of musicians functioning as "jazz ambassadors." Back on native grounds jazz musicians were also participating in seismic rearrangements of American life. Whether musicians were inventing aesthetic systems that helped communicate forcefully the "change of the century" or composing protest art that argued for "freedom now," jazz was a locus for the contingencies of American experience to be played out and for interdisciplinary, intercommunal discourses to be improvised. While it is true that many listeners and musicians alike rejected attaching jazz and politics, I think that the confrontations surrounding issues concerning avant garde musical aesthetics and the economic structures of the music business are political in and of themselves.

Thinking of Deweyan theories of linguistic utility, we can hear jazz and improvisation as linguistic/aesthetic tools for negotiating and solving social difficulties. Writing about jazz as a metaphor in fiction or criticism, Jones/Baraka, Ellison, and Baldwin attempted to negotiate the problems of race and identity while also proposing narratives for reimagining the American social arrangements and democratic political theory.

In Movement I, "Three Ways of Looking At A Yardbird: Charlie Parker and the Theorization of Jazz Improvisation in the Work of Ralph Ellison, James Baldwin, and LeRoi Jones/Amiri Baraka," I examine how these writers used Charlie Parker as a sign of Negro complexity and a symbolic guide through the contingent relationship among the illustrations and theories developed in their literary works and cultural criticism.

The alto saxophonist Charlie Parker lived within both the beautiful intricacies of bebop lyricism and the rough crucible of heroin addiction. Yusef Komunyakaa writes that Parker's jazz, with its horse-hyped, double-timed poetics, expresses "laughter and crying at the same time."[36] Komunyakaa's assertion is not a call to hear jazz as the music of dialectic oppositions; rather, for him, laughing and crying embody a wide range of musical, intellectual, and psychological contingencies at work within group or individual jazz performances. Like the innovations of the most important jazz performers of the twentieth century, Parker's improvisations are significant because they revealed more than the tensions of binaries.

Listening closely to Parker's simultaneous laughter and crying and thinking *in* jazz, to borrow Paul Berliner's title, we can hear the music's complicated emotional reality: laughing to keep from crying, crying to the point of laughter, laughing hard enough to draw tears, crying that sounds like laughter, laughter that sounds like weeping. Even more, from the liminal space between laughter and crying, jazz musicians can communicate multiple claims about emotions, experience, and being in the world. In fact, under the influence of musicians like Parker, we might hear jazz as a mode and a model for expressing the experiences of performing among multiple aesthetic impulses, multiple emotional states, and multiple psychological selves simultaneously.

Movement I

Three Ways of Looking at a Yardbird

Charlie Parker and the Theorization of Jazz Improvisation in the Work of Ralph Ellison, James Baldwin, and LeRoi Jones/Amiri Baraka

I was of three minds,
Like a tree
In which there are three blackbirds
Wallace Stevens

In early 1956, fourteen weeks into the Montgomery bus boy-cott, Ralph Ellison, living at the American Academy in Rome, wrote to Albert Murray, then stationed with the air force in Morocco, that the collective action of Negroes in Alabama revealed "just a little bit more of their complexity."[1] Interestingly, while in Rome Ellison was at work on a novel dedicated to sustaining the lineage of his "vanishing tribe," the Negroes.

Also in 1956, inspired by Irish and French modernist writers, LeRoi Jones, an air force weather gunner stationed in Puerto Rico, began developing a poetics appropriate for expressing his individual, personal complexities. Jones's early poems communicated his sense of being "out" beyond status quo American cultural sensibilities, but by the mid-1960s Jones became "Baraka," turning his modernist lyrics into poetic descriptions of the intricate connections between African American political desires and the identifying elements of blackness. Like Jones and Ellison, James Baldwin was living outside the U.S. in the mid-1950s, writing about African American identity and the shifting currents of postwar politics. Parisian life was supposed to provide Baldwin an escape from the humiliations of American racism but he found instead that his foreignness, his otherness in France, forced him to write about his intractable Americanness.

Life outside the U.S. forced each writer to interrogate the meanings of blackness, American identity, and the post–World War II political world in ways that exposed conflicts at the center of his intellectual/literary practices: How did Baldwin's desire for physical and psychological separation from American racism align with his forceful claims to the American birthright? How did Jones articulate his processes of self-awareness and his changes from postwar "outsider" artist to insider, black-nationalist aesthetician? How did Ellison account for both his sense of mid-twentieth-century Negro political complexity and his worry over the diminishing cultural presence of Negroes?

I argue in Movement I that each writer found in blues idiom culture and jazz music the necessary concepts for negotiating these questions. In particular, this movement is an investigation of how Ellison, Baldwin, and Jones/Baraka analyzed or imagined Charlie "Bird" Parker as a sign of Negro complexity or inscrutability in their works. However, these writers also proposed that Parker be read as a navigating guide through the contingencies of American identity, history, art, and democracy described in their creative and critical works.

Rather than resting on foundational notions of black identity or culture during the CRM, Ellison, Baldwin, and Jones/Baraka each theorized jazz improvisation as a demonstration of cosmopolitan blackness, an illustration of the social usefulness of Negro cultural rituals, and a way of communicating philosophical attitudes befitting the shifts in American political and social life during the 1950s and '60s. Parker represents a melodic through line that crosses their individual concerns, letting us hear the tonal similarities within their works. Writing about black intellectuals and philosophy in relationship to jazz history and performance "is not a matter of giving the music fine airs—it doesn't need them—but of saying that whatever touches our highly conscious creators of culture is apt to be reflected here."[2]

Though each writer approached Bird as "the black artist as sacrificial Negro," they charted separately defined routes toward achieving African American political, economic, and cultural freedom. Jones/Baraka, Ellison, and Baldwin communicated the terms of their pragmatist critiques of civil rights political and social changes, African American identity, black masculinity, and black cultural production through their analyses of Parker. In so doing they also displayed the political differences that separated them. We can find both the harmonies and dissonant counterplay by studying how Jones/Baraka, Baldwin, and Ellison responded to Parker and bebop.[3]

Bebop at the Center of American Politics

To understand Parker's manifold cultural significance we must situate jazz and bebop as central cultural cogs not only in postwar American cultural production but also in Cold War foreign diplomacy. In the 1950s, on the cusp of the CRM's insurgent dive into the postwar political mainstream, the State Department began sending African American jazz musicians to eastern Europe and the unaligned, postcolonial world to sing literally the praises of American democracy. Rather than dampening the burgeoning protests at home or satiating Africans and Arabs with the "rhythms" of American cultural diplomacy (two hopes of the Eisenhower administration), these jazz tours encouraged listeners to reinvent themselves according to the imperatives of improvisation. Ironically, Americans at home would be the ones to embody and perform democracy's improvisational possibilities. Baldwin, Jones/Baraka, and Ellison are crucial in this narrative, for their works countered the official government desires by encouraging their readers to consider the revolutionary political and philosophical claims laced into jazz performance.

In the 1930s Coleman Hawkins was the first significant and established artist to begin toiling with the musical formulations that would become the vocabulary of bebop. Hawkins's notion of musical progress involved the introduction of problematic and difficult chordal progressions into his improvised solos—his innovations challenged other musicians to find resolutions to those musical problems. Hawkins's progressive musical intellect made him one of the preeminent improvisers of his generation and a harbinger of changes to come.[4]

Younger musicians such as Parker, Dizzy Gillespie, Thelonious Monk, Max Roach, and Howard McGee accepted Hawkins's progressive challenge. They theorized concepts that emerged from both inherited musical traditions and the conditions of urban African American life during the 1940s. Developed in a range of locations from Kansas City dance halls to Harlem jam session parlors like Minton's Playhouse and Monroe's Uptown, bebop focused on the primacy of solo improvisation during group performance. Jam sessions featured house bands, rhythm sections (piano, bass, drums, and sometimes guitar) that created improvisational space by layering generous chord sequences over angular, second-line bomb beats and pedal point or walking bass lines.

The accelerated pace of the style was prime for the "cutting sessions," battle royals that anchored the jamming by pitting soloists against each other. The duels were meant to battle test the technical and narrative virtuosity, the musical mettle of each instrumentalist. Emulating its mother tongue, the blues, bebop is a matrix in which all musical styles (for instance, New Orleans syncopation, Ellingtonia, southwestern swing, rags, gospel, Broadway show tunes, popular songs, and contemporary classical music) are fodder for melodic quotation or technical integration into the language of bebop composition and improvisation.

Though bebop developed as a distinctly African American musical revolution it "was not a unified ideological aesthetic movement. Rather, it was an artistic challenge that was understood in a variety of ways in its social, cultural, intellectual, and creative context."[5] Bebop was not a racially exclusive musical movement;

nevertheless, it was rooted deeply in the uncomfortable realities of American racial history. Scott DeVeaux explains that bebop's politically engaged avant-garde produced a form of resistance from the underground of American culture in order to assert an "ethnic consciousness in the face of efforts by a white-controlled culture industry to co-opt and contain its subversive potential" (DeVeaux 1996, 23). For jazz musicians, the situation was particularly poignant, because music was manifestly capable of transcending racial barriers. Yet there is no escaping the fact that black musicians lived and worked in a separate and unequal world, facing obstacles and enduring indignities that set them apart from their white counterparts; race, economics, and politics were wedded in this cultural underworld.

Parker's musical innovations helped shape radical youth immediately after World War II. Parker's technical velocity, musical theories, and instinctive sense of swing helped define bebop and reshape jazz performance. Though he died mostly unsung outside of the jazz world, Parker's high modernist aesthetics and self-destructive tendencies made him an apt sacrificial figure for the narratives of Cold War culture and civil rights politics. Bird's death in March 1955 marks the pivot point during the eighteen-month period between the Supreme Court's May 1954 *Brown* decision and the beginning of the Montgomery bus boycott in December 1955. One unexpected measure of the Negro complexity Ellison thought emergent was that various groups began to use Parker symbolically.

In his analysis of Parker's iconic cultural status, Ellison offers a lucid example of his pragmatist sensibilities. Ellison's pragmatism was influenced by his personal and critical relationship with Kenneth Burke and his theories of ritual symbolism and symbolic action. But Ellison revised those theories, distancing himself from Burke by producing a vernacular analytical system whose main tool is improvisation. Examining what Burke leaves out of his theory of scapegoats, for instance, Ellison transformed Parker's shadowy cultural status into a symbolic identity by reading him through the lens of the blues idiom. Though Ellison was ultimately ambivalent about Parker and much of bebop, his critique explained much about his political ideals: Ellison believed in the maintenance of individual identity and intellectual freedom against collective group identity and political ideologies, and artistic symbolic action above the leftist political theatre of activist participation.

Recall, however, that Ellison's protagonist in *Invisible Man* hopes that the "transitional" linguistic and sartorial style of hipster-bebop culture could provide the impetus and direction for a true Harlem revolution. Spying the zoot-suited, angular black wonders on the subway platform—"African sculptures distorted in the interest of a design"[6]—the protagonist imagines them as history's "agents" or collective "ace in the hole." Describing them as dreaming the "old ancient dreams" and hearing them speak in a language full of "country glamour," invisible man thinks of the hipsters as "men out of time," soon to be gone and forgotten, but also symbols of possibility:

> [they were men] who knew (and now I began to tremble so violently I had to lean against a refuse can)—who knew but that they were the saviors, the true leaders, the bearers of something precious? The stewards of something uncomfortable, burdensome, which they hated because, living outside the realm of history, there was no one to applaud their value and they themselves failed to understand it. (Ellison 1995b, 441)

Standing outside of historical context, largely because of their invisibility, these boppers symbolically expressed the doubled language of African American life: ancient dreams of freedom communicated through the angular linguistics of urban experience. In the scene above, Ellison's narrator realizes that bebop presents models for improvising rhetorical responses to the political context and social world. But, in order for the improvising to create change, the performers must be able to understand the complexities of the sociopolitical world.

By the late 1950s, Ellison had soured on the musical innovations and potential cultural penetrations of bebop. In letters to Albert Murray, Ellison argues that bebop had boiled itself down to meaningless technical exercises, generalized antientertainment, antiwhite performance attitudes, and extended musical theses on Parker's harmonic and melodic inventions. Ellison explains that Parker's influence amounts to chalky clots of bird dropping: "If the Bird shits on you, wear it."[7]

Though Ellison acknowledges in his essay "On Bird, Bird-

Watching, and Jazz" (Ellison 1995a) that Parker stands as one of the most remarkable improvisers in jazz history, he also presents Parker as a "symbolic bird" to white audiences who have "thrice alienated" Parker as a Negro, a jazz genius, and a drug addict. Essaying as an ornithological enthusiast, Ellison situates Bird in a postwar cultural context in which white jazz audiences pluck "feathers" off Parker in the hopes of making meaning from his dead form. And though he argues in the essay that Negroes did not know Parker well, it is clear from Ellison's letters that he hears black jazz musicians emulating and imitating Parker's musical gestures, ensconcing that language firmly into African American music and the American cultural mainstream.

In his critique Ellison presents Parker as the distorted and corrupted black artist. Rather than valorizing his music's complexity, Ellison explains, Parker fanatics consumed his body and musical clichés. Accordingly, much of Parker's symbolic power comes from his station in the American underworld where, Ellison argues, the turbulent conflict between human social desires and American social institutions thrashes unchecked by social decorum or cultural status quo. Parker's symbolism is hatched below the surface of American life where "contemporary civilized values and hypocrisies are challenged by the Dionysian urges of a between-wars youth born to prosperity, conditioned by the threat of world destruction, and inspired—when not seeking total anarchy—by a need to bring social reality and our social pretensions into a more meaningful balance" (Ellison 1995a, 261). Ellison marks the American underworld as a marginal social space inhabited by black musicians and white audiences who use bebop to fund the new political and cultural vocabularies formed to diminish segregated American life while attempting to fulfill the social, economic, or political pretenses of democracy.

Braiding together thoughts on Parker, bebop, political revolution, generational cultural power, and Cold War geopolitics, Ellison's critical perspective bears a striking resemblance to a Deweyan sensibility. Dewey argues, for example, that philosophy or criticism charged, "consciously or unconsciously, by the strivings of men to achieve democracy will construe liberty as meaning a universe in which there is a real uncertainty and contingency . . . incomplete and in the making . . . made this way or that according as men judge, prize, love and labor. . . . [Democracy is] a genuine field of novelty, of real and unpredictable increments to existence, a field for experimentation and invention."[8] In this case, Ellison's critique of Bird, published in 1962, is animated by striving African Americans and their push to participate fully in American democracy. For postwar youths, Parker, master experimenter and improviser, symbolized the real and unpredictable possibilities for recreating the national sociopolitical reality.

Ellison developed his cultural reading of Parker by riffing on Burke's theory of language as symbolic action. Burke's arguments about symbolic action begin with the premise that we are symbol-using animals, creating, iterating, remembering, and experimenting in order to make languages and meanings. As vessels for language we also become symbols, acting in accordance with our created symbols when we put them to use. But Burke forgoes correspondence theories of reality, warning against reading named objects as having realities separate from the linguistic realities we construct. (It is an argument that recalls James's method and Dewey's sense of language as a tool, and anticipates Rorty's linguistic turn.) Language has dexterity that objects do not: in order to define symbols we must use other, different symbols in the naming process. So we experiment with language, generating discourses in order to name and rename the objects, ideas, actions, and truths we willfully believe in.

Burke explains that "words communicate to things the spirit that the society imposes upon the words which have come to be the 'names' of them. The things are in effect the visible tangible material embodiments of the spirit that infuses them through the medium of words."[9] Language as symbolic action mediates our ideas and the physical objects of the world, but it also establishes the possibilities and boundaries of our physical worlds. We use language to name the world and ourselves, illustrating the ways that language works *on* us. We create language to fulfill desires unmet or to squash things not useful to us any longer.

For those white youths trying to create equilibrium between American social realities and American political pretensions, Parker's vernacular improvisations inspire democratic symbolic actions: inhabitants of the American underground accept Negro performance modes as models for remaking American society.

Many of Parker's masterful compositions are based on the basic chords of American popular standards. Impressing Negro vernacular practices upon canonical musical texts, Parker revises and redefines American musical culture. Parker's improvised melodies might also be heard as models for what Tim Parrish, in Burkean fashion, calls democratic doing and undoing. Parrish argues we use language to "undo" the use of an object or idea in order to give the thing its proper "doing": "We might employ our 'technology,' say the automatic rifle or the small-pox-infested blanket or the atomic bomb, in the name of 'democracy' to destroy some other presumably hostile symbol, say the 'other Americans' or 'savages' or 'the yellow peril.' Conversely, also in the name of 'democracy,' we might come to view our prior action as wrong and seek to undo its pernicious consequences."[10] Parker's music "undoes" status quo American musical performance theories by offering new modes for "doing" or improvising American music. But we might also think of improvisation as a theoretical practice, a way of balancing social realities and political pretensions by using the blues idiom attitude to revise old vocabularies and improvise new vocabularies, realities, and political practices.

But the potential for revitalization is double-edged. When Ellison notes the "Dionysian" urges of postwar youth, he wants the multiple, contingent meanings of the "twice-born" god to be present in the text. Dionysus represents wine, the fertility of nature, and agriculture, and also ecstatic, intoxicated, spiritual experiences. One valence of the Dionysian metaphor suggests that Parker's music was a fertile offering to Americans who took the saxophonist's improvisational aesthetic as an inspiration to push particularly Negro experiences and cultural practices into mainstream sociopolitical practices. Another reading suggests that audiences imbibed Parker's heroine-laced solos as part of their ecstatic hero worship. In Ellison's analysis, the version that holds actual cultural cache is the one fueled by the powers that white youths brought with them from the mainstream into the underworld, cloaking Parker in a language that codified him as a mythological figure or idol. Bird became what Ellison called a "'white' hero" (Ellison 1995a, 262).

Interestingly, Ellison's negative analysis of the "white" Bird is still driven by a pragmatist description of language. In Ellison's contention that Parker mythologized was simultaneously deified and essentialized, making him a cultural scapegoat, we might read a pragmatism in which race matters. Ellison's argument extends Kenneth Burke's critique of gods, men, and ritual sacrifice. Goat sacrifices, for instance, were performed in primitive societies in order to escape the wrath of the gods. Burke explains, however, that in complex, sophisticated modern societies the social coordinates of the purifying function were readjusted so that actual persons, often the "'sacrificial King,'" eventually replaced goat offerings.[11] In search of a revitalizing masculine authority who could provide escape from status quo American social hierarchy, white youths turned to Bird, made him both a sacrificial bird and the "king" of bebop, and then sacrificed him in order to initiate an ecstatic spiritual and cultural rebirth in postwar America.

It would be easy to read this essay simply as an Ellisonian vivisection of Bird and his white mythologizers. However, Ellison does not valorize African American listeners and musicians for hearing Bird properly, accepting his music as linguistic innovation, and fulfilling the promise of improvisation as extramusical cultural practice. In fact, Ellison argues that Negroes who mimic Parker's model rather than revising it improvisationally are only mounting taxidermal Birds. On this point, Ellison pushes together Burke's analysis of ritual sacrifice and his theory of linguistic symbolic action: if Bird's doings and undoings, his symbolic performances, are misinterpreted, his actions and his audiences, black and white, will essentialize him. This problem is amplified, Ellison believes, by Parker's inability to corral the chaos of his consciousness into an artistic form, a truly revolutionary action.

In "Golden Age, Time Past," Ellison explains that bebop developed as a Negro musical vernacular framed as a "revolution in culture," a specific rejection of white American economic influence on jazz performance and recording (Ellison 1995a, 239). The revolutionary stance required that musicians stifle co-optation by refusing to suppress their high artistic ambitions in favor of the clowning, mugging stage performance styles that many older Negro musicians, especially Louis Armstrong, developed as part of their shows for white audiences.

Ellison argues that Parker's turn away from Armstrongesque stage performances was his attempt to remain aloof to the commodified blackness—minstrelsy—that soothed white audiences.[12]

But what Parker failed to recognize, Ellison explains, is that older jazzmen "possessed a clearer idea of the division between their identities as performers and as private individuals" (Ellison 1995a, 260). Though Negroes were not really a vanishing tribe, it is this sensibility of masking, a key cog in the group's survival, whose disappearance Ellison laments. Forgoing the showmanship of older jazz traditions, boppers like Parker, Ellison writes, participated in "a grim comedy of racial manners . . . [in which] calculated surliness and rudeness [were used to treat] the audience very much as many white merchants in poor Negro neighborhoods treat their customers, and the white audiences were shocked at first but learned quickly to accept such treatment as evidence of 'artistic' temperament" (Ellison 1995a, 260). Though Ellison is not rejecting the hope for presenting jazz and bebop as high art, he sees "the comic reversal" occurring when symbolic Negro performances are misread. While beboppers wanted to eschew low-down, "blacked-up" entertainment, they donned masks that were misinterpreted as iterations of minstrelsy. Ellison writes that, "for the jazzmen it has become a proposition of the more you win, the more you lose" (Ellison 1995a, 260).

Parker, expressing himself musically in order to achieve his "self determined identity," was shoved into an untenable slot of being at once "sub- and super-human" (Ellison 1995a, 245, 261). Because audiences and musicians misunderstood his symbolic actions, Ellison argues, Bird's self-inventing solos, powerful vernacular inventions though they were, turned him into a "fertility god, mangled by his admirers and imitators" alike (Ellison 1995a, 242). Ellison's analysis suggests that Parker's musical improvising simultaneously created metaphorical pathways into new African American identities and political territories and to his figurative (and possibly his literal) demise.

Ellison's analysis of Parker's cultural influence tells us a lot about the author's politics. Though he was finally ambivalent about bebop and Parker, preferring Armstrong's rhapsodic odes to invisibility, Ellison understood both musicians as models for using Negro vernacular practices to perform democratic symbolic actions. However, it is clear that Ellison sees bebop and Parker as limited models; he wants to replace the abstractions of say, "Chasing the Bird" or "Now's the Time," with the concrete possibilities of the novel form. Ellison believed that producing a novel was a democratic symbolic act. I will argue in Movement II that Ellison's improvised novelistic forms were meant to express his critique of twentieth-century American literature, American politics, black leadership, and Negro identity. Framed by Ellison's taste for Armstrong, Southwestern territory bands, and Southern Negro culture, both *Invisible Man* and *Juneteenth* are literary texts that perform pragmatist cultural critiques.

Parker's Blues: Identity Deferred

Even as Ellison was rejecting the music, bebop was tightening its threads in the cultural mainstream's weave and the national government was co-opting jazz for the purposes of international diplomacy. A world away from Minton's, Monroe's, and St. Nick's Pub, the Soviets were stockpiling atomic weapons like obsessed hobbyists but at home Negroes were marching, forsaking stubbornly such luxuries as the Montgomery, Alabama, public transportation system. In an attempt to promote American culture to the burgeoning and politically unaligned Third World while stifling illustrations of American apartheid, Dwight Eisenhower, a warrior and staunch segregationist, got Dizzy, as Penny Von Eschen has written. President Eisenhower requisitioned and earmarked special monies for the President's Special International Program, a provision to send jazz artists abroad as musical ambassadors for American democracy.

In one of the great comic ironies of twentieth-century American cultural history, the initial group of ambassadors was Dizzy Gillespie's big band. Gillespie, like many bebop musicians, had dodged the World War II draft board by showing "attitude" and speaking openly about shooting white American soldiers instead of Germans in cases of "mistaken identity."[13] This allowed Gillespie, the main "professor" and theorist of bebop, to define the new idiom as a clear musical intelligence. When Gillespie toured under the auspices of Eisenhower's program he gained insider status but he brought to the party a radical "outsider art." Bebop, vilified by white jazz critics and black dance audiences in the 1940s and early 1950s as the antimelody, "undanceable" music of crazy Negroes, junkies, and hipsters, had become part of the government's Cold

War strategy. Ike tried to turn the world toward the American form of democracy using Dizzy and bebop, a music that spoke of jazz aesthetics, critiqued American life, and expressed African Americans' desires for liberation from the oppressive status quo.[14]

Coming into his literary powers in the mid-1950s, James Baldwin had begun to communicate the same idiomatic aesthetics, social critiques, and argument for Negro political equality that bebop was expressing. Even now, Baldwin's fiction and literary journalism illustrates over and again how our democratic desires can be fulfilled by using "the dance-beat improvisation of experience" to create new networks of social communities and political solidarity. Baldwin used improvisation to build public, pragmatic discourse communities in which African American history and cultural expression revised the status quo political vocabulary.

Though Baldwin firmly believed in the maintenance of his individual identity and intellectual freedom, he also wanted to reframe the American public for the purposes of developing a better democratic community. Baldwin, like Ellison, believed that novels could symbolically illustrate democratic attitudes. However, Baldwin rejected Ellison's belief that the artist exhibited his democratic bona fides by producing works that acted symbolically. Baldwin understood, instead, that his role as black intellectual called upon him to *represent* his critical and political views physically. Serving as a witness to the CRM and American democracy, Baldwin was a symbolic actor improvising and performing his critiques publicly.

One instance of the confluence of fiction, cultural critique, and jazz is Baldwin's classic short story "Sonny's Blues." In Baldwin's story Charlie Parker's musical influence on Sonny's aesthetic provides the story's narrator, Sonny's unnamed brother, with the language for describing a new conception of black masculinity and the reader with a language for forming into a pious community — for reconstructing American democracy.

The story, at its basic level, is about fraternity and family history. However, the narrator explains that his responsibility to Sonny requires that he be a witness to his brother's human trial, learning the aesthetics of salvation and self-invention from the music. In a flashback, early in the story, the narrator recalls learning of Sonny's desire to be a jazz musician for the first time. Trying to grasp exactly what Sonny imagines his professional track might mean, the narrator asks if he means to be a "'good-time'" entertainer like "Louis Armstrong."[15] Angered by the comparison, Sonny proclaims that he's not interested in performing any "old-time, down home crap," but wants instead to emulate Bird, Charlie Parker, "one of the greatest jazz musicians alive" (Baldwin 1998a, 846). Again we find at the center of the text the crucial opposition of Parker and Armstrong. As a sign of the Southern, Negro past, Armstrong's antiquated sound cannot stand up to Parker's expressions of contemporary Negro reality. But Parker is also Baldwin's sign for genius and self-destructive obsession.

Even if only a shadow character within "Sonny's Blues," Parker inspires the kind of release that Baldwin finds crucial for developing a more free America. Once introduced in the story, Parker's apparition grounds the narrative within the context of bebop's emergence as the chosen language of postwar Negro artistry. As the story progresses, Sonny's rigorous piano training turns him into a "sound," one that doesn't "make any sense" to the others living with him. But the real problem is that Sonny's emulation of Parkerian artistic drive is too consuming: he becomes a heroin addict like Parker.[16]

We might think of Sonny as one of Ellison's underground youths, unable to distinguish between Parker's art and his symbolic image, and willing to accept Bird's shit as gospel. But rather than reading Parker through the white-made cloak over his humanity, as Ellison does, Baldwin reads Parker as a symbol of the tragic human trial and a mechanism for discussing improvised expressions of black manhood. Baldwin believed that bebop, as an aesthetic of self-creation and salvation, was integral to African American political transcendence. During the CRM, Baldwin argued that American citizens, modeling themselves after the black jazz musician's improvisational ethic, could finally achieve democracy in America.

Even as he was framing a reconstructed democracy, Baldwin was also imagining a new black masculinity. Baldwin often argued that part of reconstructing American democracy included addressing the historical consequences of Negro life. For the author this meant interrogating the manifold and private painful experiences of Negro men. For example, in "Sonny's Blues" bebop comes to symbolize the narrator's public discourse on the blues and black masculinity, on American racial history and Negro identity, and on the private, existential self-knowledge and public artistic/intellectual performance.

Baldwin's critique of the music stems from his concern for American social and political life. Eddie S. Glaude Jr. suggests that Baldwin "understood African Americans as intimately connected to the fragile experiment [of American democracy]. He saw it was *necessary* to embrace this flawed country even as he grasped, perhaps more clearly than most, how blocked grief altered these peculiar blues people's orientation to this place."[17] Baldwin encouraged Negroes to embrace the flawed democracy even as they understood that corrupted system as a major source of their blues. He reasoned that experimenting with blues expressions would produce the *necessary* discourse for releasing American democracy from its blocked growth. Improvising on Kenneth Burke's conception of piety, Baldwin portrays jazz performance in "Sonny's Blues" as the pathway to secular piety—the religion of memory and self-invention—and thus, instigating pious public ceremonies, rituals that translate individual, personal memories into the vocabulary of group solidarity and collective political health.

Burke's theorization of secular piety is a useful concept for understanding the role that Parker plays within Baldwin's critique of American culture in "Sonny's Blues." Piety, as Burke suggests we understand it, is not about religious ideals as such, though they can be referenced, or about ethics—what is good or bad for us. Piety is not another name for theistic beliefs or practices. As well, piety does not speak of ethics as such. Knowing that an act is pious does not tell us whether the act is good or bad for us; an adherent to a particular religion may or may not be pious. Rather, Burke writes, piety is about being loyal to the roots of our being, "[a] deep connection [to] the 'remembrance of things past.'"[18] Piety, then, is an attitude toward personal history and displays a desire to flesh things out, connecting experiences together into a succinct whole.

Baldwin understood intuitively that listening to jazz musicians like Parker improvise encourages us to reimagine our own identities and histories, to create selves drawn out from our own experiences. One of the lessons of bebop and jazz history is that the space for pious performance must be fought for. But as it is with Sonny and his brother, the pivot toward pious awareness or performance is agonistic. And that agon is against the existential self as often as it is against other physical opponents. Pious improvising layers private and public selves, social experiences and cultural history in the quest for meaning. Burke's definition of piety parallels Berliner's analyses of jazz improvisation.

Recalling Berliner's instructive definitions of improvisation and jazz as a way of life, we can hear Bird's compositions, improvised themes, and solos emerging from his specific orientation to jazz history and his personal education and experiences. Each lyrical phrase of a jazz musician's output is like a line of an ever-emerging poem about the private self engaging with the public world. Like piety, improvisation "is the artistic expression of human motivations; it rarely, if ever, appears 'pure'"(Eddy 2003, 27). When we listen to Parker improvising, for example, our imaginations are piqued because his style of attack expresses a pious attitude toward both the quest for meaning in personal experience and the performance of identity's constructedness. As a liberating god, Parker, the poet-improviser, is always pious.[19]

Given Baldwin's pious relation to Negro history and his personal experience, his choice to use jazz improvisation as a theory in his art and criticism makes sense. Jazz instrumental performance, which has most often been a masculine-oriented field, is framed by fraternal and patriarchal battles for position in the public performance spaces. Though musical cutting sessions in bebop (and physical battle royals in public) were often tests of African American manhood, bebop and jazz have always been tempered by Romantic artistic ideals. The jazz ethos, like Romanticism, claims that incorporating "feminine imagination within masculine reason" is the sign of genius; it is an aesthetic sensibility that privileges "originality, creativity, and emotional expression" (Porter 2002, 30). This insight might help us rethink what Ross Posnock calls Baldwin's "androgyny."

Thinking of Baldwin's sense of "the permeable self of nonidentity," his "imperative of 'love,'" and his homosexuality, Posnock explains that Baldwin's pragmatist inclinations rise from the dispersal of his identity into androgyny, into a practice of cosmopolitan selfhood.[20] In order to achieve a Romantic or androgynous self, one must be able to see (or hear selfhood) differently. Posnock points out that Baldwin learned from his mentor, the painter Beauford Delaney, how to see beyond "discrete definition" toward "the fact of simultaneity and connection" (Posnock 1998, 231). This way of seeing has both artistic and political dimensions for Baldwin. Many of Baldwin's fictions are about male characters learning to accept the layered, contingent nature of identity across national, racial, sexual, gendered, and psychological planes. Interestingly, some of Baldwin's collection titles speak to the author's sense of identity deferred: *Notes of a Native Son, Nobody Knows My Name, No Name in the Street*. Baldwin's "homosexuality intensified his differential vision, making him acutely sensitive to the artifice of bounded identity. . . . [His] namelessness announces his American-ness" (Posnock 1998, 231). But Baldwin's namelessness also announces his pursuit of meaning in personal experience and his desire to perform identity's constructedness; whatever is American about his name has been improvised.

While we can be sure that Baldwin's sexuality forced him to imagine identity differently, a better reading suggests that blues idiom music taught him how to join existential realization and aesthetic insight into a social hope of transforming jazz improvisation into a way of life. Baldwin figured his artistic attitude by drawing himself in league with Ray Charles, Miles Davis, and the "universal blues" they performed. Baldwin explained: "I think I really helplessly model myself on jazz musicians and try to write the way they sound. . . . I am aiming at what Henry James called 'perception at the pitch of passion.'"[21] As Scott Saul explains, "Perception at the pitch of passion is a high-toned translation of the blues riff" and it is also the name for Baldwin's own improvisation on Henry James's literary sense of simultaneity and connection (Saul 2005, 73).

"Sonny's Blues" provides a dramatization of Baldwin's pragmatism. Pushing Parkerian bopisms against Armstrong's paradigm-establishing anesthetization, Sonny is able to improvise an idiomatic solo performance. Sonny's improvised solo at the end of the story draws together the reasoned, articulate artistic statement with the personal, painful expression and performs it publicly. Sonny improvises on his dark personal history in order to recreate himself. However, his music also communicates to the narrator the universal language of joyful transcendence—the use of past experience to invent hopeful communal realities. Sonny's performance can illuminate a passage out of the blight because his improvising concentrates and enlarges his "immediate experience"; it challenges the audience to imagine that the music is also evoking meaning about their own experiences.[22]

Improvisation and illumination provide access to salvation in Baldwin's work. In Baldwin's sense of it, salvation arrives with an awareness of or an ability to "sing" the blues. The narrator realizes this intelligence as he listens to Sonny's band play in Greenwich Village: "He and his boys up there were keeping it new, at the risk of ruin, destruction, madness, and death, in order to find new ways to make us listen. For, while the tale of how we suffer, and how we are delighted, and how we may triumph is never new, it always must be heard. There isn't any other tale to tell, it's the only light we've got in all this darkness" (Baldwin 1998a, 862). Like Parker's, Sonny's sacrifice, his willingness to play his blues and expose his identity, is pious. Though he gave up the pulpit and religious piety in his teens, Baldwin developed a theory of secular piety for the American public that he hoped would lead toward the political salvation of American democracy. Parker's death forces us to be witnesses to American democracy's stunted growth and the mortal costs of mythologies about blackness and masculinity. As Dewey explains, democracy can only be consummated when "free social inquiry is indissolubly wedded to the art of full and moving communication."[23] As pious witnesses, Baldwin argues, we must also begin improvising a reconstructed or new democratic community.

Hope Honks the Revolution

When the Gillespie band traveled across the Middle East in 1956, Bird, who succumbed to the sweet murder of the heroin needle, had been dead for only fourteen months. While he was alive, Parker did not gain the notoriety of fellow boppers Gillespie, Monk, or Roach. Yet, in the jazz criticism of the last fifty-two years, Parker's musical oeuvre is often heard as the most dramatic combination of emotional expression, aesthetic innovation, intellectual rigor, and political statement.

By the early 1960s Parker's "way of melodic thinking" could be heard in jazz, rock and roll, country music, film and television scores, and symphonic works.[24] But those same critics also explain that Parker's oversized appetites for food, sweets, drink, and heroin and the oscillations of his personality from charming to cantankerous clouded the reception of his musical mastery during his life. However, with death came legend and mythology to color Parker's craftsmanship. In postwar New York City, in neighborhoods like Greenwich Village, the haven of the Beats and hipsters, and on 52nd Street, the mecca of jazz clubs, Parker was legendary as an intellectual/musical savant *and* as a greedy heroin junkie. As the anointed king outsider among all outsiders, Bird symbolized the drug-addled, "free" artistic, antisocial marginal white beatniks and hipsters wanted to inhabit.

Parker's music and life serve as models for narratives about Negro ingenuity and degradation—jazz as the music of democracy; for conceptions of Negro folk forms, like bebop, as militant cultural resistance; and for claims about Negroes' natural tendencies toward insolence and depravity. As a major figure in bebop culture, Parker, especially posthumously, presents a complex image of African American identity. Outside the coterie who invented, perpetuated, and lived within its culture, bebop was in large part misheard and misunderstood by the American public. But then bebop is at least one measure of how the rest of African American life and culture is read by Americans—at turns enticing, at others repellant, and, in either case, inscrutable to the point of being easily essentialized. Though Gillespie became a cultural ambassador and helped carry jazz into the Cold War political world, Parker became a symbol for African American identification and its complexities during the liberation movement. In choosing bebop to represent American culture abroad, Ike and the state department unwittingly presented to the world the most intricate and complex musical analysis of American reality; they served the world some Bird.

Since blues idiom improvisational music recharges traditional forms, heeding their influence through quotation and reinvention, Parker's "linguistic" innovations were present in the arrangements that Gillespie charted for the orchestra's Middle Eastern tour. As Yusef Komunyakaa imagines "Charlie could be two places at once,/ always arm-wrestling himself in the dark."[25] Parker's music, and bebop performance in general, puts the performer and the audience in multiple places simultaneously and generates layered sensibilities. Parker's sound was tragic and comic, baroque and danceable, raucous and uncultivated, intellectual and sophisticated, and often balanced its indebtedness to Negro folkways with expressions of high-toned Western modernism.

Rather than reading his simultaneities as a series of opposing binaries, we can best think of Parker's doublings—his "rebopped bebops" as Ellison calls them—as the necessary consequences of African American artistic and intellectual performance. Yet Parker's symbolism in the white underworld had nothing to do with what he influenced or expressed musically. So, after his death, when Village graffiti artists began draping New York City with the celebratory "Bird Lives," to whom exactly were they referring?

Like Baldwin's, LeRoi Jones/Amiri Baraka's pragmatism emerges in his belief that bebop was the total merger of aesthetics and social politics—Emersonian poetics and the search for blackness. Jones/Baraka argues that Parker's musical attitude, for instance, initiated a cultural transition from the diluted forms of mainstream expression back to the blues-based, Negro-engineered musical genius. Bebop innovators shrugged off stereotypical roles as Negro "entertainers," picking up and carrying, instead, the mantles of serious artistry. Parker's seriousness, Jones/Baraka explains, was not only about the kind and quality of the music, but also about the ways in which his music expressed the liberation movement's new politics of blackness.

Contrary to Ellison and Baldwin, Jones/Baraka's attention to bebop and Parker articulates a desire to unearth the foundations of African American identity. While this desire strikes essentialist notes, I argue that in Jones/Baraka's vocabulary "blackness" is a synonym of "improvisation." According to Jones/Baraka, Parker's music—his ability to play riff chords or "changes" with speed, agility, and emotion—became the avant-garde language for the political/social transformations of the CRM. Jones/Baraka argues that Parker's music inspired changes from status quo notions of identity toward conceptions of transitional, improvisational black identities. Jones/Baraka's transitional literature, like Parker's musical voicings, was forcefully spiraling toward change.

In Jones/Baraka's play *The Dutchman* (1964), Clay, the male lead, muses that while Parker's musical message is "Up your ass, feeble-minded ofay! Up your ass," his misguided critics are "there talking about the tortured genius of Charlie Parker." Had Parker "walked up to East 67th Street and killed the first ten white people he saw," he would not have needed to play a single note of music.[26] But what Parker did was improvise musical "violence" instead of murdering white people. As with Ellison's and Baldwin's visions of the American scene, Jones/Baraka's claim depends on the notion that jazz improvisation can transform masculine violence into symbolic democratic performance.

Parker is a "crazy nigger turning [his back] on sanity," Clay argues (Jones/Baraka 1999, 97). Refusing sanity and the false comforts of "Plutonic citizenship," Parker is able to keep his music mainlined to the blues. Instead of integrating into American society in the name of hegemonic majorities, Negro artists like Parker asserted citizenship in the sound of the music. Parker's blues idiom improvisations speak of "citizenship" and "freedom" untethered from their political status quo definitions.

In Parker's powerful soloing we hear the invention of bebop's poetics. His performances illustrate an interesting revision of Emerson's strong poet. Emerson argues that "the poets made all the words, and therefore language is the archives of history, and if we must say it, a sort of tomb of the muses."[27] Parker introduced technical concepts and lyrical phrases that expanded popular and classical musical vocabulary and his recordings archive our cultural history in the middle of the twentieth century. In *Dutchman* Jones/Baraka wants to argue that in our cultural context, where symbol making is culture making, Bird's music ushers us toward new thoughts, unlocks us from the status quo "and admits us to a new scene" where we accept our culture as poetic and invent a new discourse that acts accordingly (Emerson 1960, 236).

The strongest poets, Emerson argues, never stop exploring the "double meaning, or shall I say the quadruple or the centuple or much more manifold meaning of every sensuous fact" (Emerson 1960, 223). Emerson's suggestion is an apt description of Parker's very ability (as in his introductory statement and mid-track solo on the classic recording of "Parker's Mood")[28] to sensually stroke an improvised figure or elegantly embellish a composed phrase, riding up and down scales exposing the "manifold" meanings of musical facts. Our strong poets also remind us lesser language actors that "man is only half himself, the other half is his expression" (Emerson 1960, 223). In Jones/Baraka's play, Clay's critique of

Parker's impetus (expressing himself instead of murdering others) and challenge (expressing musical truth to the powerful status quo) extends another Emersonian conception: because poets show us that using symbols has emancipating power, they are liberating gods. Clay believes that his liberation has begun in his acceptance of Parker's bebop poetics.

It is interesting to think of Richard Rorty's vision of our poeticized culture as an extension not only of Emerson's notion of the poet as the sayer, namer, and representative of beauty, but also of Jones/Baraka's claims about Parker's emancipating poetics. Rorty, writing in near-Burkean fashion, explains that accepting some conception of linguistic symbolic action will free us to produce a culture that would not insist that "we find the real wall behind the painted ones, the real touchstones of truth as opposed to touchstones which are merely cultural artifacts. It would be a culture which, precisely by appreciating that *all* touchstones are artifacts, would take as its goal the creation of ever more various and multicolored artifacts."[29] Rather than accepting the "sanity" of "the real" or "the truth", Parker provides us access to a musical vocabulary that encourages us to imagine and improvise ever varied, multicolored truths.

This is what Jones/Baraka means in the story "Screamers" when he writes that Parker's language is Negro universal, Negro classical: his listeners wake up "whispering [Parker's signature tune] 'Ornithology' in blank verse."[30] Parker's iambic lyricism communicates a tough American Negro pragmatism. In "Screamers" Jones/Baraka imagines an extension of Parker in the character Lynn Hope. Hope's performance flows from the forces of nationalist political energy. Hope's repeated "honking" creates a musical message, the sonic pulse of revolution, and he marches his band and a club full of dancers into the streets of Newark where the music is "made to destroy the ghetto" (Jones/Baraka 2000, 186). The insurrection is a collective, creative protest—soul changes stomped out in the middle of the street. The structure of the story develops from the looping, repeated riffs and associative musings of the narrator's mind. "The sound [of those musings and of Hope's honking]," explains Jones/Baraka's narrator, "itself became a basis for thought" (Jones/Baraka 2000, 184). The sound becomes a thought practice, a new philosophical/political paradigm — music as symbolic action and instigation for collective political action.

While Jones/Baraka dramatizes these concepts for the stage, we can also find the elements of his philopolitical attitude at work in his jazz criticism. An obvious place to read this is Jones/Baraka's critique of John Coltrane, an acolyte and heir to Parker's legacy, and a former bandmate/student of both Gillespie and Monk. One of Jones/Baraka's main arguments about jazz is that improvisation is about performing the self in transition and/or transformation. Two representative examples that Jones/Baraka would bring to our attention from Coltrane's oeuvre are his solos on Thelonious Monk's "Trinkle, Tinkle"(1957) and on the classic Coltrane Quartet's recording of Rodgers and Hammerstein's "My Favorite Things" (1960). The two solos, performed on tenor and soprano saxophones respectively, play out Coltrane's transition from boppish inclinations to the definition of his *sound,* the generative thematic and conceptual style of the post-bebop avant-garde.

In 1957, working with Monk's band during its famous summer-long stay at the Five Spot in Manhattan, Coltrane learned that playing with the piano maestro demanded awareness all the time because a musician could suddenly feel as if he'd "stepped into an empty elevator shaft."[31] Pushed by Monk to perform under the pressure of his compositions and shaking loose the influence of Lester Young, Dexter Gordon, and Parker, Coltrane learned to play away from dominant notes, find the power of altered changes, and realize the "simple truths" of minor chords. On stage and on record, Coltrane learned to play more freely when Monk left him without piano accompaniment, forcing him to rely on the rhythm section's buoyancy and tenor saxophone's harmonics.

In the early 1960s when Coltrane introduced the soprano saxophone to his repertoire and recordings, he, along with alto saxophonist Ornette Coleman and the pianist Cecil Taylor, had begun expanding bebop's lessons into a full-on re-evaluation of jazz performance. Taylor, Coleman, and Coltrane did not find bebop or its gospel sister, hard bop, musically finite; they found in bop's lessons opportunities for inventing new performance techniques and connections to new musical systems. However, rather than hearing the postwar jazz avant-garde as improvisers on traditional elements, jazz critics thought these musicians were blowing ideas into the air like so many dandelion spores: they fertilized petite, flowering weeds, but not full, lush, varietal gardens.[32]

What many critics missed at mid-century was that Coltrane's introduction of the soprano sax to avant-garde performance invoked Sidney Bechet's mastery of the horn while also turning jazz toward Eastern promises: "My Favorite Things" is both exotic and ancient-sounding.[33] The soprano sax suits Coltrane's proclivities, writes Jones/Baraka, because the horn allows him to turn "his attention to that old problem in jazz of improvising on a simple and terribly strict melodic line."[34] But Coltrane, exploring his tutorials in bebop, spawns a new musical attack and new ways of constructing his improvised solos on "My Favorite Things" while still referring to "old problems" of jazz. Coltrane's muscular performances asserted a new African American sensibility born of the tumultuous and dangerous political times of the freedom struggle.

In "Screamers" Hope's play is meant to evoke both Parker and Coltrane as models for merging jazz, improvisation, and collective political action. He creates charivari and instigates liberating movement—swaying, swinging, stomping, and marching. Hope's music finds presence in the bodies of dancers and they become a black body politic. Jones/Baraka imagines Hope's musical figures as inspiration for individual improvisations worked out in unison; as Brent Hayes Edwards suggests, the music is a "telling inarticulacy" that signifies.[35] Hope's improvisations signify, as John Dewey might argue, that the "junction of the new and the old is not a mere composition of forces, but is a re-creation in which the present impulsion gets form and solidity while the old, the 'stored,' material is literally revived, given new life and soul through having to meet a new situation."[36] Through the confluence of Hope's improvisational riffing and the narrator's musings, Jones/Baraka reimagines Dewey's vision as a newer political force. Jazz aligns well with pragmatism because both require a rigorous understanding of disciplinary traditions that are enlivened through borrowing from other traditions or systems. However, Hope's honk has a historical resonance that takes us toward pragmatism with a black difference. Improvisation, then, is a synonym for Deweyan experimentation wherein secondary racial identity/racial antiessentialism can stand in for antimetaphysical attitudes.

If the sound itself is the spark of a new self, a new philosophy, then Hope's repeated riff is like the blues holler or field holler that Jones/Baraka has called the initiation or assertion of African American citizenship:

> There were no formal stories about the Negro's existence in America passed down in any pure African tongue. The stories, myths, moral examples, etc., given in African were about Africa. When America became important enough to the African to be passed on, in those *formal* renditions, to the young, those renditions were in some kind of Afro-American language. And finally, when a man looked up in some anonymous field and shouted, 'Oh Ahm tired a dis mess,/ Oh, yes Ahm so tired a dis mess,' you can be sure he was an American.[37]

The "blues shout" is the signal of and for change; the noise creates a fissure, an improvisational space for self-naming or renaming, or the invention of an new self altogether. In "Screamers" the poet/improviser symbolizes the possibility of his social desires. We should read Lynn Hope's (and his name points to authorial wishes) action in "Screamers" as a fictional dramatization of improvisation's hopefulness, its philopolitical promise.

As I will argue in Movement IV, in his transitional poems, Jones/Baraka illustrates how we produce new instruments for dealing with old problems. Like Parker or Coltrane, Jones/Baraka uses poetry to display the shifts or transformations of his selves. Just as bebop and hard bop introduce the total merger of musical innovation and social politics, Jones/Baraka imagines that his poetic innovations, his improvisations of self, merge with and change the nature of the cultural and political networks we live within. Following Dewey's themes of art as experience, Jones/Baraka draws poetry and jazz improvisation together so that he can simultaneously exercise the culture's diverse and contradictory parts while poeticizing the spiraling self in transition. Jones/Baraka provides the American public with a poetics for transforming American culture and politics with the inclusion of improvisational African American identities.

Black Is, Black Ain't

Violence, Black Masculinity, and the Novel as Democratic Symbol

As Ralph Ellison explains, one of the dangerous realities of African American life before the 1950s and 1960s was "the persistence of racial violence and unavailability of legal protection" (Ellison 1995b, xv–xvi).[1] The violence perpetuated on Negroes was a consistent barrier to their integration into the bounty of American life. In his novel *Invisible Man,* Ellison examines the connections among racial violence, black male identity, and the ironies of American democracy. The protagonist must run a physical and psychological gauntlet in his search for personal identity. The novel's drama is produced by the protagonist's awareness of his own tragicomic existential status. Ellison uses the blues to trigger a succession of symbolic events on the protagonist's journey. By way of the character, Ellison is able to illustrate that "the making of self . . . is linked to the making of history."[2]

Ellison wants the novel to highlight the conflicts between American democratic and American social realities. He underlines the protagonist's narrative of personal realization and philosophical change with violent acts meant to illustrate the rejection of Negroes as Americans and humans. Invisible man must engage cooperatively but antagonistically with the barriers and dangers of the political and cultural system. John Callahan calls Ellison's vision (and the protagonist's negotiations) "moral historicism." But C. Vann Woodward's term "ironic historicism" brings us closer to Ellison's blues. The ironic historian must observe and recount with detachment and sympathy. He "must be able to appreciate both elements in the incongruity that go to make up the ironic situation, both the virtue and the vice to which pretensions of virtue lead."[3] Ellison's version of ironic historicism blends the novel with blues idiom insight to frame a tragicomic interpretation of African American identity and American culture. Ellison the ironist argues that a close, honest examination of Negro life exposes our national moral predicament: American democracy is pregnant with its contradictions (Ellison 1995a, 704).

Thinking of Ellison's protagonist/narrator as an actor in a pragmatist drama, taking in the narrative of his plight, we, listener/readers, also learn that our personal stories are connected to his. Just as the blues idiom soloist makes her story the audience's narrative, Ellison's ironic history becomes the national story. As Ellison creates the protagonist's history and name, rather than eradicating blackness, he forces the audience to read from the Negro's perspective. Richard Rorty explains that the ironist philosopher is a nominalist and a historicist, an antiessentialist storyteller. So too is *Invisible Man*'s blues idiom narrator. However, Ellison's irony explains something different from Rorty's. Rorty's ironist tells individual and private stories but refuses to interrogate the implications of those realizations on public, sociopolitical hopes. Ellison's ironic historicist, his protagonist/narrator, argues that his private existential shifts carry larger implications for American Negro sociopolitical hopes and the national desire to achieve American democracy.

My reading of *Invisible Man* challenges Rorty's pragmatic perspective of "Western liberal ethnocentrism." Rorty's Deweyan sense of social hope obscures what Woodward calls the "tragic aspects and ironic implications" of American history in favor of the "national legend of success and victory." What Woodward might suggest about Rorty's ardent desire to maintain one's philosophical changes as an exclusively private enterprise is that it perpetuates an "infant illusion of American innocence and virtue" (Woodward 1993, 209).[4] Ellison tells us that social hopes and private changes are deeply connected where American democracy, American history, and Negro identity are concerned. The blues idiom provides pragmatism with a difference: it allows us to acknowledge the social, public significance of private improvisations of the self.

Blues idiom pragmatism is also about aesthetics: invisible man's journey to improvised selfhood is a metaphor for Ellison's process of improvising on the traditions of American literature and the novel. The chief significance of *Invisible Man*, Ellison writes, is "its experimental attitude, and its attempt to return to the mood of personal moral responsibility for democracy which typified the best of our nineteenth-century fiction. . . . That period took a much greater responsibility for the condition of democracy."[5] Like a trumpeter working through the catalog of sounds, concepts, and styles of the jazz trumpet tradition, Ellison works the American literary canon to place himself within it while simultaneously creating new narrative possibilities from traditional elements. Ellison's process recreates and expands the tradition's boundaries.

Ellison's jazz and literary criticism paired with his fiction provides a formidable intellectual statement about blackness, identity, American culture, and democracy. In order to negotiate these multiple interests Ellison introduced his theory of literary improvisation onto his palette of tropes, techniques, and concepts. For instance, in *Invisible Man* Ellison riffs on his definition of the blues, improvising various scenes of symbolic tragicomic violence meant to communicate his claims about history, blackness, and democracy at once. Ellison believed in the cathartic qualities of blues idiom expression and, in a revision of Du Bois, wanted his novels to disseminate ideas about the practice of artful American living. Ellison's version of art as propaganda narrates Negro experience (identity, history, and culture) as the epitome of America's high principles and the sacred political documents—the Constitution and the Declaration of Independence. I'll begin by analyzing Ellison's use of violence and the mixture of private ironies and public hopes, race, and masculinity in the short story "Flying Home." This early story introduced themes of masculine violence and tragicomedy that Ellison subsequently improvised upon and polished in *Invisible Man*.

I

Leaning back on his elbows, his throbbing ankle broken, Todd, the protagonist of "Flying Home," thinks, "If I were a prizefighter I would be more human. Not a monkey doing tricks, but a man."[6] A Tuskegee Airman learning to fly but not piloting combat missions during World War II, Todd must come to terms with the dangerous psychological and physical terrain that Negro men must travel en route to achievement. Ellison's story interrogates the consequential dangers of Todd's falling behind the black veil of Southern agrarian life after he attempts to fly too steeply, too quickly away from blackness.[7]

Knocked back one hundred years when a buzzard clips his hatch shield, Todd, who represents technological advancement, modernist sensibility, and theoretical understanding, enters an earthly "storm of blood and blackness" when he comes to after his crash (Ellison 1996, 155). Jefferson, a Negro sharecropper present when the pilot awakens, represents the kind of blackness Todd is trying to fly over, transcend. Jefferson attempts to console the pilot by recounting his own attempts at flying. A natural born "liar," Jefferson's story of death and heavenly flight becomes a symbol to Todd. In his moment of death, Jefferson explains, he arrives in heaven and quickly earns his wings. Once tested, Jefferson begins to fly across heaven with speed and agility but without adopting the harness required of Negro angels. The harness is meant to make flying harder for black angels; even heaven is segregated! Adept with his soaring, Jefferson even learns to speed along on one wing. But his skill and rapidity are too much for the white angels to countenance. Already guilty of flying without the harness, Jefferson is expelled from heaven by Saint Peter. On his descent, rather than going to hell with Satan, Jefferson is given a parachute and a map of Alabama (a place not altogether different from hell for Negroes).

The story-within-the-story acts as a metaphor for Todd's hopes of escaping the harnesses that keep him from transcending race and proving his worthiness to his white superiors in the Air Corps. While Todd recognizes the tragedy of his own fall in Jefferson's story, he cannot understand why Jefferson finds the personal tale of heavenly rejection so humorous. The joke comes from Jefferson's awareness that his blackness is not a real harness, a real physical impediment. The traps of racial order are artificial instead of innate. Rather than feeling braced by essentialist notions of blackness, Jefferson exclaims that absent his harness, he was "the flyin'est son-of-a-bitch what ever hit heaven" (Ellison 1996, 160).

Jefferson's lie about heaven is coupled with a dangerous truth: the unpredictable attitude of Graves, on whose land the plane has crashed.

The danger that the white landowner poses dashes Todd's hope that the Air Corps will notice that he is missing and come to his rescue. Upon hearing Jefferson tell of Graves's rash and oft-unprovoked cruelty, Todd has the sensation of "being caught in a white neighborhood after dark" (Ellison 1996, 168). Even more stunning for Todd is that Jefferson is able to bifurcate himself in his speech on Graves. One Jefferson "shook with fits of belly laughter" while the other one "looked on with detachment" (Ellison 1996, 169). Graves's unpredictability is affirmed when he shows up not with medical doctors or paramedics but with attendants from the asylum from which his brother has recently escaped. Straightjacketed and dumbfounded, Todd lies speechless as Graves ignores all relevant or logical ideas about the plane, claiming instead that the pilot must be crazy because "you caint let the nigguh git up that high without his going crazy. The nigguh brain ain't built right for high altitude" (Ellison 1996, 171). Jefferson's joke and Graves's farcical philosophy are amplified when Graves plants his boot in the center of Todd's chest, stifling his protestations and sending him into a spasm of eye-bulging coughing that surprisingly induces laughter. Todd's convulsion of laughter becomes his "sole salvation in an insane world of outrage and humiliation. It brought a certain relief" (Ellison 1996, 172).

Todd laughs to keep from crying. He has evaded acknowledging his blackness or his proximity to violence in order to "avoid the unsettling risk of seeing [his] own 'impurities,'" the places where his self spills beyond its tight boundaries.[8] Todd evades this tragic knowledge "out of an effort to postpone completing that identity which [he is] compelled nonetheless to seek" (Ellison 1995a, 714). While Todd cannot exempt himself from Southern racial violence or essentialism by flying over them, he can achieve personal identity by confronting the African American history he wants to escape. In so doing, Todd also learns the joke built into Jefferson's bifurcation: black identity acknowledges the irrationality and masking involved in racial identification by sincerely performing detachment from essentialism. Todd can also overcome the harnesses that racial violence and essentialized blackness place on him. His violent, tragic fall helps him consider what blackness is and what blackness ain't.

"Flying Home" presents Ellison's theory of African American psychology. Todd's explosion of laughter at the end of the story reveals that "our weaknesses have a strength built into them, ready for reappropriation" (Eddy 2003, 9). Todd's confrontation with his fears—of being connected to Southern rural blackness and of the random power of white racist violence—helps him develop a clear vision of the harnesses he has placed on himself. While the strait-jacket literally clips his limbs, keeps him from physically flying, Graves's boot thrust kick-starts the blues tragicomedy. Todd's tragedy stems from his belief that he has bypassed the traps of blackness and racial violence; his tragedy charges him to improvise a usable identity. Todd sees the comedy in his situation when the chaos reveals the disconnection between his desire to be acknowledged as a human being and the irrational denial of his humanity within American society. Laughter becomes Todd's salve; laughter becomes the will to persevere or survive. Ellison argues that there is a "subtle triumph hidden in such laughter . . . more affirmative than raw anger [because it provides] a vague but intriguing new perspective" (Ellison 1995b, xv–xvi).

The mixture of tragedy and farce fascinated Ellison, and his work actually seems to burst from the liminal space between those poles. Tragicomedy allows Ellison to improvise the terms of his critical vision rather than rely on the standard language for interpreting African American life or American democracy. Ellison turned away from sociology, for instance, because its concepts placed the onus on the Negro's brown skin, rendering him "un-visible—whether at high noon in Macy's window or illuminated by flaming torches and flashbulbs while undergoing the ritual sacrifice that was dedicated to the ideal of white supremacy" (Ellison 1995b, xv). Sociology cannot help Ellison examine artistically or critically the surreal disconnections between American political ideals and the realities of black American life. While mid-twentieth-century sociologists were suggesting that racism worked because one's "blackness" can be seen, Ellison argued that racism worked because it denied both American history and Negroes' humanity. Graves denies Todd's humanity in order to maintain the Southern sociopolitical status quo that held that Negroes were not part of American technological progress or the struggle to defend democratic principles. The denial initiates Todd's blues; he gains, we might imagine, a second self, like Jefferson, in order to act out the symbolic gap between himself as sacrificial figure and himself as human.

II

Invisible Man is framed by the protagonist's passage through acts of ritualized violence, beginning with pugilistic confrontation and ending with castration. In the prologue the protagonist relates an anecdote about coming to blows with a white man who has bumped into him on a city sidewalk. The "inner eyes" of white folks, the protagonist/narrator explains early on, are developed to not see him, to render him invisible. Although there are advantages to not being seen, the narrator suggests, invisibility can also make you "doubt if you really exist." The protagonist's suspicions spur his resentment and prompt him to "begin to bump people back." "Let me confess," invisible man continues, "[you feel] that way most of the time. You ache with the need to convince yourself that you do exist in the real world, that you're a part of all the sound and anguish, and you strike out with your fists, you curse and you swear to make them recognize you. And, alas, it's seldom successful" (Ellison 1995b, 4).

After being bumped and cursed on the sidewalk, the protagonist repeatedly head butts his white assailant, dropping him to his knees. With the "tall blond man" bloodied and semiconscious, the narrator demands an apology; he demands to be recognized as a human: "[I was] holding him in the collar with one hand, and opening the knife with my teeth—when it occurred to me that the man had not seen me, actually; that he, as far as he knew, was in the midst of a walking nightmare! And I stopped my blade, slicing the air as I pushed him away, letting him fall back to the street. . . . He lay there, moaning on the asphalt; a man almost killed by a phantom" (Ellison 1995b, 4). The blues edges out as the white man, with a knife at his jugular, refuses to see (visually or psychologically) the protagonist as human.[9] The blues edges out as invisible man offers his opponent choices: recognize the protagonist's humanity or be stripped of his own. Unnerved by the prospects of all the choices the protagonist turns to flee, laughing, amused by the "crazy discovery" that he may have freed the blond man to waking life by introducing him to death.

Feeling "both disgusted and ashamed" after the near-slashing, the protagonist is enlivened by a "picture [of the blond man] in the Daily News, beneath a caption stating that he had been 'mugged.'" "Poor fool, poor blind fool," he thinks with sincere compassion, "mugged by an invisible man" (Ellison 1996, 5). Irony chimes in Ellison's scene, in his narrator's laughter and "sincere compassion." The protagonist's realization is ironic and bluesy because it couples the near-tragedy of murder with the near-comedy of his insight. Without the catharsis of the death scene, invisible man is left only with laughter and the willingness to see what the white man cannot. Accepting his invisibility the protagonist discovers light in the underground, he gives birth to his form, he becomes a thinker-tinker, he comes to life—which is to say he becomes aware of his possibilities as an improviser.

Another way to read this scene is as a moment of Ellisonian ironic drama—"antagonistic cooperation."[10] Many critics have read Ellison's concept as a theory of reader-writer relations. I argue, however, that critics might also profit from this corollary reading: antagonistic cooperation is a theorization of the "violence" that the black novelist must act out on the American imagination, the American literary tradition, and Negro stereotypes. Antagonistic cooperation is also an apt description for the experiences of Negroes engaging with a sociopolitical system whose definitions of freedom and democracy have been shaped by the presence of black Americans; yet the system is hostile to their full participation in the citizenry (Ellison 1995a, 493).

Cooperation requires, for instance, that the white man in the scene above must mentally and physically (visually) recognize the humanity of invisible man. However, since that recognition does not rise up, the protagonist is left to make a choice: he must either cooperate by fulfilling the stereotype of blackness, taking the man's life, or by drifting back into the blond man's dreamy landscape, asserting his humanity only to himself. The narrator is *forced to act* in either case, making himself visible in separate negative realities. His "against-the-grain" cooperation triggers blues idiom improvisation.

As a tool for negotiating, transcending, or redescribing the consequences of his plight, improvisation is not simply what William James calls the "go-between" or "smoother-over of transitions."[11] Rather, improvisation points out the implicitly "cruel contradiction" of blues idiom music, especially jazz. The music, Ellison argues, is directed by the "violent" interaction of the personal assertions of the individual musicians "within and against" the group performance.

> Each true jazz moment (as distinct from the uninspired commercial performance) springs from a contest in which each artist challenges all the rest; each solo flight, or improvisation, represents (like successive canvases of a painter) a definition of his identity as individual, as a member of the collectivity and as a link in the chain of tradition. Thus, because jazz finds its very life in an endless improvisation upon traditional materials, the jazzman must lose his identity even as he finds it; how often do we see even the most famous of jazz artists being devoured alive by the imitators, and shamelessly, in the public spotlight. (Ellison 1995a, 267)

To achieve identity musicians must contend with personal desires, traditional group initiatives, and performance contexts. But this identity is mercurial, elusive, and, once presented, a mark for contest. Ellison's interpretation of improvisation in jazz performance can be read as a model for the contest between the individual and the communal group. Just as Ingrid Monson's version of cultural identity provides a useful counter to Walter Benn Michaels's rejection of it, Ellison's picture of jazz takes us another step beyond the pluralist knot: the improvised mark is a useful place to begin thinking about identity formation and the evasion of racial essentialism because identity is lost even as it forms. The process has no end and no metaphysical foundation.

In *Invisible Man* violence similar to that of the jazz context forces the protagonist to improvise his "visibility"—an identity worthy of contestation within Harlem and in America at large. The protagonist's self-invention is also symbolic of the novelist's necessary improvisations. As I suggested earlier, *Invisible Man* can be productively read as Ellison's struggle with the literary tradition and his struggle for identity. As a specific literary form, however, the novel is not known to be amenable to the tutored spontaneity of jazz improvisation. Novelists have shaped the form around careful scripting, polished set pieces and scenes, and highly structured systems of metaphors and symbols. I want to propose, in the case of *Invisible Man,* that Ellison's particular style of reference and revision be read as literary improvisation. In fact, Ellison's approach embodies a pragmatic critical attitude in that jazz provides the author with a practice that is at once culture/art producing and cultural criticism. Improvising on the literary tradition through (sometimes thinly) veiled quotation on American culture's history through exaggerated symbols, and on Negro experience through specific reference to black folk culture, Ellison hoped to accomplish in *Invisible Man* "an assertion of identity that could, through expressing the ideals of democratic society, remain at once cultural and political."[12]

As the improviser works within the tradition, he remakes it; the process is as much about developing a critical sensibility as it is about developing an autonomous aesthetic. The novelist, in Ellison's case, is critic and artist simultaneously. As a critic Ellison displayed his ambivalence about twentieth-century white American novelists and their abilities (or willingness) to represent African American experience. As a novelist Ellison engaged and cooperated with a narrative tradition that often characterizes blackness or Negroness as inarticulate inhumanity and the manifest corruption of American purity. Like Todd, Ellison's response to this gut punch is tragedy-tinged laughter: *Invisible Man* is a jocular protest.

While the blues evokes a near-tragic, near-comic lyricism, Ellison's joke is dissonant. Playing his novel within Western and American literature, Ellison created a confrontational discourse, asserting his voice and narrative disruptively against the grain of tradition's composition and definition. "Discourse" is a crucial term here because, as Teju Olaniyan explains, it refers not only to a practice we impose on things but also "a violence . . . that we do to and impose on human beings."[13] Rather than play up Deweyan narratives of smooth pragmatic progress, Ellison's pragmatism charges us to understand American democratic growth as a violent, dissonant process. As Kenneth Burke might say, *Invisible Man* is a long, improvised solo written across the jugular veins of the American imagination and the American literary tradition.[14]

The violence surrounding the protagonist's becoming points to Ellison's belief that the formation of America's social and political principles are played out on the black male body. As he explains in the essay "Twentieth Century Fiction and the Black Mask of Humanity," we cannot escape the presence or meaning of blackness when we discuss American literature, American identity, or American democracy; the black body is at the center of those discussions:

> [O]n the moral level I propose that we view the whole of American life as a drama acted out upon the body of a Negro giant, who, lying trussed up like Gulliver, forms the stage and the scene upon which the action unfolds. If we examine the beginnings of the Colonies the application of this view is not in its economic connotations at least too far-fetched or too difficult to see. For then the Negro's body was exploited as amorally as the soil and climate. It was later, when men drew up a plan for a democratic way of life, that the Negro began to exert an influence upon America's moral consciousness. Gradually he was recognized as the human factor placed outside the democratic master plan, a human natural resource who, so that the white man could become more human, was elected to undergo a process of institutionalized dehumanization. (Ellison 1995a, 85)

Even with his invocation of Swift, Ellison's proposal is neither modest nor satirical. Instead, Ellison suggests that the project of American democracy is suspect because its practice has been a linguistic correlative of white supremacy. The "institutionalized dehumanization" of African Americans, Ellison argues, is both a political and literary problem in American history. American literary authors have helped corrupt the spirit of democracy by treading in stereotypes of Negroes. *Invisible Man* describes both the violence on the route to identity and on the route to literary efficacy. The author uses *Invisible Man* to confront American literature in the hope of carving space in the symbolic discourse for African American humanity. The protagonist's memoir amounts to the political description of nationhood wherein quintessential American identity is Negro and thus improvisational.

Ellison sets the pace of the novel by invoking Louis Armstrong early in the work. Armstrong's improvisations express the philosophical qualities of invisibility. Satchmo negotiates the violence and tragicomedy surrounding black masculinity by improvising from the liminal spaces of his experience. Picking up on Armstrong's sense of swing, the narrator realizes that "invisibility . . . gives one a slightly different sense of time, you're never quite on the beat. Sometimes you're ahead and sometimes behind. Instead of the swift and imperceptible flowing of time, you are aware of its nodes, those points where time stands still or from which it leaps ahead. And you slip into the breaks and look around. That's what you hear vaguely in Louis' music" (Ellison 1995b, 8). Swing provides an alternative sensibility to the cultural and political status quo.

Returning to his theme of violence, Ellison marks the disorder that arrives when a yokel can step inside a superior opponent's "sense of time," knocking the prizefighter, "science, speed and footwork as cold as a well-digger's posterior" (Ellison 1995b, 8). The gangly surprise and classical humor of this image brings out the elegance of improvisational response.[15] Ellison's scene encompasses several old American metaphors—the story of the tortoise and the hare, the con man and the homeboy, the country mouse and the city mouse, Brer fox and Brer rabbit. Yet, "all those metaphors of innocence and experience collapse into the image of the prizefighter's confrontation with his opposite, his nemesis, the very antithesis of himself" (Early 1994, 5). The struggle between antagonist and antithesis elaborates the symbolic action not only of American folklore but also the drama of the American's struggle for individual identity. As in the fight with the blond man, this use of boxing is a symbolic representation of antagonistic cooperation.

In the opening of *Invisible Man* boxing and jazz mix together potently. For instance, when the protagonist expresses his disgust and shame for attacking the blond man, his self-flagellation is a sly riff on Richard Wright's own battle royal in *Black Boy*. As we shall see, Wright's memoir provides Ellison with the "chord changes" for developing the scenes of the battle royal in *Invisible Man*. In the novel's opening chapter, "The Battle Royal," Ellison concentrates all the spectacular effects and social ramifications of lynching into the context of the ad hoc prizefight. Battle royals, boxing matches set up to pit large groups of black boys against one another in "fights to the finish," were promoted throughout the American South during the twentieth century. These bloody melees blend sadistic, racist, and ritualistic desires as black boys engage in brutal physical combat for white entertainment. In Ellison's version he blindfolds the boys to play his themes of blindness and invisibility in the context of white viewership.

After successfully presenting a graduation day speech, invisible man is invited to speak to the town's leading white citizens at a private smoker where he will re-present his speech. The narrator explains that as a young man he had fashioned himself in the mode of Booker T. Washington and his oration preached "humility" as the "secret, indeed, the very essence of progress" (Ellison 1995b, 23). This sentiment is the antithesis of the battle royal scenario. The protagonist knows that the chaos of the fight will detract from his own individual performance of order and acquiescence. Ellison's description of the party is surreal and dreamy: a moaning clarinet, unabashed drunkenness, bluish cigar smoke, half-naked black boys, grotesque, glossy, and disfigured white men, a boxing match and a speech, and the full frontal nudity of a white female burlesque dancer. The naked blond woman raises the sexual undercurrent of the proceedings above the flood level. As in lynching spectacles, the battle royal is underwritten by myths of black male physical and sexual potency, and myths of sanctified white womanhood.

The "spectacle of lynching" was used to disenfranchise Negro citizens, to emphasize the limits of Negro social and professional mobility, to construct and accentuate the power of a white racial identity, and finally, as an illegal means to exterminate black citizens. Lynching is built on a platform of sadistic and lurid sexual connotations. The concept of black sexual depravity, "the specter of the black beast seized by uncontrollable savage sexual passions," triggers the violence. Meanwhile, "the inhumanity, depravity, bestiality, and savagery practiced by white participants in lynchings [is] justified in the name of humanity, morality, justice, civilization, and Christianity."[16] White men lynched black men and women in the name of protecting white womanhood. In turn, lynching solidified an ethos of whiteness as a priori "American" identity. Lynching "the black beast rapist" helped affirm the ascension of the "glorified white woman," an old American myth iterated and amplified since Reconstruction.[17]

From this perspective, a fear of or desire to protect white femininity becomes a fear of/desire to destroy black masculinity. Grace Hale writes, "Lynching helped reconcile the ambiguity of gender difference at the heart of a society in which the primary boundary was the color line. The gender lines within the whiteness made by the culture of segregation were less than clearly drawn. . . . [W]hite supremacy always carried with it the possibility of strengthening the white woman as it emasculated, often literally, the black man" (Hale 1998, 233). Lynching is an exaggeration of the microinteraction of American racial hierarchy. Not only could white men transgress the lines of racial segregation and sexual difference ("enacting the 'whiteness' segregation simultaneously created and undermined"), they could also eliminate their "violent" Negro others without reason.

Ellison heightens the tension of the battle royal by making the sexuality—the sexual parts—of the white woman visible and available to both young black men and the white city fathers. The dancer is both the object of and impetus for the white men's sadistic voyeurism. The "influential" men goad, cajole, and threaten the black boys to look (and not to look) at the woman gyrating and slithering to the clarinet's musical direction.

The sight of the white woman incites fainting, crying, moaning, desire, hatred, and fear amongst the Negro teens. The narrator realizes what the dancer's body symbolizes for all parties and his thoughts exhibit the dialectics of the blues as he reads the scene from inside the chaos:

> I wanted at one and the same time to run from the room, to sink through the floor, or go to her and cover her from my eyes and the eyes of the others with my body; to feel the soft thighs, to caress her and destroy her, to love her and murder her, to hide from her, and yet to stroke where below the small American flag tattooed upon her belly her thighs formed a capital V. I had a notion that of all in the room she saw only me with her impersonal eyes. (Ellison 1995b, 19)

This scene, driven by sex and trauma, is also underwritten by the same threat of and desire for miscegenation that drives lynching rituals. The protagonist's desire and hatred amplifies the theory that miscegenation threatens the status quo of white male social dominance. The narrator's words could also represent the wishes of the white men and their ambivalent feelings for both the white woman and those black boys. The U.S. flag tattooed above the dancer's pubic area is the banner of American white male identity; the white leaders present understand that their victory and identity depends on protecting her sexuality as well as having the power to ritualistically display her and sadistically consume her. The white men, to whom license beyond reproach is accorded, lose control of their sexual urges and attack the dancer. For the black boys the woman's naked body symbolizes the lust and disgust of the battle royal. Not only will their black bodies manifest the sexual desires of the white men, their bodies also represent the impulse for the violent, murderous urges of the group of white leaders. As the narrator explains, "the harder we fought the more threatening the men became" (Ellison 1995b, 24).

At its heart, ritualized lynching was consumer driven. The executions almost always involved torture to heighten the theatrical aspects of the event. The dismemberment of bodies and dispersal of souvenir parts (genitalia, joint and bone fragments, and skin were all often torn from the living victim before the hanging or burning took its desired effect) added to the "marketability" of the "lynching carnivals." This aspect is made comical in Ellison's scene when, following the bout, the fighters are presented with the chance to scurry for the prize money, counterfeit currency strewn on an electrified mat. Even with the blindfolds off the black boys cannot see that both the money and the mat are extensions of the battle royal ritual. The events of the battle royal symbolize the Negro's negotiation of America writ large: Negro citizens are pitted against one another in a blind battle for individual space, for the opportunity to reap some small benefit from the privileges of second-class American citizenship. However, even the chance for financial gain is charged with faulty promises; what you get is shockingly inadequate. Compounding this tilted socioeconomic scale are the dehumanizing effects of the narratives girding the battle royal itself. The white town leaders assume that the Negro boys are depraved. Worse yet is the narrator's attempt to speak his valedictory speech through bruised and bloodied lips. In a fit to be heard above the din of the drunken city fathers, the protagonist slips in his speech and refers loudly to the need for "social equality."

The narrator's call for social equality is a shot in the dark, but it speaks to the emergence of his own recognizable humanity. Like lynching, staged battles and bouts effectively present the white viewers as normal by effectively dehumanizing the black participants (or victims). Lynching is also at work in Ellison's conceptual framework. Ellison's fiction works through the conundrums at the heart of American life — the contradiction built into the collision of the Constitutional contract with the chaotic groping for identity, whether individual or group. On one hand, lynching works as the extreme, particularly Southern, eradicating act used first for defining regional whiteness and on the other hand, it represents the defense of the national ethos of whiteness as "American."

Robin Wiegman argues that "the implicit whiteness and maleness of the original American citizen is thus itself protected by national identity. In constituting the citizen through the value system of disembodied abstraction, the white male is 'freed' from the corporeality that might otherwise impede his insertion into the larger body of national identity."[18] Negroes, on the other hand, must contend with socially imposed traps framed by blackness. What lynching does is reassert the social trap of blackness in order to prevent black people from entering the citizenry and disembodied abstraction. Through the lynching scenario, violent sacrifice of black bodies protects psychologically and politically "the economic and social coherency of the nation" (Wiegman 1993, 223).

In two other apprentice stories, "Party Down at the Square" and "The Birthmark," Ellison uses burning or disfigured black bodies to symbolize the grave difficulties Negroes have expressing their contingencies or social hopes in the South. Of particular interest is the way that Ellison presents male genitalia as symbols for American masculinity and citizenship. In "The Birthmark" the patrolman refuses to allow Matt and Clara to declare their brother Willie's death a lynching. Consequently, this becomes a legalized murder, a legally protected disenfranchisement. Willie loses his identity when Matt, looking for the telling birthmark below Willie's navel notices "a bloody mound of torn flesh and hair" where the mark should have been.

Ellison shapes "Party Down at the Square" around a lynching. The scene is fire and brimstone. Set in the middle of a rainstorm, besides the lynching party, an airline jet nearly crash lands in the town square as the "funeral pyre" lights up the night sky. When the mob returns its attention to the burning "Bacote nigger," the victim pleads, "will somebody please cut my throat like a Christian?" In response, a crowd member, Jed Williams, hollers back, "Sorry, ain't no Christians around tonight. Ain't no Jew-boys neither. We're just one hundred percent Americans." Ironically, the sheriff, who is present for the air traffic accident, does not halt the lynching; the victim has no legal protection as a citizen or a Christian. Rather than the twentieth century leading to the decommodification of the black body, technologically modern America recodifies it as the boundary of citizenship and economic possibility. The black body returns to its chattel status through lynching.[19]

III

Ellison works through some of these same concerns in his essay "Richard Wright's Blues." There, Ellison presents his crystalline definition of the blues—near-tragic, near-comic autobiographical chronicle of personal catastrophe expressed lyrically—and argues that the blues is distinctly humanist and poetic. He affirms this interpretation by contextualizing the importance of Wright's memoir within a frame of works by Joyce, Nehru, Dostoevsky, George Moore, and Rousseau. Ellison's critical point is to make the story of Wright's rise out of Mississippi part of an international literary tradition: the oppressed national or colonial insider who transcends race, ethnicity, or class status to become the epitome of national ideals while providing a crucial critique or rebuke of the political system working against him.

For Ellison there are two kinds of political commentary at play in Wright's memoir: One is Wright's ideological, Marxist-inflected reading of African American life in the rural South and urban North. The other commentary is cultural and symbolic—the blues. Given his comparative context Ellison's contention is that the blues "is the strongest affirmation" that Negroes have the capacity to make cultural products that can stand on the world stage (Ellison 1995a, 143).[20] However, the blues also exposes specific social and historical difficulties about black life. "Blues expressiveness," Adam Gussow writes, "is grounded in, and significantly shaped by, the encounter of working-class black folk with violence in the Jim Crow South, and with versions of that violence later encountered by, and propagated by, black folk who migrated North."[21] Ellison's blues is a steely literary theory, one that he subsequently places at the heart of *Invisible Man*'s literary system. But in the essay, Ellison excavates the violence threaded into Wright's memoir and uses the blues to critique both Wright's expertise and the political problems in American Negro life.

In his memoir Wright illustrates his own "crazy discovery"

when, as a teenager, a white coworker pushes him to believe that another young black man, Harrison, wants to kill him. Olin, a white lens crafter, warns Wright that Harrison, who works across the street from the lab, wants to plant a blade in him. Olin also, with the aid of Harrison's boss, perpetrates the reverse lie on Harrison. The two boys meet and proclaim no ill will for each other. They realize that Olin is the real threat, yet they watch each other with anxious eyes.

When the white workers at the optical laboratory concoct the homicidal scenario for Wright and Harrison their aim is to turn the lynching ritual into intraracial murder. However, the wariness of the two teenagers foils the plan and the workers opt to stage a boxing match. Wright describes these events so that readers become aware of the "psychological scrimmage" at work beneath the battle. Wright agrees to fight Harrison; realizing the ramifications of his acquiescence later he explains, "I grew ashamed of what I had agreed to do and wanted to back out of the fight, but I was afraid that they would be angry if I tried to. I felt that if white men tried to persuade two black boys to stab each other for no reason save their own pleasure, then it would not be difficult for them to aim a wanton blow at a black boy in a fit of anger, in a passing mood of frustration."[22] Like Ellison's protagonist, Wright is forced to choose between two dangerous realities. But fear of brutal retaliation from the whites, including potentially his death, forces Wright to perform the charade, though the "self" Wright presents in the fight is not a version of his choosing.

On the day of the fight only white men, save the fighters, are present for the proceedings. Beforehand, Wright and Harrison conspire to fix the fight, protecting each other from real harm. However, as Wright prepares to do battle his fright is heightened by worries over Harrison's loyalty. The white audience, smoking and yelling obscenities, encourages the two fighters to draw blood with each blow and crush each other's genitalia:

> The shame and anger we felt for having allowed ourselves to be duped crept into our blows and blood ran into our eyes, half blinding us. The hate we felt for the men whom we had tried to cheat went into the blows we threw at each other. . . . [After the fight] I could not look at Harrison. I hated him and I hated myself. . . . I heard of other fights being staged between other black boys, and

each time I heard those plans falling from the lips of white men in the factory I eased out of earshot. I felt that I had done something unclean, something for which I could never properly atone. (Wright 1995, 264–65)

The participants and the viewers are entangled in the racial gestalt. The two Negro opponents are so rife with shame and anger that they view each other as surrogates for the white men they actually want to rebuke. But the psychological effect imprisons them in a well of intimate hatred. Though invisible man escapes with only disgust, Wright, duped and half blind, is trapped by self-hatred. Ironically, Wright's feelings are driven by what Ellison calls the "irrepressible moral reality of the Negro" (Ellison 1995a, 90). Wright's effort to accept Negro stereotypes as true in order to "seek out the human truth which [the stereotypes hide]" is a model for Ellison's own literary practice: the opening sequences of *Invisible Man* are improvisations on Wright's blues (Ellison 1995a, 98).

Not surprisingly, Ellison counters his "quotation" of Wright with references to another Southern writer, William Faulkner. From Faulkner, Ellison gains an apt model for diagnosing the crippling power of racial violence on white Americans, riffing on his illustration of Southern depravity in *Absalom, Absalom!* (1936). In *Absalom, Absalom!* Thomas Sutpen promotes bouts between his black slaves for the amusement of his white male neighbors. However, Faulkner wants the deprivations to work across racial lines so he puts Sutpen in the final, main-event matches. Sutpen's participation symbolizes his misgivings about his own social status (if not his racial status).[23]

Rosa Coldfield, who narrates Sutpen's legend to Quentin Compson, explains that in these barnyard brawls two of Sutpen's Negroes would fight

not like white men fight, with rules and weapons, but like negroes fight to hurt one another quick and bad. . . . [Sometimes the two were] a white one and a black one, both naked to the waist and gouging at one another's eyes as if their skins should not only have been the same color but should have been covered with fur too. Yes. It seems that on certain occasions, perhaps at the end of the evening, the spectacle, as a grand finale or perhaps as a matter of sheer deadly forethought toward the retention of supremacy, domination, [Sutpen] would enter the ring with one of the negroes himself.[24]

Coldfield's recollection creates an image of a furious Sutpen, fighting not like a white man, but as a beast waging battle against his internalized other. After watching several bouts the racial gestalt awakens in Sutpen, forcing a confrontation between his two selves in a death match. One imagines Sutpen's body speckled with the blood and sweat of the slave he battles in this scene standing a stark contrast to the glowing alabaster skin tone of Ellen Sutpen (his wife). Whiteness, however, cannot save the Sutpen children from their blood ties to "blackness." Faulkner's point about Sutpen's racial conflict is that it is sexual and natal in its origin. Faulkner knows that nothing underscores and undercuts the problematic myth of Southern white supremacy better than miscegenation, sexual or cultural.

Sutpen's desire for union with black bodies and repellent hatred of blackness is tragicomic because it suggests "the struggles of a sensibility at war with itself."[25] Ellison's novel parallels the tension in Faulkner's as his protagonist confronts his "blind" white assailant and demands acknowledgment, but the act is fraught with menace; slashing the man's throat, though an effort of self-preservation, is also suicidal. The fighters in Ellison's battle royal are stand-ins for the white patrons, yet their collective inability to win the fight, gather their rewards, or speak about social equality keeps them from achieving identities within or against the community.

The opening bouts in *Invisible Man* initiate readers to invisible man's confrontation with the white world's blindness and the spectacle of the battle royal. But the end of the memoir proper leaves readers with the consequences of blindness and spectacle: the protagonist's castration dream. After falling into the underground, the protagonist dreams of being hunted by his "benefactors." Invisible man's dream of castration finalizes the lynching ritual in the novel. It helps the author describe the crisis of black intellectual and political action in the midst of ideological essentialism—whether that ideology belongs to the white establishment, the Brotherhood, or black nationalism. The protagonist imagines subverting the illusions and mythologies of Brother Jack and Tobitt, Norton and Bledsoe, Emerson and Ras with laughter. Laughter becomes the protagonist's subconscious acknowledgment of the complex relationship between self-identification and Negro social action.

This is particularly important in the context of *Invisible Man* because even in the protagonist's private, underground hibernation the hopefulness of infinite American possibilities is tempered by the dream of his castration. The protagonist's castration is meant to recall the rituals of the lynch mob and "marks" his body as disenfranchised of both masculinity and citizenship. But invisible man's laughter reshapes the end of the illusion; the freedom from myth turns into a concrete image of American possibility. Not only do the protagonist's bloody testicles constitute the future generations of his assailants, they are, as the narrator describes to the mob, "your universe, and that drip-drop upon the water you hear is all the history you've made, all you're going to make" (Ellison 1995b, 570). The image is a way to slip the yoke of dehumanization and turn the joke back onto the essentializers.

However, in order for the castration to have impact we must read it as a corollary to the opening fights of the novel. Dismemberment of the black male body in the context of the lynching ceremony worked to deny black men any part of the abstract American patriarchal myth connected to whiteness as well as masculinity and citizenship. This final act also cycles us back to "The Battle Royal." Together these two episodes provide the symbolic "underground" narrative to Ellison's dominant picaresque narrative. Ellison's protagonist travels into the urban North hoping to shed all the backward and negative elements of the Southern Negro cultural and political experience. But Ellison encourages his readers to see that these elements cannot be shed because they work on both the physical and the psychological levels of the narrator's experience. Even more, by joining all of his antagonists together in this dream, Ellison moves the problems from the South to the North, making them national difficulties and not regional ones. Ellison builds a series of antithetical pairs—injustice and civil rights, abstract democratic ambitions (for equality and individuality) and the demoralizing reality of racial violence and essentialism, private philosophical changes and public social hopes—around his protagonist in order to play a game of dialectics on the black male body. The movement back and forth between the warring ideals helps to draw out both the ironies of American democracy and those that belong to processes of self-identification. The joke is that invisible man realizes that what has happened to him as a black man will eventually become the whole nation's lot. Invisible man resists the tragic elements of the blues because of his "improvisational dexterity and a salvific sense of absurdity" (Gussow 2003, 151).

IV

As if lynching were not absurd enough, Ellison continues his improvising by introducing masking and minstrelsy in the novel.[26] Ellison weaves ritualized lynching and the burnt-cork comedy of minstrelsy into antagonistic cooperation. This conjunction gives another presence to blues tragicomedy. Minstrelsy and blackface performances by white actors complicate the lineage of whiteness. Blacking up is a way of negotiating the latent anxieties of cultural and sanguine miscegenation, but rather than eliminating blackness, minstrelsy makes blackness elemental to the construction of a white American ethos.

In order to inject his work effectively with the mood of moral responsibility, Ellison knew that revealing the philosophical concerns hidden behind the habitations of the mask would be of the utmost importance. Ellison realized that the grease-painted minstrel masks worn by whites as cosmetic concealer of identity and cleanser of black humanity revealed more about whiteness than they disguised. In fact, burnt cork, as Ellison suggests in his novel, cannot mask as much as the brown-skin facial features that naturally mask Negroes' private identities. That mask is like a reversed photo solarization of minstrelsy: the reflection of whiteness in blackness, blackness in whiteness. In the scheme of *Invisible Man* Ellison utilizes this understanding to conceptualize his philosophy.

The goal of African American writers has always been partly a humanistic one: to present Negro life through a vision of human reality by whatever philosophical or ideological means. Rather than rely on the Communist Party ideologies that he and Richard Wright learned in the 1930s, what he might have called in Wright's work the "victimhood of Naturalism," Ellison promoted his own "anti-ideology" ideology. Thomas Schaub explains that the "idea that human existence is intrinsically ambiguous is itself an ideology," and so, "Ellison used [that ideological mode] as a self-limiting device so that any articulated vision would always be inherently modest, aware of itself as a necessary fiction."[27]

The roots of minstrelsy reside in nineteenth-century anxieties about race and gender (anxieties that still gird up our contemporary cultural surface). Blackface performance is part of an iconography that includes clowning, transvestitism, and political protest and demonstration—not to mention "racial" rioting. Before T. D. Rice and minstrelsy per se, blackface was used as a way of disguising whiteness (or emphasizing it) for dramaturgical purposes. Blackface (and even "redface") was often used as part of protest action. And during special workman's and seasonal holiday parades blackface paint was used to give white participants performative license for outrageous public behavior.

During the antidraft, antiwar, and antiabolition demonstrations of the 1850s and 1860s whites used blackface to amplify their disputes. The masquerading whites often attacked black citizens during these protests.[28] Much of this action was located in northeastern industrial cities. Interestingly, the rise of "blackface fun" falls in chronological line with the advent of abolitionism in the North. These coterminous actions are not mere coincidence; their contradictory yet simultaneous eruptions highlight the complex black center of whiteness. Eric Lott writes that "minstrel representations, then, were not continuous with either earlier blackface figures or the deployment of blackface in rioting and revelry; although in certain cases there clearly were borrowings and affinities, these were scarcely all structurally 'the same.'" These traditions do illustrate that blackface performance contains "an unstable or indeed contradictory power, linked to social and political conflicts, that issues from the weak, the uncanny, the outside." The slippery political shadings of the traditional uses of blackface during the nineteenth century are instructive because they express "a derisive celebration of the power of blackness; blacks for a moment, ambiguously, on top" (Lott 1994, 29).

In his essay "Change the Joke and Slip the Yoke," Ellison describes the multifarious meanings hidden behind the "darky entertainer" of American culture. The essay is a response to Stanley Edgar Hyman's critique of the Negro literary tradition and its relationship to African American folklore. Hyman also includes in his piece an interpretation of Ellison's use of the "trickster" figure in *Invisible Man*.[29] However, according to Ellison, the characteristics that Hyman associates with the trickster figure actually belong to blackface minstrelsy. Ellison writes that minstrelsy "does not find its popularity among Negroes but among whites; and although it resembles the role of the clown familiar to Negro variety-house audiences, it derives not from the Negro but from the Anglo-Saxon branch of American folklore. In other words, this 'darky entertainer' is white" (Ellison 1995a, 101). Ellison's piece makes a significant distinction between the protean bliss of masking that he finds in Negro folklore and Hyman's minstrel-inflected understanding of the trickster. In Ellison's symbolic structure, a mask of brown skin is more powerful than the negative, essentializing burnt cork–covered visage.

The masks worn by some of Ellison's characters—Bledsoe and Trueblood—are minstrel masks. However, those masks are ironic weapons in Ellison's hands; blackface concentrates all the disparate meanings of blackness behind a veil of clownish theatrics. Ellison knew that janiform masks could be used to free Negroes from the restraints built into the American social system. When Negroes performed the minstrel shuffle on stage they could only do so by "blacking up" further so as to fulfill the grotesque needs of white audiences—here one is reminded of the indelible image of the "blackened" Negro vaudevillian, Bert Williams. The black mask as American icon covered the implications of a chaotic Negro humanity. Ellison writes that

> being "highly pigmented," as the sociologists say, it was our Negro "misfortune" to be caught up associatively in the negative side of this basic dualism of the white folk mind, and to be shackled to almost everything it would repress from conscience and consciousness. . . . Because these things are bound up with their notions of chaos it is almost impossible for many whites to consider questions of sex, women, economic opportunity, the national identity, historic change, social justice—even the "criminality" implicit in the broadening of freedom itself—without summoning malignant images of black men into consciousness. (Ellison 1995a, 102)

In other words, "the mask [is] the thing (the 'thing' in more ways than one)" (Ellison 1995a, 103) The mask veils Negro humanity and helps repress a recognition or awareness amongst white folks that their own sexual proclivities, dehumanizing acts, and moral complexities are pushed behind the action of the Jim Crow jump.

When Negroes assume the minstrel role for profit, the self-immolating, scapegoat role, that kind of blacked-up performance signals its own malignancy and relieves the surface level culpability of white folks' watching (or reading). Note Houston Baker's crucial reading of Booker T. Washington's rhetorical "darky act" in *Up From Slavery*. Baker suggests that Washington's own nonsensical tones and types serve first as "mastery of form" and secondly become a "deformation of mastery," in his appropriations of the minstrel image for social gain.[30] Ellison's characterizations of Trueblood and Bledsoe are examples of deformation of mastery. The irony of their performances, the powerful joke at the heart of the mess, is that "blackness" masks the instability of whiteness. Both racial constructs are illusory but black masks stabilize and determine racial perimeters.

Ellison's focus on the appropriations of the minstrel mask early in the novel sets up his late turn to "the righteous daddy," B. P. Rinehart. Rinehart is an improvisation, an experiment, an expression of possibilities outside of essentialism. When the protagonist dons the green-tinted sunglasses and a hipster's hat, he unknowingly becomes Rinehart. Rinehart is emblematic of the improvisational spirit that Ellison sees as the irony of masking. Rinehart's multifarious roles in Harlem allow invisible man to roam freely through the village. Disguised as Rinehart, the narrator's view of the community is enhanced by a super stereo-optic perspective. Mistaken identity is not the point; rather, the emphasis turns on the protagonist's ability to use masking, invisibility, and improvisation in his favor.

Though the disguise is fashioned to elude Ras's thugs, it also provides invisible man with more powerful insight into his own individual status. The sunglasses literally help invisible man to see the protean bliss of invisibility, to "BEHOLD THE INVISIBLE," as Reverend Rinehart's leaflet proclaims. Rinehart uses his mask to work around the conventions of identity. He is able to create his own identity by refusing a determined, absolutist version of social representation. Invisible man realizes the power of masking when he too refuses to find "proper political classification" or label for Rinehart and his situation:

His world was possibility and he knew it. He was years ahead of me and I was a fool. I must have been crazy and blind. The world in which we lived was without boundaries. A vast seething, hot world of fluidity, and Rine the rascal was at home. . . . I was both depressed and fascinated. I wanted to know Rinehart and yet, I thought, I'm upset because I know I don't have to know him, that simply becoming aware of his existence, being mistaken for him, is enough to convince me that Rinehart is real. . . . Too little was known, too much was in the dark. . . . My entire body started to itch, as though I had just been removed from a plaster cast and was unused to the new freedom of movement. (Ellison 1995b, 498)

Rinehart provides the protagonist with possibilities that were always available. On the surface however, this realization seems to be part of a process of self identification that can only happen in the North, as if philosophical awareness can only happen in a place where segregation and, more particularly, lynching are not sanctioned civic practices. In the trajectory of the storyteller's journey from the South to Harlem and then back south, underground, he seems to suggest to his audience of listeners (readers) that these possibilities are only available in the North. "Bliss Proteus Rinehart, sharpie and 'spiritual technologist,'" Lawrence Jackson writes,

> obtains instant recognition from Harlemites by his trademark sunglasses and from sporting literally the broadest hat on the Broadway. Rinehart is myth and dash, being and non-being, a well-known Harlemite who experiences life in competing modalities, a man who crosses boundaries sacred and secular, an image of confrontation and reserve, a man whose life is a continuum of intensity. He holds the offices of numbers runner, pimp, gambler, preacher, nurturer of the spiritual and material comforts, arbiter of dreams.[31]

However, the author (hiding behind the mask of his protagonist) subverts that message by using Rinehart's many roles in Harlem to recall the narrative possibilities that "blues-singing" characters like Barbee (the blind, Homeric "Founder's Day" speaker whose myth-perpetuating poem makes a hero of both the school founder and the president, Bledsoe) or Trueblood (whose story of "moving without moving" becomes a financial coup) used to manipulate the circumstances of segregation in the South. Ellison's message says that even in the South where "everyone knows you," the Rinehart form of improvisational masking is available; it is a form of invention that extends the intellectual tradition that the protagonist names in the prologue, "thinker-tinker." Improvising new masks or narratives expresses the truths of experience and the ambiguities of blackness otherwise denied by political forces outside of the individual.

Rinehart's masking is the key to his visceral social presence. Although he is a mouthpiece for the Brotherhood, invisible man is part of a political engine that does not accommodate improvisational identities. Rinehart's multiangled perspective is exactly the kind of democratic possibility that Ellison tries to promote in the novel. Pondering his newly found power, invisible man takes note of his own easy movements from behind the mask:

> [T]he notion was frightening, for now the world seemed to flow before my eyes. All boundaries down, freedom was not only the recognition of necessity, it was the recognition of possibility. . . . I caught a brief glimpse of the possibilities posed by Rinehart's multiple personalities. . . . I had been trying simply to turn them into a disguise but they had become a political instrument instead. . . . It was too simple, and yet they had already opened up a new section of reality for me. (Ellison 1995b, 499)

Jackson suggests that the key improvisation in the last third of the novel develops when Invisible Man recognizes that the hipster or "sharpie" style is a viable, radical politics of the margin. Jackson explains that in 1930s and 1940s Harlem, "hipsters and zoot-suiters were recognized as important underground actors, whose language and style teemed with potential" (Jackson 1999, 67).

Among the prominent "sharpies" during the 1940s when Ellison was devising and writing his novel were the purveyors and innovators of the bebop sound and style, Gillespie and Monk, for instance. Like those musicians, invisible man realizes that by improvising and interpolating different cultural perspectives he can create new political space for himself in Harlem and in America. Bebop music and the sharpie style presented young black men with a quintessentially Negro performative sensibility. However, as I examined in Movement I, Ellison believed that musicians like Parker misunderstood the power of masking and were sacrificed by the ardor of white audiences. Ellison believed that beboppers and sharpies failed to recognized that their significant powers rested in their abilities to portray the imperatives of cultural improvisation and philosophical experimentation, Rhinehartism, through masking.

Masking as Rinehart, even if accidental, is an improvisational move that allows invisible man a new freedom and a more lucid conception of identity. The awareness of things unseen, of visible invisibility leads the protagonist to rebel; "after years of trying to adopt the opinions of others I finally rebelled. I am an invisible man" (Ellison 1995b, 573). But this invisibility is not inactivity. The acceptance of invisibility carries with it the responsibility to be politically and philosophically astute in the social realm. Invisible man must *act* out his social responsibility because he is only "invisible, not blind."

Rinehart not only makes us aware of the protean quality of identity, he (the character we never see, in fact) structures the entire novel. Rinehart enacts the play of language (allegory and metaphor) and the process of improvisation as experience (masking, unmasking, and joking). Ellison's allegorical/metaphorical play is an attempt to invent a new position of subjectivity. That is, the name "Rinehart" cloaks a subjectivity that is both the "rind" and the "heart," a subject position that is in fact always in the process of moving away from both. "Rinehart" is another name for the Derridean "mark," the site where context and experience, in the action of naming and wordplay, become metaphorical.

Ellison's model for this symbolic action is not postmodern or poststructural or Burkean; the jazz musicians of his youth taught Ellison that improvisation is the American's most significant tool. Growing up in Oklahoma City, Ellison believed that the city was a place where "anything and everything was to be found" and fashioning identities as "Renaissance" men was possible for him and his cohort of friends (Ellison 1995a, 50). The play of this "Renaissance" ideal is crucial to Ellison's identity because the term highlights both the cultural era of his adolescence, the New Negro movement or Harlem Renaissance, and, with equal weight, the importance of European high culture to his personal development. However, Ellison and his group found the best example of Renaissance—and freedom—in the jazz tradition and the lifestyles of Oklahoma City jazz musicians.

Oklahoma City was a crucible for the southwestern jazz tradition. The city was a training center for musicians working to merge the country blues with urbane, urban dance rhythms. However, as Ellison explains throughout his jazz criticism, the jazz tradition is always bolstered and advanced by musicians who can expand the tradition by creating individualized personal styles of play and by invoking the techniques of various musical ideas and traditions (including European classical composition) within the context of group performance. Many of the musicians who performed in Oklahoma City bands like the famous Blue Devils Orchestra went on to become beacons in the national tradition because of their abilities to improvise idiosyncratic personal statements or compositional theories while maintaining the ritual traditions of jazz performance.

From his childhood bedroom Ellison could hear jazz and blues music coming from the clubs of Deep Second, the famous entertainment block on Oklahoma City's East Side. In those joints, rigorously trained and technically superior jazzmen like Hot Lips Page, Count Basie, and Lester Young used their knowledge of multiple musical traditions to blaze new jazz territories. The music was also significant for its part in a sequence that framed an "institutional form." After church and school, Ellison remarks, "the blues, the singer, the band and the dancers formed the vital whole" of the public jazz dance, a ritual practice of African American communal life in Oklahoma City (Ellison 1995a, 275). This "third institution," Ellison argues, promotes the idea of "jazz as experience" rather than "jazz as entertainment" (Ellison 1995a, 269). Jazz as entertainment removes jazz from its communal, ritualized station within black life, packaging its history so as to ignore "the most fundamental knowledge of the dynamics of stylistic growth which has been acquired from studies in other branches of music and from our knowledge of the growth of other art forms" (Ellison 1995a, 270). Jazz as experience rejects the clichés of commodification, asserting instead the "irrepressibly human over all circumstance, whether created by others or by one's own human failings. [It is] the only consistent art in the United States which constantly remind[s] us of our limitations while encouraging us to see how far we can actually go" (Ellison 1995a, 277).

Southwestern territory bands figure importantly in Ellison's estimations. Whether nationally known or locals from, for instance, Texas, Missouri, and Oklahoma, the musicians played for "themselves and for the black community, using the continuous sessions as a way to test their manhood and their instrumental proficiency."[32] It is no wonder then that Ellison's best jazz writing is about the Oklahoma City–bred musicians Jimmy Rushing and Charlie Christian. Rushing and Christian energized their musical powers by tapping their encyclopedic musical intelligences and stylizing them within the specifically African American performance tradition. These musicians were models for artistic performance and masculinity that would later embolden Ellison the writer. In the Oklahoma City of his youth, Ellison saw and heard musicians "creating out of tradition, imagination and the sounds and emotions around them a freer, more complex and driving form of jazz" (Ellison 1995a, 51). The music gave a soundtrack to Ellison's youthful exploration of "human versatility and possibility" in the face of segregation and racist obstacles "erected to restrict" him from participating "in the life of the country" (Ellison 1995a, 52).

In New York City, having turned from neophyte musician to apprentice writer, Ellison recalled those models of Renaissance artistry and demanded from himself the highest "personal discipline and creative quality" (Ellison 1995a, 58). More importantly, Ellison notices that the musical tradition drives performers to strike a "delicate balance between strong individual personality and the group" (Ellison 1995a, 228). Jazz calls for discipline and technical mastery but it also requires that the artist "achieve his creativity within its frame. He must learn the best of the past, and add to it his personal vision" (Ellison 1995a, 229). The Renaissance ideal developed in Oklahoma City charged Ellison, the young writer, to improvise within the literary tradition in order to overcome segregation of the word, "the most insidious and least understood form" of segregation (Ellison 1995a, 81). Ellison recognized that exploring human versatility and possibility in writing required that he, like those Oklahoma City jazzmen, push his discipline and creativity to absorb the sounds and emotions of American culture in order to produce a freer, more complex and driving form of the novel. Ellison's jazz-literary attitude prompted him to invest in the tradition of the novel while reinventing that tradition by adding his idiosyncratic novelistic vision to it.

Ellison's territorial education presents jazz and literary artistry as a conflict between "received traditions (constraints imposed by an institution)" and the " materials from an improviser's past (autobiography)."[33] The artist works in his discipline "cognizant that he is, as it were, already 'written' by [ideologies]" (Jarrett 1998, 90). This understanding of identity disrupts distinctions between what is self-effacing and what is self-indulgent. "Rinehart" as a name, as a sign, does not designate an identity (or a character)—rather it marks "a terrain where the idiomatic and the ideological blur" (Jarrett 1998, 90). Nomenclature and irony are related to each other by improvisation; in *Invisible Man* ironic self-naming is a way of asserting both racial experience and ambivalent identity—each blurs into the other. Naming yourself always forces a choice: "One must either embrace or deny undecidability: reject ultimate distinctions between *rind* and *heart* (for they are always purchased at the cost of violence) or reject the 'vast seething, hot world of fluidity' (for it is gained only at the expense of stabile [essentialized] identity)" (Jarrett 1998, 84–85). In "Harvard Blues" Jimmy Rushing sings, "Rinehart, Rinehart / I'm a most indifferent guy!"[34]

Rinehart symbolizes the action of naming the self: "Our names, being the gift of others, must be made our own" (Ellison 1995b, 192). We accomplish this by taking possession of our names and acting them out. Our actions name us and the spirit of the name is in our actions. When invisible man accepts the promise of his self-naming, invisibility comes to mean an awareness of the infinite possibilities of being. However, that naming also acknowledges how the black American experience sits at the center of socially responsible American citizenship and in the spirit of the words American democracy.

V

For two years Ralph Ellison used the light in Rome to illuminate his ideas on jazz and literature. As a fellow at the American Academy, having earned the Rome Prize, Ellison used his time (September 1955 to September 1957) to work in a focused manner on his second novel. As with his theoretical essays and review essays and *Invisible Man* in the 1940s, Ellison made his initial public steps with the new novel via criticism. Even though he was writing in Europe, the African American freedom movement, postwar American social and moral shifts, and the role of the American writer in the conversations on those matters became Ellison's paramount concerns. Though he left radicalism for others, Ellison still maintained a hard anger about the circumstances surrounding the plight of Negroes in Harlem and across the South.

In the funny, enlightening, and intellectual letters exchanged between Albert Murray and Ellison, the two novelists pronounce their mutual disgust with the Southern senators and congressmen attempting to run end around the Supreme Court and the *Brown* decision. During Ellison's fellowship the CRM's initial lurching steps onto the national stage became a confident, resilient gait. But Ellison was troubled by the gap between the Negro struggle for full citizenship and white Southerners' battles to cement the racial hierarchy, what he saw as a corruption of democracy. Just as disruptive as this gap was the "protection" that many Southern politicians received from the national press, in venues such as *Time* magazine. In a letter dated August 1957, Ellison wrote to Albert Murray about his displeasure with a celebratory *Time* profile of Richard Russell,[35] a senator from Georgia: "There is something so immoral and rotten in those [Southern politicians] that any attempt to perfume them leads to the corruption of language; and if Russell of Georgia is the most skillful man in the Senate then it's because most of our political leaders don't have the guts to oppose him and are too busy fattening on the swill he's allowed to brew out of democracy. Now I read that Joe MC is being praised in the Senate."[36] The final jab at Representative Joseph McCarthy of Wisconsin, famous for his zealous work on the House Un-American Activities Committee, is telling. The House and Senate were both corrupted in Ellison's eyes for both Russell and McCarthy degraded "democracy" by rejecting the spirit of the word in favor of their own personal distorting definitions.

Six weeks later, in early October 1957, in his first letter to Murray upon his return to New York City from Rome, Ellison's previous anger had become acidic. Not back a week and complaining that the racial tumult had already given him a gaseous stomach, Ellison refused to entertain even a sentence on Orval Faubus, Little Rock, Arkansas, and the desegregation of Central High School, though he did call for the Southern congressional delegation to be charged with treason. In the end, Ellison argued, "tolerating those guys is as bad as tolerating communist subversion, for they are just as damaging" (Ellison and Murray 2000, 178). These two moments are a far cry from the hopeful tone that Ellison's letters carried just eighteen months earlier when he wrote with glee that the Montgomery Bus Boycott had white people in such a lather that even Northern white patrons were pulling their donations from Tuskegee Institute. Clearly, Ellison writes, this reveals "that their intention was to bribe the school into staying third-class. But hell, they forgot to bribe the preachers! I saw some of them look like the old, steady, mush-mouthed, chicken-hawk variety; real wrinkle-headed bible pounders. . . . But they're talking sense and acting!" (Ellison and Murray 2000, 116).

The Southern black ministers, facing down violence-triggered tragicomedies by improvising realities and identities that tied their private philosophical ironies to their public political hopes, had inspired the vision for Ellison's second novel. Though we do not yet have the full text of that novel, we do have a snapshot of it: *Juneteenth*, a novel about race, religion, and national identity. The narrative focuses on Reverend Alonzo "Daddy" Hickman, a former jazz trombonist turned revival minister, who is forced by circumstance to raise a young white boy he names Bliss. Bliss flees that fold, working as a roving filmmaker at one point and eventually becoming Adam Sunraider, a race-baiting Northern senator.

At the beginning of *Juneteenth* readers learn that Sunraider is hit by an assassin's bullet on the Senate floor. Sunraider is rushed to the hospital with Hickman standing vigil at his bedside. The novel is built as a call and response exchange between Hickman's oral narration and Sunraider's subconscious narrating, as he floats in and out of a coma. The interchanging narrative explains Bliss's growth in the church, Hickman's motivations for pushing Bliss to the pulpit, Bliss's escape from the church and blackness, and his stumbling attempts to name himself outside of blackness. Hickman and Sunraider must both face the painful consequences of Bliss's rejection of the love, comfort, and protection of black life in favor of performing a spiritually empty brand of white masculinity, what Barry Shank calls "the blackface construction of whiteness."[37] Hickman's failure stems from his inability to let Bliss make his own name. Sunraider's fall stems from his decision to not maintain his relationship to the ritual practices of black life and his refusal to develop a spiritual sensibility. As a word "Sunraider" puts us in mind of Icarus, who flew too high and fell too fast; as a character he is kin to Todd the pilot in "Flying Home." Sunraider and Todd hope to reject their personal histories and transcend race but fall tragically because of their imprudence, or what Kenneth Burke would call their impiety toward history.

If, as Ellison describes in "Society, Morality, and the Novel" (a treatise on authorial responsibilities written during his Italian sojourn), the novel as a rhetorical gesture must persuade readers to accept the novelist's projection of an experience, what is the author telling us about his protagonists in the second novel? Clues for answering this question are spelled out in Ellison's arguments about the novel as a literary form. Ellison explains that American novelists are at their best when diagnosing problems of identity. Even more, American literary ideas are "bound up with our problem of nationhood" (Ellison 1995a, 704). Ellison's implication is that definitions of "American" and "America" are still being debated. Written in 1956, this claim points to an America in the first throes of massive social shifts.

Ellison's best critical insights often arrived when he was defining the formal elements of novel writing and jazz performance. The most significant part of an artist's development, Ellison argues, is the definition of technical skills specific to the chosen medium of expression. Jazz performance and literary novel making demand technical prowess; and both forms share qualities of plasticity. In order to accentuate the possibilities of these forms (the stretchable, flexible, amorphous, protean possibilities), artists must be able to create while simultaneously acting as historians of their formal traditions and as prophets imagining future innovations of those forms.

In order to manage the fine balance between maintenance and innovation, jazz musicians, for instance, sharpened improvisation (obbligato, embellishment) into an art. Since blues idiom music is at the hub of Negro ritual experience, the impulse to improvise, to maintain and innovate, is a celebration of human experience. This is also the novelist's impulse. As Ellison argues in "The World and the Jug," novels "arise of an impulse to celebrate human life and therefore are ritualistic and ceremonial at their core. Thus they would preserve as they destroy, affirm as they reject" (Ellison

1995a, 161–62). In Ellison's works dialectic confliction of preservation/destruction and affirmation/rejection is bound up with the problems of nation and identity defining.

As he imagines in "Tell It Like It Is," the social role of black novelist demands dexterity with dialectics. In the essay, a piece that is part letter, part Freudian dream analysis, and part memoir, Ellison recounts his dream of riding in an open wagon with his mother on their way to his father's funeral. In the dream the body lies draped and prepared for the final rites. In the chaos of the funeral procession Ellison loses his mother and his father's body becomes Abraham Lincoln's body. Lincoln's corpse, dangling from the carriage, is dropped, defiled, and damaged by a raging, drunken mob. The burden of finally carrying Lincoln to his resting place is put to several "ragged Negroes." In this dream, Lincoln, the father of the twentieth century, as Ellison calls him, is a sacrificial figure. However, his public rites, his passage and safe burial, are corrupted by the ingratitude of the mob. Here, Ellison has transposed Burke's critique of sacrifice, tragedy, and identity into the story of the Negro's struggle for full citizenship. The mob defiles the body so as to mangle the history that Lincoln's assassination represents. The American mob refuses piety in favor of what they believe is a new national identity. That is, by sacrificing the "father" they can create a new lineage. However, Burke argues that this attitude is misplaced because the hope for transformation through patricide is really a tragic suicide. "A thorough job of symbolic rebirth would require the revision of one's ancestral past itself—quite as mystics hold that in becoming wholly transformed one not only can alter the course of the future but can even remake the past (the crudest act of the sort being such revision of the past as we get in official Nazi historiography)."[38] With his funereal garb ripped and tattered, a beer stein clamped on his head, and a corncob pipe jammed between his lips, Lincoln doesn't look like a sacrificial king. By disrupting the public rite, an impious act, the American public can ignore history in favor of a historiography that tells of victory and progress, the very problem Woodward warns of at the beginning of this movement.

In the dream Ellison is "a slave who could read," and he sees that the preservation of the national memory is the burden of Negroes. The responsibility of American history falls not only to those four Negroes carrying Lincoln, but also to Ellison, who, as novelist and improviser, must be a "trapped and impotent observer" of political shifts. While many critics have chastised Ellison for his refusal to perform a more forceful public role during the CRM, it is worth noting that even in the shadows of the public, as critical observer/novelist, Ellison was able to produce symbolic acts that charted the intellectual and cultural failings of the nation better than most other literary works of the period.

Cultural and political questions about what is and who is American arise in the mid-twentieth century from white America's collective refusal to face the significant complexities of the nineteenth century. When Ellison was writing these ideas in the 1950s, the nineteenth century's underground battles were returning to the national stage — segregation, lynching, race riots, political revolutions, integrationist ideologies, essentialist nationalist ideologies, racial identity. He knew that whatever his second novel did it would have to investigate "the impact of change upon personality," a reality that Americans wanted to ignore (Ellison 1995a, 698). Ellison's investigation of psychological change illustrates "one of the enduring functions of the American novel, which is that of defining the national types as it evolves in the turbulence of change, and giving the American experience, as it unfolds in its diverse parts and regions, imaginative integration and moral continuity" (Ellison 1995a, 703). One measure of this effort is Ellison's invocation of Southern Negro rituals and innovation of formal possibilities in *Juneteenth*.

It seems clear that Ellison's merger of jazz and the novel was an attempt to produce a politically symbolic artistic representation of the consequences of America's unfinished process of identification. But the significance of Ellison's literary artifact, the unfinished second novel, may in fact lie in its formal uniqueness rather than the quality of the writing or the narrative as such. Ellison expanded the form of the novel by playing through several styles concurrently: third-person omniscient narration, first-person stream of consciousness, dream sequences, surreal images, dialogic narration, unannounced turns in narrative voice. When we take into account the stories that Ellison published individually between the work's inception and the posthumous publication of *Juneteenth* (including the exceptional piece "Cadillac Flambé"), we find the author employing devices such as reportage, the epistle, the interview, and antiphony to produce "a vision of the complexity and diversity of the total [American] experience (Ellison 1995a, 764).[39] Ellison intended the second novel to range across all contingent narrative possibilities, improvising on the "maximum freedoms" of the novel form, but also attempting, ultimately, to explode the form (Ellison 1995a, 763).

I want to argue here that Ellison eschewed traditional linearity in *Juneteenth* in favor of an exploded form that conveyed the contingency of narrative forms and a holistic literary attitude.[40] One of the main complaints that critics have had about *Juneteenth* is that it lacks narrative or formal coherence. While we can see the author interpolating elements of Joycean and Faulknerian theories of literary consciousness in *Juneteenth*, it is not a replication of the syncopated narratological improvisation (the riffs, for example, on Wright and Faulkner's novels) that informs *Invisible Man*. While, as John K. Young has suggested provocatively, readers might benefit from thinking of *Juneteenth* as an improvised posthumous collaboration between Ellison and his literary executor, John Callahan, the advice doesn't bring us closer to the formal innovations I find implicit in the writing.[41]

Basic examples of Ellison's formal play are available in the portrayal of his protagonists in the pulpit. "Daddy" Hickman shepherds young Bliss into the ministry, teaching him the musical power of call and response oration. For example during a Juneteenth holiday service, as they work the pulpit, Bliss plays "call and response" with Hickman, questioning him about and imploring him to narrate the Negro journey from Africa to America to liberation: "We were chained, young brothers, in steel. We were chained, young sisters, in ignorance. We were schoolless, toolless, cabinless—owned . . ." Bliss calls out to the congregation and Daddy Hickman. "Amen, Reveren Bliss," Hickman responds, "We were owned and faced with the awe-inspiring labor of transforming God's Word into a lantern so that in the darkness we'd know where we were."[42] This history lesson has twofold significance: 1) Hickman can communicate the narrative that he believes is Bliss's inheritance (he hopes to raise a white child through blackness, shaping Bliss to be a champion for Negroes) and 2) Ellison can bring a specific Negro history and a particular Negro folk form to bear on the novel form.

As we learn early in the novel though, after Bliss runs away from Hickman's guidance, eventually becoming Sunraider, he only accepts the performance style, not the Word or the liberation narrative, as his birthright. Beth Eddy suggests the senator's rejection of Negro history and denigration of Negro culture is impious (Eddy 2003, 103). But Bliss/Sunraider's impiety is complicated by the fact that under Hickman's tutelage he learns how to perform and mask but is given little of the spiritual education necessary to keep the performance from becoming the singular projection of his identity. In the logic of the novel, Bliss's miseducation begins when Hickman places him inside a false coffin as part of an elaborate resurrection scene during a revival meeting. Dressed in a white suit and boxed within a black performance, young Bliss never develops an identity beyond the masking itself. Whereas Bliss Proteus Rinehart is a model for Negro identity as improvisational in *Invisible Man*, in *Juneteenth* Bliss is a model for the inability to escape the narratives of essentialism. Ellison had to invent a form that presents the escapes from behind the mask that Bliss's narrative cannot.

Since Ellison's imperative is to use the novel as a tool for social/cultural critique, a symbolic action, he had to create a form that would allow him to "change all the stories up" about American nationhood and identity, history and blackness (Iyer 2004, 395). Vijay Iyer's analysis of storytelling in jazz performance is crucial here. Describing a transcription of an audio recording of a John Coltrane studio session on which the players muse about the process of creating a specific feeling in play, Iyer explains that the musicians come to the conclusion that by asserting the chord changes in his solo, Coltrane can tell his own story. In fact, one player argues that "(the) changes *themselves* is some kind of story" (Iyer 2004, 394). Iyer argues that this claim illustrates that narrativity in jazz performance places philosophical importance on both the music and "'in' the moment-to-moment act of making the changes . . . it implies a shift in emphasis from top-down notions of overarching coherence to bottom-up views of narrativity *emerging* from the minute laborious acts that make up musical activity" (Iyer 2004, 395). Iyer proposes that the stories the improvisers tell are revealed not as simple linear narratives, but as "fractured, exploded" ones. Even more, jazz is a music of embodiment; that is, improvised musical narratives have sonorous and kinesthetic properties that are fixed to bodily feeling, performance.

Ellison's play with the various points of view and narrative techniques was an attempt to tell the story of race, nation, and identity differently. Again, it is clear that the performance demands for novelists and jazz improvisers are different. However, it is worth noting that Ellison's sense of play emerges from the same tensions that blues idiom improvisation does: the "opposition of freedom and necessity, of spontaneity and order."[43] Though his characters misuse the folk forms and rituals he invokes within, for example, Ellison can use call and response and masking as framing devices for the novel's concept.

Late in *Juneteenth*, for instance, Sunraider, unconscious and dreaming, imagines hunting in a deep wood and realizes that "surprise, speed and camouflage are the faith, hope and charity of escape, and the essence of strategy. Yes, and scenes dictate masks and masks scenes. Therefore the destructive element offers its own protective sanctuary. . . . To imaginate is to integrate negatives and positives into a viable program supporting one's own sense of value. . . . Therefore freedom is a willful blending of opposites, a conscious mixing of ungreen, unbrown things and thoughts into a brown-green shade. . . . Where's the light? What's the tune? What's the time" (Ellison 1999, 328). After years of defying the realities of mixture in the American context, especially the commingling of Negroes and whites, the senator is confronted by his own suppressed psychological awareness that masking and context define each other. Sunraider's definition of freedom as the blending of opposites, the integration of negatives and positives, brings us back to Ellison's theory that the novel as a form is meant to preserve and destroy the literary tradition, affirm and reject the culture.

Ellison's notion that the novel is a symbolic act of artistic and political significance and his conception of it as an instrument upon which to improvise coalesce around John Dewey's argument about *play* in art: "The very existence of a work of art is evidence that there is no such opposition between the spontaneity of the self and objective order and law. In art, the *playful* attitude becomes interest in the transformation of material to serve the purpose of a developing experience. Desire and need can be fulfilled only through objective material, and therefore playfulness is also interest in an object" (Dewey 1980, 279). Thinking of the collision of styles in the larger second novel project and its slimmer version in *Juneteenth*, we might imagine that Ellison was playing opposites in order to give birth to a form, a body shaped out of Negro culture, that would also give birth to a new America.

With child preachers, improvisation, and new Americas in mind, we turn next, in Movement III, to an examination of James Baldwin and the various positions he inhabited in order to move between the shadow world of the literary intellectual and the active world of the witness/chronicler during the CRM. While Ellison worked to establish the complex exchanges of African American masculinity, Baldwin drew on jazz to aid his deconstruction of masculinity.

Cutting Session
Baldwin as Prizefighting Intellectual, Baldwin as Improvising Intellectual

The boxing ring is the ultimate focus on masculinity in America, the two-fisted testing ground of manhood, and the heavy weight champion, as a symbol, is the real Mr. America. **Eldridge Cleaver**

I "The Fight"

When James Baldwin covered the 1962 heavyweight championship bout between Floyd Patterson and Sonny Liston his literary career was nearing its apex. But in "The Fight," Baldwin's only essay on boxing, he wrote as if cornered by the semiotics of the match. Rather than write a sports profile about the athletes or their feats, Baldwin retreated to a position that combined elements of the disinterested, objective reporter with those of what we have come to know as New Journalism. Baldwin realized that the Patterson / Liston fight carried political implications given the representations of masculinity and blackness embodied by the two fighters—the angry, "inarticulate" Liston, as Baldwin named him, versus the complex, liberal, "good Negro," Patterson.

Noting his own wariness about whom to side with, Baldwin wrote, "I felt terribly ambivalent, as many Negroes do these days, since we are all trying to decide, in one way or another, which attitude, in our terrible American dilemma, is the most effective: the disciplined sweetness of Floyd, or the outspoken intransigence of

Liston" (Baldwin 1989, 333). Remarkable here is Baldwin's willingness to implicate himself in his critique of the political routes symbolized by each fighter. Even more, in the midst of the CRM heavyweight prizefighting came to symbolize the American discourse on identity and race, masculinity and democracy.[1]

Baldwin understood that the CRM hinged on definitions of American masculinity and African American identity.[2] In "The Fight" he tips his hand about the definitions that he favors by creating an analogue between himself and Patterson. While watching Patterson at his training camp, Baldwin describes the fighter's rope-jumping technique as "very beautiful and gleaming," and the fighter reminds the author of a "boy saint helplessly dancing [as] seen through the steaming window of a store front church."[3] The latter remark is an allusion to the characters and setting of Baldwin's first novel, the roman a clef *Go Tell It on the Mountain*, and to his personal history as a boy preacher in Harlem during the 1930s. As far as Baldwin was concerned, the fight's potential to shift the defining terms of masculinity or black identity rested on Patterson's victory.

A Patterson victory, the retention of his title, would have meant that the fight game (and Baldwin's aesthetic of love, redemption, and self-creation) could also retain its representation of moral, egalitarian ideals; in 1962 Patterson was an avatar of American democratic possibilities. Liston, with his aura of boiling rage and criminality, his ineloquent brutishness, was read as the antithesis of boxing's romantic ideals; he was the very stereotype of Negro depravity. A Liston victory would have turned the representation of blackness and Negro masculinity away from the integrationist attitudes of the CRM and back toward essentializing, racist narratives of black identity.

In his analysis of the fight's promise, Baldwin sees his own philosophical dilemmas embodied by Patterson and the extreme consequences of those dilemmas impressed on Liston's person. Though Baldwin's political allegiances are entangled with Patterson's, he also understands something of Liston's longing "for respect and responsibility" (Baldwin 1989, 333). Liston's inarticulate machinations remind Baldwin of the unspeakable pain, the brutal marginalization of generations of silently aching black men. Liston had had more happen to him than he knew how to express and he was "inarticulate in a particularly Negro way—he has a long tale to tell which no one wants to hear" (Baldwin 1989, 333). While Patterson may be Baldwin's political parallel, it is for Liston that Baldwin wordsmiths, musters a vocabulary, a narrative. Baldwin feels some thick connection to Liston since his vocation demands that he provide eloquent, truthful representations of American Negroes; Baldwin gives voice to the barely audible, seething rage brought on by marginalization from the sociopolitical and economic mainstream.

By the end of the piece, it becomes evident to Baldwin (and his readers) that his relationships to Patterson and Liston are fraught with the complexities of the historical moment: the process of achieving political parity for American Negroes. As Baldwin explains near the end of "The Fight," Patterson and Liston represent two different moral positions, two different political visions, that all Americans are forced to choose between. Whichever representation Americans accept, Baldwin argues, they must deal with their responsibilities as citizens. Primarily, explains Baldwin, these responsibilities are the creation of a real, equitable democratic American life and the willingness to reject stereotypes of blackness in favor of complex Negro identities. The failure to accept those complicated, contingent responsibilities, for black and white Americans alike, Baldwin suggests, will lead ultimately to gross political and humanistic failures.

Movement III analyzes the contingencies among American masculinity, American citizenship, and African American identity. I illustrate in the following pages how Baldwin used the essay form as an improvisational space for demonstrating these connections and for sparring with his intellectual/literary "family relations" like Harriet Beecher Stowe, William Faulkner, Richard Wright, and Norman Mailer, his chief nemesis upon his return to the U.S. cultural milieu.[4]

In his battle with Mailer, for instance, Baldwin recontextualized masculinity in an effort to forward a new conception of American democracy. Displaying a pious attitude toward American racial history, Baldwin's essays also framed a new American citizenry or public. Eschewing what Richard Rorty calls the "inherited narratives" of the American social context, the newly formed public, Baldwin hoped, would radically transform the practice of American democracy. In what follows I will illustrate and extend Robert Reid-Pharr's provocative argument that achieving African American identity is a "constant process of choosing blackness [and] choosing a relationship to American history that privileges critique without insisting upon the destruction of either state or society."[5] Following Baldwin, I argue that Americans could achieve radical democracy by learning to improvise narratives of self-becoming that also communicate the power of what John Dewey calls the American "great community."

While Baldwin's essays emphasize his brand of improvisational pragmatist cultural critique, in short stories like "This Morning, This Evening, So Soon" and "Sonny's Blues" Baldwin dramatizes his theory of improvisational masculine identity. The two unnamed narrators of these stories use jazz as a model for the processes of achieving selfhood and creating Deweyan great community. Rather than speak the author's cultural critiques about American masculinity and democracy, Baldwin's narrators exemplify the new American citizenship by *performing* African American identity and black manhood. That is, Baldwin constructs his narrators so as to emphasize their pious attitudes toward familial history and their efforts to redescribe black male identity. Rejecting American gender norms and American masculine ideals, the narrators improvise and perform black manhood. As I argue later, Baldwin's essays, like "The Fight," punched out creative cultural space for his fictional characters to fill in with improvised narratives about manhood, democracy, and African American identity.

II The Black Intellectual as Prizefighter

Baldwin's ambivalence in "The Fight" is notable because his attitude, though leaning in the direction of Patterson, allowed him the space to evoke a prophecy about "the American dilemma." While Baldwin sense a wrathful agony in Liston's silence, younger cultural and political radicals like LeRoi Jones and Eldridge Cleaver saw Liston as the symbol for a new urgent militancy, a raging black masculinity.[6] Even though the full effect of the CRM's paradigm shift toward the various forms of black political and cultural nationalism was at least four years away in 1962, when Baldwin describes himself as being "depressed" about the possibilities of a Liston victory, or as having a "deepened depression" at the sight of a fallen and knocked out Patterson looking "terribly small" at the feet of Liston, one senses that Baldwin's depression lies in seeing that his own "sweet discipline" is doomed against the brute power of the mythologies of masculinity and essentialized blackness. Moreover, Baldwin's depression is an extension of his ambivalence about having to choose from only two representations of black masculinity that are regrettably narrow yet inextricably yoked.

"The Fight" presents Baldwin at a philosophical crossroads: although he was completely invested in the fight for Negro political equality, Baldwin's style of expressing his cultural critiques was in flux. Though he chose not to include "The Fight" in any essay collections, the piece confronts powerfully the complexities of American democracy, African American identity, and intellectual work. In fact, "The Fight" begs us to reexamine earlier Baldwin essays such as "Many Thousands Gone," "A Question of Identity," "The Discovery of What It Means to Be an American," and "The Black Boy Looks at the White Boy" in which the author accepts the rudiments of gender and racial essentialisms in order to perform disciplined deconstructions of them.

When he left for France in 1948, Baldwin was ambivalent about his American citizenship; his alienation from the social system, he believed, impeded his creative powers. Desiring to serve as a witness to the CRM, Baldwin returned to the United States after eight years living in Paris. Events such as the Montgomery Bus Boycott and the desegregation of public schools in Southern cities like Charlotte, North Carolina, and Little Rock, Arkansas, charged him to repatriate. So, in 1957 Baldwin began an extended period of continual drift, swinging back and forth between Europe and America, between Greenwich Village and Harlem, between narrating the processes of individual identification and interrogating conceptions of group solidarity, racial and political. His movement among these positions, geographical, psychological, philosophical, is another striking example of antagonistic cooperation.[7]

Baldwin's pragmatist vision and his willingness to fight for improvisational space distinguish his civil rights era essays. He displays his pragmatic critical approach in essays about the political, social, and psychological contexts that also trapped him intellectually and existentially: masculinity, America, and blackness. Just as

Patterson and Liston (and later Cassius Clay/Muhammad Ali) were inclined to accept the brutality of their sport in order to elude it or deliver it, Baldwin accepted his intellectual prisons in order to design escape routes from them. As Baldwin argues in the essay "Equal in Paris," engaging the various humiliations that Western cultures impose on the black male psyche is a form of antagonistic cooperation.[8]

African American intellectuals wage political and cultural battles in order to communicate the complexities of being both black and American. For instance, one claim about the final message of *Invisible Man* is that "there are no real victories for the black fighter, for the prizefight into which the fighter is both coerced and seduced is itself an utter corruption and distortion of democratic values and American individualism."[9] The seductive and coercive nature of that fight speaks to both the affirming possibilities and the self-denying actualities of black intellectual work; the critic is forced to essentialize "blackness" so as to publicly demystify essentialist notions of Negro life in the hopes of creating better access for all citizens to the American political mainstream.[10] While Ellison's novel gives us the black intellectual as fighter in the ring, Baldwin actualizes this characterization by performing the role publicly.

Baldwin's essays accentuate a striking style of black intellectual practice: the black intellectual as prizefighter. Aligning Baldwin's belletristic approach with boxing is not as strange as it might appear. In his essays the author cooperates antagonistically with his intellectual foils in order to engage in a discourse on antiessentialist self-identification and the formation of a public or community to challenge the American cultural and political status quo and develop a new definition of democracy. Tejumola Olaniyan's description of "discourse" as violence imposed upon bodies and languages is useful here: Baldwin as prizefighter helps us to locate both his body (and his criticism) at the center of the discourse that trusses the "incessant battles for the framing and definition of 'reality.'"[11] The most significant battles of postwar American life involve the nature and definition of American citizenship and of Negro participation in that institution. And, as Richard Wright once opined, these citizenship battles are really battles between Negroes and whites over the nature of reality.

III Recontextualizing American Masculinity

Baldwin realized that his identity was partially a product of the forceful assertion of the white American will upon his body—the negation of his humanity. In his essay "A Question of Identity" Baldwin explains that once the exiled or alienated American demands something from his past, from his suppressed memory, he will recognize himself, he "discovers his own country and brings to an end [his] alienation [from his] American [self]."[12] Baldwin's description also illustrates a convention of boxing: while many suggest that boxing is a "matter of one fighter asserting himself forcefully over another," boxing is also a "matter of accepting that what you become rests in the hands of others. Or in the hands of orchestrated circumstance."[13] However, as the American "demands" something of his "suppressed memory" he is also working against the grain of those forceful assertions or orchestrated circumstances, in antagonistic cooperation with them, in order to assert his own self-identified Americanness. Baldwin probes his own grievous wounds, his own biography, in order to reveal the contingencies and ambiguities of human experiences.

Baldwin's probing recalls Kenneth Burke's theory of piety. Piety, Burke writes, is a "desire to round things out, to fit experiences together into a unified whole. Piety is the sense of what properly goes with what" (Burke 1954, 74). In the play for unification and proper matching, Burke argues, piety is a quest for meaning. But, as Beth Eddy argues, piety also "has to do with an attitude toward history—one's own history" (Eddy 2003, 27). Baldwin's attitude toward his own "suppressed memory" is an attempt to interrogate American racial history in order to fit his experiences as a black man and as an American into a unified whole. But Baldwin's quest for meaning also involved addressing the forced assertions of American racism and accepting how the hands of others or orchestrated circumstances had shaped him. Baldwin's sense of "what properly goes with what" included fighting against the grain of the American status quo.

Baldwin understood, however, that his analyses might be rejected by the very public he hoped would respond to them. In the American social frame intellectual critique is suspect because it seemingly contradicts American notions of masculine certainty and production. In Europe, Baldwin writes, "the American writer . . . is released, first of all, from the necessity of apologizing for himself. It is not until he *is* released from the habit of flexing his muscles and proving that he is just a 'regular guy' that he realizes how crippling this habit has been." While in Paris Baldwin does not have to pretend to be something he is not because the artist doesn't suffer under the same suspicions held against him in America. Baldwin claims that the American writer fights his way "to one of the lowest rungs on the American social ladder," a position achieved through stubborn work ethic, only to realize that he "probably *has* been a 'regular fellow' for much of his adult life, and it is not easy for him to step out of that lukewarm bath" (Baldwin 1998b, 139).

When Baldwin writes about the "muscle-flexing habit" of the "regular guy" he's describing the American desire for anti-intellectual masculine action, *doing*. American masculinity, argues Baldwin, is framed by the capitalist ethos of production and consumption. But Baldwin was interested in a masculine ethos that challenges capitalism aesthetically, intellectually, and analytically. Like the Beats, he saw postwar American culture becoming more tightly governed by corporate structures and the sway of America's international economic power. However, the ability to serve close critique does not eliminate the status quo or "lukewarm" social definitions of gender ethos.

Baldwin pulled together the contingencies of the fight: he had to accept the masculinist corporate terms of production and consumption in order to defeat or even address their relationship to the status quo of American life. But the contingent relationship between gender ideals and the social/cultural status quo also illustrated for Baldwin the occupational hazard of black intellectual prizefighting: his essays expressed a desire for an escape from the racial and gender status quo while also elucidating an awareness that this desire might go unmet unless the language of the discourse was seeded with new meanings (for older terms like masculinity) or fleshed out with a new vocabulary.

Burke argues in classical pragmatist fashion that in the quest for meaning new meanings for older vocabulary terms are created, not breaking completely our relationships to old meanings, but certainly reweaving those meanings as our beliefs shift. For instance, American political contexts and social environments were forced open by civil rights advocates; rather than eliminating the democratic vocabulary, Baldwin redescribed the key terms of the vocabulary to include African American experiences. Baldwin's pious redescriptions or recontextualizations were also an attempt to construct a "public," an American audience willing to probe the national history, analyzing the suppressed elements of Negro history while orienting themselves loyally to the sources of their individual identities.

In his cultural criticism Baldwin recontextualizes key terms of American discourse by creating narratives that either redescribe identity, redescribe community, or redescribe the relation of the two. These redescriptions illustrate the process of replacing inherited contingencies with self-made contingencies. Rorty suggests that the more an individual or a society accepts powerful widespread changes, such as, say, the CRM, "the more use [an individual or society] has for a notion of 'a new context'" (Rorty 1991, 94). While this context can be a new classification or a new vocabulary, a new personal or social purpose, Baldwin wants to recontextualize terms like "democracy" and "citizenship." For Rorty, recontextualization is a way of explaining contingency, self-creation, and affiliation. Baldwin recontextualizes by performing or representing new definitions of democracy and citizenship, American masculinity, and Negro identity.

Recontextualizing black intellectual practice as prizefighting draws attention to the performance of Baldwin's body seduced by the promise of political and cultural gains (the full benefits of American citizenship, economic parity) while simultaneously "infighting" against coercive, essentialist narratives about African American identity. As Eldridge Cleaver explains in this movement's epigraph, the spectacle of the prizefight dramatizes the contingent relationship between conceptions of American masculinity and national identity. The prizefighting metaphor makes "black intellectual" into a performance of the contingencies among intellectual work, the construction of American masculinity, American citizenship, and anti-essentialist conceptions of Negro identity.

IV Baldwin and Mailer Trade Twelves

In Baldwin's analysis of black masculinity, the damage exacted on the black male body and psyche is a reality that "white men do not want to know" (Baldwin 1998b, 208). This is not the "Negro reality" that Norman Mailer offers in "The White Negro" (1957). There, Mailer explains the phenomenon of the hipster or the Beat, the social and aesthetic pose that grew out of the Greenwich Village (mostly white) intellectual crowd during the late 1940s and 1950s. Mailer theorizes that this pose or style is an attempt to embody "the Negro" ethos. Mailer suggests that because of the marginal social and political status that Negroes are accorded (in post–World War II America), they must negotiate the American scene with an innate ability for grace under pressure. According to Mailer's logic, since Negroes must live on the margin with violence and oppression every day, their culture owns the mythical masculine power that mainstream white American culture once had but now has lost or has, at least, repressed. Further, Mailer's philosophy says that since the black male body is socially marginal, it has license to sexually consume other bodies for the purpose of asserting an illicit power or irresponsibility; the goal is to achieve one "apocalyptic" orgasm after another.

The Negro male, particularly the Negro jazz musician, was the symbol of Beat generation aesthetics because he provided the marginal, revolutionary, and radical cultural position that they covet. In "The White Negro" Mailer describes the Negro margin as the space where white masculine vigor can be replenished and the diminished vitality of American culture revived. "It is no accident," writes Mailer, "that the source of Hip is the Negro, for he has been living on the margin between totalitarianism and democracy for two centuries. But the presence of Hip as a working philosophy in the sub-worlds of American life is probably due to jazz, and its knifelike entrance into culture, its subtle but so penetrating influence on an avant-garde generation."[14] To paraphrase Allen Ginsberg: angelheaded hipsters walking the Negro streets, contemplating jazz indeed! Absent from Mailer's evaluation is any discussion of the root motivations for bebop's emergence, the development of the new musical vocabulary of Gillespie, Monk, and Parker, or how those musical changes implied changes in Negro culture and experience. Like Ginsberg, Mailer is all too happy to sanctify the efforts of the Beats without contemplating the Negroes living with, for, or through jazz.

In this metaphorical boxing match between Mailer's critique of the Beat attitude and Negro masculinity and Baldwin's critique of American masculinity and the cultural status quo, modern jazz, especially bebop, is the soundtrack. Jazz is crucial to both Mailer's analysis and Baldwin's response to it. Mailer's reading of the sexual freedoms on the margin seems defensible given jazz's conception in Storyville, the turn-of-the-century red-light district of New Orleans. Tales of the jazz musician as pimp or hustler have been prevalent since Jelly Roll Morton began his performance career in brothels and made his ends meet by pimping prostitutes. By the middle of the century, when Mailer was formulating his conceptions, crucial late modernist musicians like Miles Davis and Charles Mingus bragged about their own pimping.[15] But their "muscle-flexing" masculine economics and their high art performances clash in the same ways that Baldwin explains the crisis surrounding the American writer's position on the social ladder.

Mingus's version of "pimping" had less to do with "working girls" than with his aggressive mixture of revolutionary ideals and radical philosophy. His pimping was a "commentary on and alternative to victimization by the music industry" (Porter 2002, 143). While this concept of pimping illuminates the heterosexual and masculine codes long associated with jazz performance, Mingus's pimping is also a metaphor for Romantic notions of self-invention and improvisation. Eric Porter explains that the Romantic core of black male jazz performance is laced through with female attributes. Jazz musicians like Mingus developed personal aesthetics that favored "feminine" sensibilities, such as "originality, creativity, and emotional expression" while also tapping into an "androcentric artistic modernism as they constructed themselves as 'serious artists.' As in earlier decades, musicians' ideas about their own artistry went hand in hand with economic relationships with women" (Porter 2002, 80).

Just as it was for Duke Ellington, music was Mingus's mistress. Mingus's pimpery was a means to personal liberation from both the economic system colluding against his artistry and the social structure trapping him racially. Baldwin's theory seems a useful lens here: in order to explode the codes of muscle-flexing American masculinity, Mingus must accept those codes. In his autobiography, *Beneath the Underdog,* Mingus imagines that pimping gives him a financial exit from the society, allowing him to become a member of "the raceless people of the earth."[16] One imagines the people who have been "raced" within other societies are the ones who populate Mingus's dream society of raceless citizens. I think Mingus's concept also suggests one hidden factor of jazz performance: even though jazz musicians function within the Negro engineered blues idiom, the imperative of improvisation forces them to express aesthetic concepts that resist essentialist ideologies.

Though Mailer's formulations of hip and of "the Negro" are built on themes of hustling and pimping, alternative economies, the control of female bodies, and the assertion of violent masculine power, he could not imagine the metaphorical pimping that Mingus plays in his music. Mailer's notions are difficult to stomach because they rely on a vision of the black male body as a barely bridled, pathological orgasm machine. While Mailer shrewdly analyzes the flaws of Northern liberalism in "The White Negro," he fails to examine how his critique renders black masculinity an absolute, primitive state.

Mailer ignores that the white male hipster has a choice to make (albeit a rather banal choice) about his social position in the center or on the margin; it is a choice that is really only available to those who will always have access to the center. When "The White Negro" was published Negroes did not have the luxury of choosing between the center and the periphery; they had been forced into the political and social margin by the racist structures implicit in American democratic practice at the time. As opposed to Mailer's analysis, Baldwin's writing illustrates another set of choices waiting to be deliberated—another set of responsibilities waiting to be accepted. Baldwin's criticism battles the essentialist thinking behind Mailer's vision of black masculinity by exposing "what a strangely perishing thing" masculinity actually is.[17]

Baldwin's first counter to Mailer's vision reveals the antiessentialist possibilities available below the surface of the American social framework. Writing in 1959, Baldwin proclaims in the essay "The Discovery of What It Means to Be an American" that "American writers do not have a fixed society to describe. The only society they know is one in which nothing is fixed and in which the individual must fight for his identity. This is a rich confusion, indeed, and it creates for the American writer unprecedented opportunities" (Baldwin 1998b, 142). However, the author is also aware that the opportunities for imagining a "complex" American reality are equal to the tensions built into the thickness of American mythologies. Baldwin writes that "in a society much given to smashing taboos without thereby managing to be liberated from them," removing ourselves from determined slots "will be no easy matter." Here Baldwin describes a complex reality that Mailer had declined to consider: in the process of shedding old vocabularies, meanings, or identities in order to accept new ones, the quest for meaning is a rich confusion, not a search for better orgasms (Baldwin 1998b, 142).

In 1961 Baldwin targeted Mailer's theory of Negro masculinity more directly with his essay "The Black Boy Looks at the White Boy." The essay begins in Paris, 1956, when Baldwin first encounters Mailer. The Harlem-reared Baldwin describes his meeting with the Brooklyn-bred Mailer as "two lean cats, one white and one black . . . circling around each other. . . . We were trapped in our roles and our attitudes: the toughest kid on the block was meeting the toughest kid on the block" (Baldwin 1998, 270). Baldwin's image evokes a potential brawl; it is also predatory and sexualized.

The crucial aspect of this moment in the essay is that Baldwin accepts that their role-playing is identity construction shaped by the hands of the other. Rather than taking on Mailer's version of Negro essence as potently honed sexuality, thus innocent and free of modernity, Baldwin (writing five years after the first meeting and with chilling self-exposure) throws analytical jabs at the meanings that gird American masculinity and label black masculinity libidinal: "I think that I know something about the American masculinity which most men of my generation do not know because they have not been menaced by it in the way that I have been. It is still true, alas, that to be an American Negro male is also to be a kind of walking phallic symbol: which means that one pays, in one's own personality, for the sexual insecurity of others. The relationship, therefore, of a black boy to a white boy is a very complex thing" (Baldwin 1998b, 269–70). Framed as a memoir, this essay spins into recontextualizing social criticism. Negro marginality is prerequisite for Mailer's analysis of power and, subsequently, for the white hipster to have access to a "knife-like" masculine power source. Mailer's theory depends on phallic fantasies, while Baldwin's depends on exploding the phallic phantom that menaces him; he reweaves the meaning of black masculinity.

Yet Baldwin's acute realization does not allow him to easily escape this racial prison. "The world," Baldwin writes, "tends to trap and immobilize you in the role you play; and it is not always easy — in fact, it is always extremely hard — to maintain a kind of watchful, mocking distance between oneself as one appears to be and oneself as one actually is" (Baldwin 1998b, 271). Baldwin's rhetorical approach, oscillating between offensive and counter-punching stances, embraces the ambiguity of a double awareness — he understands the imperatives for both purposefully exposing the myth of Negro sexual potency and cautiously embracing the reality that the social world immobilizes him in phallic status.

Baldwin's ambiguities — figured, if you will, as the liberal, religious Patterson versus the angry, inarticulate Liston; the analytical writer versus the muscle-flexing consumer culture; the Negro as walking phallus versus the Negro as thinking man; the "watchful, mocking distance between oneself as one appears to be and oneself as one actually is" — oppose Mailer's supine acceptance of the masculine order and racial essentialism. Mailer's desire to know "how power . . . really works, in detail" keeps him from gaining sincere knowledge of what it means to be hip or black, or what meanings can come from jazz (Baldwin 1998b, 279).

Baldwin knows power and its workings; without such intelligence, he claims in the piece, he would be dead. The author argues that Mailer cannot earn any knowledge of Negro lives or of the cultural pose of "coolness" or "hip-ness" because he fails to understand that "cool" is a Negro-invented defensive stance that wards off menace by facing it or performing it. "To become a Negro man, let alone a Negro artist," Baldwin explains, "one had to make oneself up as one went along. This had to be done in the not-at-all-metaphorical teeth of the world's determination to destroy you. . . . Now this is true for everyone, but, in the case of a Negro, this truth is absolutely naked: if he deludes himself about it, he will die. This is not the way this truth presents itself to white men" (Baldwin 1998b, 279). Baldwin recognizes that his discourse with Mailer is about the nature of reality. His response to Mailer reclaims jazz as an expression of Negro experience rather than fodder for the rejuvenation of white masculinity. The jazz artist expresses the naked truth of Negro survival through improvisation.

For the ethnic inhabitants of the colored margin, difference is a rigid hierarchy of power and agency. But the delusion embedded in "The White Negro" is that the margin is the seat of power because it is different from the mainstream; however the slip in Mailer's theory is that for those with the power of agency, "difference is an exercise of choice."[18] Importantly, as a member of the generation of black, mostly male, artists who created bebop culture, Baldwin understood that the Negro male's imperative of self-invention motivated writers and jazz musicians alike. Unlike Mailer's, Baldwin's theory of American masculinity made him privy to both the expressions of joy and freedom and the expressions of terror and anxiousness contained in bebop. The music's knife-like qualities bear witness to the psychological traumas of being young, black, and male in America. Baldwin knew that "bebop was a mass performance of a male identity crisis" (Early 1989, 309). And improvisation fashioned artistically embraces the ambiguities of Negro consciousness while exposing paths out of trauma and away from essentialized masculine and black identities.

For the marginalized black subject, difference has been forced onto the body rather than chosen. Baldwin's insistence that self-creation is the key to survival in the American context is another rendering of pugilistic engagement. While boxing may be an apt metaphor for Baldwin's intellectual attitude, jazz improvisation becomes Baldwin's metaphor for self-invention and Negro experience. Jazz and boxing intersect as crucial sources for the construction of African American intellectual attitudes during the CRM.

V Framing the Public, Imagining a New Democracy: The Essay as Cutting Contest and Jam Session

While Baldwin presents an ethic of self-invention in "The Black Boy Looks at the White Boy," he doesn't extend that theory to explain jazz improvisation as self-invention. However, the essay does provide us with a lead back to the performance, if not the explanation, of improvisation as identity. Baldwin explains late in the essay that his revenge against the mortal power of racism will be the achievement of a "power which outlasts kingdoms" (Baldwin 1998, 279). Baldwin's will to power, I believe, is performed in the rhetorical strategies he employs. He needs a style that performs both pugilistic attitude and improvisational identity. Borrowing from the lyrical strategies of the blues, Baldwin uses first-person narration and personal experience to inculcate his audience with his critical riffs on Mailer's myth of Negro masculinity.

When he countered Mailer, Baldwin had begun to use the essay form to connect his private hope of achieving lasting power to his social hope for political equality. In many pieces Baldwin positions his reading audience at the center of his critical efforts by enticing them to be both spectators and, importantly, participants in his battles. Baldwin's penchant for the first person voice and autobiographical writing creates space for his analysis of race and masculinity in the American context. The autobiographer's "instinctive knowledge" of the effect of the narrative on the reader leads her "to exploit its potential for reference to endow that principal referent, the self, with a reality it might not otherwise enjoy." Autobiographical writing activates "specular reciprocity" matching the "author as reader" to the "reader as author," forcing the reader into the authorial consciousness. The reader/writer consciousness parallel, intrinsic to the experience of reading the autobiographical text, potentially makes readers "autobiographers themselves."[19]

Whether using the first-person singular or plural to level his critiques, Baldwin wrote to create a parallel between himself and his audience. In his early essays, like "Everybody's Protest Novel" and "Many Thousands Gone," Baldwin (writing almost exclusively for white and Jewish liberal intellectual magazines such as *Commentary* and *Partisan Review*) explored the use of the first-person plural as a strategy for incorporating his readers within his cultural critique.[20] For instance, in "Many Thousands Gone" Baldwin explains precisely that "our dehumanization of the Negro then is indivisible from our dehumanization of ourselves: the loss of our own identity is the price we pay for our annulment of his" (Baldwin 1998b, 20). Baldwin makes himself and his readers culpable for the irresolution of (our) American racial difficulties. As the author explains in both essays, the inability to overcome old racial hierarchies (white over black, master over slave) in favor of the possibilities for self-identification leaves us "clutching at the straws" of racial essentialism. Baldwin's approach deconstructs the "homogenous innocence" of whiteness, forcing his liberal white readership to shift their perspectives to his: the challenge of a Negro's vision of American reality.

The author's use of the first person plural crowds the ring, so to speak. Baldwin's strategy collapses the distance between the authorial, autobiographical stance and the position of the absent reader. This leveling action turns Baldwin's private realizations into public discourse. Here the power of autobiographical writing and the imperative of boxing are drawn together: the fighters are engaged in mutually assured creation and re-creation. Baldwin created discourse by drawing his referential self parallel to his readers' consciousnesses, his vision became theirs; readers were forced into the fray. Once inside the critical space—the ring or the cutting session—Baldwin directs them to look at the false essences of "blackness" and masculinity, and see themselves in the same spot where he uses his own body as an example of a new philosophical reality—the American Negro as thinking man.

However, the first-person singular dominates rhetorically in Baldwin's second essay collection, *Nobody Knows My Name.* Building upon the critical authority on display in *Notes of a Native Son,* Baldwin forgoes the embrace of the first-person plural to refocus readers with his philosophical vision. Once the audience accepts Baldwin's critical analyses, they fall under the purview of his analytical gaze. Writing on the cusp of the CRM's northern shift, Baldwin's "I" forces intellectual confrontation across the author/reader divide. For instance, in the essay "East River, Downtown: Postscript to a Letter from Harlem," Baldwin, explaining the "riots" held outside the United Nations following the assassination of Patrice Lumumba, responds pointedly to the liberal white Northeastern interpretation of the young, angry, black protesters: "What I find appalling—and really dangerous—is the American assumption that the Negro is so contented with his lot [in the United States] that only the cynical agents of a foreign power can rouse him to protest. It is a notion which contains a gratuitous insult, implying as it does, that Negroes can make no move unless they are manipulated. It forcibly suggests that the Southern attitude toward the Negro is also, essentially, the national attitude" (Baldwin 1998b, 181). Baldwin, speaking for himself rather than the representative American "we," matches the insult of the Negro's easy political malleability with the ultimate insult against Northern liberals. Though Baldwin's swift alignment attaches the racist Southern attitude to Northern white sensibility, that move only sets up his actual punch: Baldwin illustrates that the blind assumption of Negro contentedness is both "a cruel injustice" and a "grave national liability" (Baldwin 1998b, 181). Baldwin's combination builds an emphatic political claim, namely that first-class citizenship for Negroes is imperative for the fullest realization of American democracy.

The simplistic quality of Baldwin's argument disguises his radicalism. In his essays, Baldwin consistently disrupted the American status quo by tracing the "workings of race consciousness at [multiple] levels of American experience."[21] Rather than accept Mailer's claims about the Negro margin or black masculinity, or claims about the Negro's political manipulation, Baldwin acknowledges the "inescapable tension" between maintaining the status quo and the hope of creating a new American reality. But Baldwin's radical intellectual attitude stems from his willingness to describe (and redescribe) and then attempt the philosophical shifts required to escape the racial ideals that govern American life in favor of "the promise of multiracial democracy" (Balfour 2001, 138).

For Baldwin the realization of this multiracial democracy appeared to be far off in 1961. Speaking of the panic that Northern whites experienced as the processes of social and political integration disintegrated the racial status quo, Baldwin declared in "East River, Downtown" that white America's heightened fears stemmed from being unprepared for the risks involved in extending the benefits of citizenship to Negroes. While Northerners "proffer their indignation about the South as a kind of badge, as proof of good intentions," Negroes, urged by "pain and rage—and pity," refuse to trust whites, knowing that their panic and indignation are parts of a "long history of moral evasion." The inability of white Americans to risk ending the racial or political status quo has had an "unhealthy effect on the total life of the country, and has eroded whatever respect [Negroes] may once have felt for white people" (Baldwin 1998b, 183). Baldwin's political analysis reminds me of John Dewey's claim that democracy "is not an alternative to other principles of associated life. It is the idea of community life itself."[22] The principles and health of American democracy, the American community itself, cannot be actualized without dismantling the status quo racial order and gender role definitions.

VI Discovering What It Means to Be a Black Man: Improvising Manhood and the Great Community

While Baldwin's pugilistic approach forwarded new ideas about American masculinity and African American identity, his critical efforts did not imaginatively illustrate the escape routes he ultimately wanted his audience to pursue. Instead, Baldwin's fiction dramatized the possibility of self-creation through improvisation. Like Ellison, Baldwin found the roots of African American political and cultural philosophies in Negro musical forms. While Ellison projected but ultimately rejected the potential for a new political ethos in zoot-suited beboppers, Baldwin imagined that bebop aestheticized the processes of American spiritual and psychological reconciliation.

Just as musicians like Charlie Parker generated musical intelligence from the blues, Baldwin generated psychological ballast from the blues. In "The Discovery of What It Means to Be an American" Baldwin explains that his education in Americanness developed from his immersion in the blues of Bessie Smith. Smith forces Baldwin to acknowledge the psychological verities of his experience. Listening closely to her tone and her phrasing, Baldwin learns to acknowledge his "pickaninny" self; she helps him reconcile "being a 'nigger'" (Baldwin 1998b, 138). Naming himself "nigger" gives Baldwin claim to the truths about Southern experiences evident in Smith's blues and in black American history. Baldwin's blues memory directs him to reconcile with his familial history in the South.

As Southern resistance to the Supreme Court's rejection of segregation became increasingly acrimonious and violent, many African American writers and musicians began to filter political commentary into their works. Orval Faubus's obstinate stand against the integration of Little Rock Central High School in 1957 was part of Baldwin's inspiration to return to the United States from Paris as a witness/scribe. One musician who attempted to reconcile blues idiom music, Negro history, and the Southern political moment was the band leader, bassist, and composer Charles Mingus. On the album *Mingus Ah Um* Mingus and the Jazz Workshop parodied Faubus's infamous rejection of social change with the tune "Fables of Faubus." Like Baldwin's essays, Mingus's music is cosmopolitan. A composition cobbled together from vaudevillian show themes, the blues, modern theories of composition, Count Basie swing time and call and response framings, Duke Ellington / Billy Strayhorn arrangement aesthetic, and bebop progressions, "Fables" is a sonic intimation of the black artist's imperative to perform several musical / intellectual tasks simultaneously in order to communicate his aesthetic or critical vision.

Mingus's arrangement of the opening section sets the mood for the tune by coupling a limping, slithering tenor and alto saxophone duet with a melodic brass statement that creates an introductory call to "send in the clowns." The main theme is striking because it points at once to Mingus's purposely crude syncopations and his elegant, Ellingtonian harmonies. All the while, Mingus sews the faltering, dueling parts together with thick bass plucks that steady the main musical movements through counterpoint. During the solo breaks the rhythm section shifts between a loping, gangly gait and an urbane, swinging blues stroll. In the same way that Baldwin's use of first-person perspectives massages the rhetorical tonalities of his critiques, Mingus's bass lines conduct the attitudinal turns between lockstep group sensibilities and the freedoms of solo improvisation.

The sliding rhythmic meters articulate Mingus's reading of the strange maneuverings involved in maintaining older, musical orders when complex cultural possibilities demand new expressive forms. The rhythmic and stylistic blending— clowning, circus music, and hip, sophisticated jazz—delineates the cultural and political rearrangements afoot in the American South, from segregation to the exciting uncertainties of the CRM. Mingus's merger of Ellingtonia, Kansas City swing, and bebop explodes the stuttering, ragged opening themes; his cosmopolitan group responds to Faubus's fable of white supremacy by mocking his folly with combative yet eloquent intelligence. Mingus's meaty solo also provides a sonic model for the kind of performance we imagine Creole giving in Baldwin's "Sonny's Blues." As Creole does in his performance with

Sonny, Mingus creates blues idiom music that helps us "leave the shoreline and strike out for the deep water"[23] where the complexities of black masculinity, American citizenship, jazz performance, and Negro identity are swirling in the dramatic social and political sea changes of the civil rights era.[24]

Baldwin's favor for the blues and interest in the Southern black past are prevalent concerns in both "Sonny's Blues" and "This Morning, This Evening, So Soon" ("This Morning"). Both stories are filled with references to the "old folks," those Southern Negroes who moved northward during the Great Migration to populate urban sectors like Harlem. The stories are narrated by unnamed black men focused on tightening family ties against the traumas of black masculine performance in the American context. In both pieces Baldwin examines the power of improvisation to create escape passages from the traps of American masculinity and essentialized blackness.

Gathering his Paris-based, biracial, trinational family, the protagonist/narrator of "This Morning" is taking them to the United States where he will embark on a Hollywood film career. The narrator fears that the return to the United States will ruin his young son's life. Without the conditioning of Southern experience, the narrator worries, the dangers of being black and male in the United States will crush his son, Paul, psychologically, possibly mortally. While acting is the protagonist's new performance mode, he establishes his reputation as a jazz singer. And it is the combination of acting and jazz improvisation that leads the character to understand the source of his son's salvation.

In the story, his imminent return to the United States is propelled by the growth of his pious attitudes. He realizes that he must ultimately "perform" black masculinity for his son's salvation. While "Sonny's Blues" frames the jazz world as a masculine community, "This Morning" illustrates the world of black music and musicians as a hybrid one. The narrator of "This Morning" sings music that floats out from "the margins of high art, folk expression, and commodified mass culture as well as from the collision between working-class and bourgeois orientations and African American and European American musical cultures" (Porter 2002, 28). At those points of impact Baldwin introduces the complex, sensual aspects of black manhood.

One way into this frame is to note that Baldwin's choice to make his protagonist a singer rather than an instrumentalist elides the strict androcentrism of the jazz world. While male jazz singers have been prevalent and important to the jazz tradition, female singers have been dominant innovators in the lineage.[25] The narrator performs his masculinity in relation to an arts tradition that is markedly female. While he has achieved identity in Paris, the challenge becomes about his ability to perform this hybrid masculinity in the U.S. frame.

Early in the story, when the narrator recalls his initial voyage from France to New York City (and eventually to Alabama, his home state) after several years in Paris, the Atlantic Ocean is a liminal space where the masks of American identities can be dropped, allowing the white patrons to take pleasure in his presence. Their friendliness, however, "was not intended to suggest" the possibility of friendship. On the ship to America the narrator regards "an eerie and unnerving irreality about everything [his white shipmates] said and did, as though they were all members of the same team and were acting on orders from some invincibly cheerful and tirelessly inventive coach" (Baldwin 1998b, 878). While we often believe in "the universality of musical expression," especially the power of the improvisational tradition, Baldwin makes us see the limitations of "jazz" as a category in this instance. While jazz can be, at its best, an expression of the artist's "inner self" it is "also a commodity created by the music industry to conform to its idea of the tastes of a mass audience" (Porter 2002, 107). Mixing the commercial and existential, the narrator's musical choices describe a critical perspective.

Invited to perform on the penultimate evening of the voyage, the narrator recalls how nearness to the American shoreline brought the singer and his listeners into recognizable, prescribed roles:

> Nothing was more familiar to them than the sight of a dark boy, singing, and there were few things on earth more necessary. It was under cover of darkness, my own darkness, that I could sing for them of the joys, passions, and terrors they smuggled about them like steadily depreciating contraband. Under cover of the midnight fiction that I was unlike them because I was black, they could stealthily gaze at those treasures which they had been mysteriously

forbidden to possess and were never permitted to declare. (Baldwin 1998b, 878–79)

The protagonist/narrator's performance is multilayered. The sight of him onstage fulfills two qualifications for the American audience members: familiarity and necessity. The valence of familiarity suggests that the audience on board the ship, a group who the protagonist intimates is white, can only understand their identities in relationship to the performance of blackness. The valence of necessity amplifies the previous idea, claiming that the operation of the racial status quo or the hierarchical structure of the social arrangement can only function when the agents maintain their roles. Interestingly, the narrator claims that in this role play he is protected by his "own darkness." Baldwin, here, points toward the kind of masking that Ellison would find potent and pointedly Negro. That is, Baldwin's protagonist is able to escape the clutches of the racial status quo, "the midnight fiction" of his assumed difference and inferiority, while simultaneously observing its machinations and performing within it.

The most striking element of the narrator's analysis arrives when he notices the audience gazing at him, at "those treasures" which they are "forbidden" to possess or declare. Those treasures recall Baldwin's claim that in American culture black men are characterized as walking phallic symbols; the erroneous belief is that the potency of blackness lies in Negro genitalia. Possession in Baldwin's usage implies both the sense of ownership and that of amorous stake. In either sense, whites have refused to "declare" their positions in the legacy of owning (and emasculating) black men or their desire to lay loving, sexual claim to black male bodies. This instance of observational dexterity illustrates the protagonist/narrator's movements away from the accepted vocabulary on race and gender in the American context.

Singing a combination of folk and gospel tunes the narrator is able to present a consumable commodity while weaving his performance into a political commentary directed toward his audience. Rather than end his set with a rendition of Billie Holiday's "Strange Fruit," the protagonist decides to end the show with Mahalia Jackson's "Great Getting Up Morning." The choice is subtle: instead of emphasizing his critique of the American experience with a fairly recognizable Tin Pan Alley protest song, the narrator leans on the blues idiom tradition, singing a gospel tune that calls upon the audience to prepare for the "comin' of judgment." Baldwin turns the lyrical concept from a heavenly inclination toward an earthly one, intimating, on one hand, the coming changes of the civil rights era and on the other hand, the material realities of the narrator's re-entry to the American scene.

When the ship docks and the narrator steps on shore, returning to the United States means donning old masks of Negro performance. But no longer an expert performing on native grounds, the narrator has forgotten how to address the white customs inspectors, how to pitch his voice between "curtness and servility," which end of the "razor's edge of a pickaninny's smile" to display. Standing on gangplank between the ship and the Port of New York, the narrator considers the song "When Will I Ever Get to Be a Man?" (Baldwin 1998a, 882). Indeed, this crucial question implies another one about the narrator's return to America: what kind of man can he become?

These questions are central to Baldwin's cultural critical focus and they remind me of his classic assessment of blues idiom musical forms in *The Fire Next Time:* "In all jazz, and especially the blues there is something tart and ironic, authoritative and double-edged."[26] What white Americans miss in the blues, according to Baldwin, is what those who have been "down the line" understand: the blues expresses an ironic and sensual philosophy of life (Baldwin 1998b, 311). Sensuality is not a connotation of "quivering dusky maidens or priapic black studs." Rather, it refers to a "much simpler and much less fanciful" concept. "To be sensual," writes Baldwin, "is to respect and rejoice in the force of life, of life itself, and to be *present* in all that one does, from the effort of loving to the breaking of bread" (Baldwin 1998b, 311). Baldwin's explanation of sensuality stands as the expression of an element of his own intellectual vision. One who has been "down the line," one who has been present in the workings of experience, can then use those experiences as a way of coming to terms with the contingencies of identification. Sensuality and presence burn away the over-baked illusion of American freedom as an expression of masculine strength or sexual power. Celebrating the sensuality of the black body is one way to outlast kingdoms, to take *revenge*. Surviving the claustrophobic tenets of phallic symbolism, the African American male embraces and celebrates his body. Baldwin's definition of masculinity replaces the oppressive virility that Mailer promotes in the images of "the Negro."

Writing about his fictional characterizations of homosexual masculinity, Barbara Judson and Andrew Shin explain that although Baldwin rejected the aggressive virility of white liberal intelligentsia and radical black vanguard,

> he did celebrate the male body, not as juggernaut of power but as sensorium of comfort—the body as harbor and refuge . . . enjoying an amorphous, passive sexuality. . . . Baldwin's emphasis on the pleasures of nurturance as opposed to mastery was anathema to black radicals who feared and despised such imagery as a return to childish dependence, a soft-pedaling of agency and activism. But Baldwin repudiates masculine autonomy as the instrument of a repressive social order by reveling in the sensate . . . a convergence of bodies that opposes the formulations of white liberalism and black radicalism.[27]

Clearly it is important to see Baldwin's elaborations on the "sensate" qualities of the body as an avant-garde queer theoretical analysis.[28] However, it is also important to read Baldwin's conception of sensuality in terms of the powerful residue of the historically governed social codes that are impressed on all black bodies, male or female, queer and straight. Baldwin's sense of masculine sensuality is meant to disrupt heteronormative narratives of gender and sexuality, making room for a new philosophical awareness of the communion of the body (the sensual self) and identity (the constructed self). We can read this disruption and new awareness arising for the protagonist in "This Morning."

Preparing for his second trip to the United States, now as a movie star with a family in tow, the narrator of "This Morning" struggles with his fear about Paul's plight in the American racial theater. While the narrator's Paris is a "place where people were too busy with their own lives, *their private lives,* to make fantasies about mine, to set up walls around mine," the U.S. context is a place where white citizens "scarcely know that there is such a thing as history and so, naturally, imagine that they can escape [it] scot-free" (Baldwin 1998a, 891, 887).

Touring the cafes of St. Germain with Vidal, the director of his French film, the narrator meets a group of American Negro students. They bring news of desegregation in the South, white Southerners fighting to maintain the status quo, and the burgeoning black liberation movement. Sitting at the famous bohemian cafe Les Deux Magots singing gospel songs with these students, the narrator spies an old friend, Boona, a down-and-out Tunisian prizefighter, looking on. Fighting days over, Boona stews in Paris, unemployed and unable to return to Tunisia to take part in the independence movement afoot there.

Baldwin implies a connection between Boona's inability to return to North Africa and the narrator's worries about taking Paul back to North America. This is another point of cultural collision: while the students suggest to the narrator the possibility that black children might be able to become men and women in America, Boona, lost in cultural translation, signifies the possible psychological plight for the fighter who stays too long away from home. Getting by on thrift and thievery, Boona has been effectively emasculated by Parisian life. Late in the story, when Boona is accused of stealing from one of the students, the protagonist realizes that in the hierarchy of world politics and the beginning of the postcolonial era, American Negroes look to the exiled ex-fighter like the "luckier gangsters in a world run by gangsters" (Baldwin 1998a, 904). To Boona, out of luck and out of work, an unwanted African in Paris, the narrator and the young black students appear to be outside of or beyond the fray of racial hierarchies and colonial oppression simply by being able to move freely between the United States and France. Though the narrator understands the cause of Boona's misreading, it seems to instigate a realization about his imminent return to America.

Returning home early the next morning, the narrator retrieves his son from a neighbor's apartment and prepares the boy for the journey to the new world. Taking the lift to their apartment, the narrator explains, "I open the cage and we step inside. . . . I press the button and the cage, holding my son and me, goes up" (Baldwin 1998a, 907). Though Baldwin does not allow his protagonist to speak his understanding clearly, he does place them within a cage of masculinity. Heeding the call of the Negro liberation movement, the narrator takes up Boona's mantle as prizefighter, if only metaphorically, and joins it with his improvisational attitude as a way of steeling himself against the old forms of masculinity waiting in America. Rather than turn away from the demands of the new America burgeoning, the father and son accept the cage of masculinity in order to "go up" above it, transcending it, and in the process, improvise selves that defy and redefine masculinity.

As we've seen in "This Morning," in "Sonny's Blues," jazz performance creates access to familial past. As the logic of both narrations illustrates, only jazz improvisation can illuminate passages out of the blight. Sonny is the protagonist in absentia because his actions and his musical performance at the end of the piece drive the narrator's compulsion to story-tell. But the narrator of "Sonny's Blues" has the power to imagine his own familial history by establishing access to that past through a shading of light and dark. It is a history shaded darkly by danger with few light patches of safety.

Remembering his childhood and the powerful quietude of Sunday evenings the narrator explains that "the silence, the darkness coming, and the darkness in the faces [of the old folks] frightens the child obscurely. He hopes that the hand which strokes his forehead will never stop—will never die" (Baldwin 1998a, 841). But death is exactly what is at work between the fading day and the wattage of the lamp-brightened room. "The darkness outside," Baldwin writes "is what the old folks have been talking about. It's what they've come from" (Baldwin 1998a, 841–42). The darkness, amorphous and silent, is actually the palpable danger of violence, Southern violence perpetrated against black bodies. Baldwin unfolds the narrator's memory to dramatize the dangers of evening tide and darkness: the story of his uncle's death.

In telling the story of the uncle's murder, the narrator's mother draws on the Sunday silence to emphasize the dangers that encroach upon black masculinity. The silence and darkness of those Sundays pull the reading audience into the dark Southland of the Negro past. A victim of hit-and-run, the silent and long-dead uncle was run over by a car full of white men, whooping, hollering, drunk, and bent on having some mortal "fun" with any black male bystander. Baldwin makes this unnamed uncle a fun-loving, guitar-playing bluesman to emphasize the cultural context. For Baldwin the blues signifies danger as well as Negro resistance or survival.

When the car plows over the uncle, Baldwin makes the assault a symbol for all murderous crimes against black men. The narrator listens as his mother explains, "Your father heard his brother scream when the car rolled over him, and he heard the wood of that guitar when it give, and he heard them strings go flying, and he heard them white men shouting, and the car kept on a-going and it ain't stopped till this day. And, time your father got down the hill, his brother weren't nothing but blood and pulp" (Baldwin 1998a, 843–44). The story is important within the larger frame of the narrative because it instigates the fraternal responsibility that the narrator takes toward Sonny. As well, the story of their father and uncle mirrors the later brother bond between the narrator and Sonny. Baldwin's narrative palimpsest forces his audience to read both brotherly relationships back within the context of the South. The narrator must do all he can to save Sonny from the darkness falling across his body.

Written in late 1955 and early 1956 while Baldwin was living mostly in Paris, "Sonny's Blues" coincides with his initial interrogations of the Southern experience. Baldwin's first hard foray into the South came in his "position paper," "Faulkner and Desegregation" (1956).[29] A Harlem native, Baldwin had yet to make any extended trips to the South at the time that both pieces were conceived. His sense of the South was conjecture, and he made his arguments by extrapolating from his general awareness of the Negro condition there and by grafting to it his sense of Negro life in the North; his impressions of the South struck chords that improvised on themes of Negro experience in Harlem. (This explains one element of the yoked brother narratives in "Sonny's Blues.")

Baldwin's discourse on Faulkner draws out two concepts that become significant to his overall theory of Negro experience. According to Baldwin, Faulkner, as a national figure, is representative of both the Southern and the national white consciousness.[30] As Baldwin reads it, the condition of the American consciousness is knotted up by the desire to maintain the status quo and the piecemeal shift toward a new social and political order.[31] In Faulkner's case, famously, this means standing armed in the Mississippi streets to combat any outside influences charging in to rile the Negroes to revolt against the social hierarchy.

Like a critic interpreting a fictional character's psychological condition, Baldwin reads Faulkner's advice to "go slow" as a desperate effort to cling to a mystical sense of the South. This sensibility concedes the moral wrongness of Southern violence against Negroes, but sees the South as a beleaguered dream world or kingdom, making it "unjust to discuss Southern society in the same terms in which one would discuss any other society" (Baldwin 1998b, 210). But Baldwin's most telling critique explains that Faulkner is torn between maintaining constitutional principles of freedom and Southern principles of racial hierarchy.

Although Faulkner's books, like *Absalom, Absalom!* and *Go Down, Moses,* upset the very racial mythologies that Southern sensibilities rest on, he also understood that the maintenance of Southern society demanded the defense of the notions of racial purity and white-masculine power. Baldwin understood the defensive pose but also saw another set of corrupting positions behind it. On his first visits to the Deep South in 1957, Baldwin writes that the "Northern Negro," like himself, sees "that his ancestors are both white and black. The white men, flesh of his flesh, hate him for this reason. On the other hand, there is scarcely any way for him to join the black community in the South: for both he and this community are in the grip of the immense illusion that their state is more miserable than his own" (Baldwin 1998b, 197). Finally, Baldwin argues, this conflation of hatred, power, and martyrdom leads to the national delusion that American military and economic power gives the nation privilege over all other nation-states. This delusion is the last shred of the "great dream" of America.

In "Nobody Knows My Name: A Letter From the South," Baldwin explains that belief in the American dream "prevents us from making America what we say we want it to be" (Baldwin 1998b, 198). Baldwin supplements this point by imagining that the Georgia red soil he sees as his plane descends into Atlanta "has acquired its color from the blood that had dripped down from the trees. My mind was filled with the image of a black man, younger than I, perhaps, or my own age, hanging from a tree, while white men watched him and cut his sex from him with a knife" (Baldwin 1998b, 198). Baldwin's descent into the South is shrouded by the specters of lynching, past and recent, as he ticks off names like the Scottsboro Boys and Emmett Till. Picking up where invisible man's castration dream leaves off, Baldwin suggests that the bitter interracial history of the South (and the nation) is consistently hidden by the illusions of white masculine superiority, by the literal and figurative emasculation of black men, and by a refusal to pay the psychological toll of acknowledging such a history.

These histories of lynching and emasculation lie beneath the construction of "Sonny's Blues" and "This Morning." Baldwin explains that while he cannot imagine the things endured by Southern Negroes, those Negro migrants had not been able to imagine what awaited them in Harlem. The realities of the South and Harlem are different but the mortal dangers are parallel. Thus the narrator and Sonny have the potential of reliving in Harlem the Southern trauma of their father and uncle.

As well, Baldwin finds that the material world turns on the dynamics of Southern racial hierarchy and white Northerners' indignation, both designed to evade Negro humanity. "This failure to look reality in the face," Baldwin explains, "diminishes a nation as it diminishes a person, and it can only be described as unmanly" (Baldwin 1998, 208). This is a daring intellectual claim because it forces Baldwin to forward a redescription of what is masculine. His analyses of Negro experiences in the South and descriptions of Negro life in Harlem tell him that the black men are stronger than the white because they have nurtured a wisdom born from watching the nation fail its own principles. Baldwin develops tension in "Sonny's Blues," for instance, by explicitly dramatizing the physical and psychological dangers imbedded in Negro experiences while also redescribing masculinity in opposition to Mailer's rigid, phallic notion of the Negro margin.

Like Ellison, Baldwin understands the symbolic power of invoking racial violence in his fiction. However, in "Sonny's Blues" Baldwin shifts the emphasis from Ellisonian symbolic action to his own sense of pious action. As many critics attest, salvation is a key concept in Baldwin's work. "Sonny's Blues" draws together references to the blues and to African American spiritual practices to create the context for salvation. Baldwin's effort in this short story is much like Mingus's most significant arrangements and orchestrations in that it specifically invokes gospel and the blues, tying together the religious and the secular. But reading Baldwin and listening to Mingus, keeping in mind the social and political contexts of the CRM, we imagine and hear music that veers from a strictly religious sense of piety toward Burke's sense of secular therapy. Piety, like James's notion of truth, "must both lean on old truth and grasp new fact" (James 1987, 514). More importantly, pious action redescribes tradition in order to make it appropriate to new ideas and circumstance, broadening the tradition and its possibilities. Thus, jazz improvisation is a name for piety.

Baldwin turns away from religious resolution in "Sonny's Blues" by replacing Christian salvation with blues idiom salvation. The narrator begins to understand salvation when he spies Sonny listening to a street revival across from their apartment building. The singers perform "The Old Ship of Zion." The audience and the singers form a bond, but not because of the gospel group's easy access to holiness or because they've been sanctified. Rather, the listeners gathered around the group because "very little divided" them from the singers; the audience members knew "too much about [the singers], knew where they lived, and how" (Baldwin 1998a, 853). Crossing over to Zion, "being saved" happens for those willing to address their histories, improvising new identities from that pious awareness.

At the end of the story, Sonny performs his own "crossover" before a club audience after a long rehab-induced hiatus. The final number of his set is "Am I Blue?." David Yaffe suggests that Baldwin's choice of the Harry Akst/Grant Clarke tune illustrates an allegiance with certain Jewish artists and thinkers through jazz. But rather than pointing to the ecumenical or interracial qualities of jazz, I think that Baldwin is marking the imperative of blues idiom contexts to encourage the reinvention of standardized texts.[32] When Creole takes his turn in the break, soloing in the middle of "Am I Blue?," the blues he improvises for Sonny is a new composition that departs from the Akst and Clarke song structure. Creole's new song structure amplifies the anaphoric element built into the classic blues lyric form while imploring Sonny to respond with his own invention. The improvised exchange between the two musicians pushes the blues toward a secular spirituality, putting everyone listening (including the narrator), regardless of racial background, back into a specifically black cultural context.

As Sonny collects the notes and narrates his solo, he performs the history of his being, its pains and pleasures. The solo is the narration of self-reinvention, but the act is also redemption by improvisation. Listening and watching his brother, the narrator is also redeemed by his spontaneous musical education. He shifts from knowing only that "not many people ever really hear [jazz]" to understanding that jazz musicians must shape the cacophony emerging from the inaudible void, "imposing order on it as it hits the air" (Baldwin 1998a, 861). Sonny's play tells the narrator something orally unspeakable about music, about private personal histories and spirituality; the improvising on the bandstand is "terrible because it has no words, and triumphant, too, for that same reason. And his triumph, when he triumphs, is ours" (Baldwin 1998a, 861). Sonny's pious address of his experience spurs him to improvise. However, his play connects the audience together intimately, enticing them to also engage with their own narratives piously. In this regard Baldwin's vision of the performance is ceremonial, ritualized. Perhaps we would benefit in reading this moment in the story as Baldwin's attempt to articulate the conditions of community making.

Consider Sonny performing, his aesthetic shaped by Charlie Parker and bebop, the musicians improvising on the changes in the music. But as Iyer explains in Movement II, the changes are themselves the story. Dewey argues that in order for democracy to be actualized in the American context the public must be realized; but neither the public nor democracy can emerge until we change from being a great society to a great community. Society is the product of political arrangements, a grouping engineered by the nation-state. But community, according to Dewey, is the life of multi-group association freed from "restrictive and disturbing elements." The democratic community that Dewey imagines is one in which "everybody thinks that it is human solidarity, rather than knowledge of something not merely human, that really matters."[33] Dewey suggests that "communication can alone create a great community," but the dissemination of news and information are not enough to constitute it (Dewey 1927, 142).

Given that sign and symbol exchange sutures our collective experience, it is only art, Dewey argues, that can "break through the crust of conventionalized and routine consciousness" (Dewey 1927, 183). Influenced by Emerson's attraction to the low element of American culture, Dewey argues that the common things, not rare and remote things, "are the means with which the deeper levels of life are touched so that they spring up as desire and thought. This process is art. Poetry, the drama, the novel, are proofs that the problem of [presenting the news of change] is not insoluble. Artists have always been the real purveyors of news, for it is not the outward happening in itself which is new, but the kindling by it of emotion, perception and appreciation" (Dewey 1927, 184). Baldwin's understanding of the jazz moment, Sonny's meaning-producing improvised solo, is suffused with Dewey's pragmatist insight on art and community formation.

Jazz is significant, Baldwin suggests in "Sonny's Blues," because musicians improvise realities out of the inaudible darkness of African American history. Baldwin's effort is similarly significant because, as Keith Byerman writes, his linguistic aesthetic is limited in comparison to the musical aesthetic the story describes.[34] While the narrator's language communicates a balanced intellectual interpretation of the music, we must imagine how the improvising actually traverses the silent void, how it fulfills the promise of freedom:

> Freedom lurked around us and I understood, at last, that [Sonny] could help us to be free if we would listen, that in his face now, I heard what he had gone through, and would continue to go through until he came to rest in earth. He had made it his: that long line, of which we knew only Mama and Daddy. And he was giving it back, as everything must be given back, so that, passing through death, it can live forever. I saw my mother's face again, and felt, for the first time, how the stones of the road she had walked on must have bruised her feet. I saw the moonlit road where my father's brother died. And it brought something else back to me, and carried me past it, I saw my little girl again and felt Isabel's tears again, and I felt my own tears begin to rise. And I was yet aware that this was only a moment, that the world waited outside, as hungry as a tiger, and the trouble stretched above us, longer than the sky. (Baldwin 1998a, 863)

As opposed to the dark fears of the old folks, the darkness of the club allows the narrator to hear jazz's emancipatory properties. In their improvised discourse, Sonny, Creole, and the band perform from the shadow of the hungry tiger, but that effort to "say something" is the beginning of community formation. Sonny's solo portrays a pious attitude toward his musical and personal histories, encouraging the narrator to hear the family history and the old fears of darkness in the music. The audience is also charged to listen to the "news" of Sonny's experience (the common human suffering described in the musical changes), learning to transcend that painful experience through his lyrical effort. Sonny's artistry cannot squelch the voracious hunger of the world, but in facing the darkness and the void his musical narrative creates freedom and community.

The improvised expression of suffering, community, and freedom inspires Baldwin's closing—Sonny sipping Scotch and milk from "the very cup of trembling." The glass and its contents unfurl various ambiguities because their meanings veer from the intent of the Biblical verses Baldwin invokes. The drink contains the promise of both nourishment (milk) and destruction (whiskey), and with no Biblical reference to the cup of trembling remaining in the possession of Israel, Sonny is left between grace and suffering (in this sense, we might also read the narrator of "This Morning" also sipping from Sonny's cup of trembling).[35] Sonny's music carries us to the fine dialectic between sacred and secular piety. While avoiding a saccharine optimism—improvisation as religious salve—Baldwin charges readers to negotiate the tensions of self-identification and personal history improvisationally. Rather than saving us religiously or pointing to the improvising artist as national savior, Baldwin's image directs us to imagine Sonny's jazz and the narrator's pious attitude toward his personal history as models for democratic sensibilities.

Sonny also performs a Negro masculinity that escapes Mailer's racial trap. As Baldwin explains to Mailer, the black jazz musicians look free and cool because Negro men, under constant threat from the teeth of the hungry world, must make themselves up as they experience the world. As Baldwin explains, "whatever white people do not know about Negroes reveals, precisely and inexorably, what they do not know about themselves" (Baldwin 1998b, 312). Without knowledge of black life or the acknowledgment of Negro citizenship it is impossible to actually achieve American democracy. And, without acknowledging Negro humanity, white Americans can never realize their own human conditions. Baldwin argues, however, that Americans are chained together in this compromise: "[Negroes] cannot be free until [whites] are free" (Baldwin 1998b, 295). Baldwin's vision of white American freedom can only arrive as a product of a tough Negro philosophy: "We, with love, shall force our [white] brothers to see themselves as they are, to cease fleeing from reality, and begin to change it. . . . We can make America what America must become" (Baldwin 1998b, 294). Because they continually engage personal and group histories to invent themselves, Negro blues people provide models for our collective democratic salvation.

Fred Moten, writing about Baldwin's self-representation in the documentary film *The Price of the Ticket,* argues that the blues idiom tradition is one in which the development of society is the focus of the art and that blues idiom music

> disrupts and reorganizes the forms of sensual expression in the interest of the development. But it is also the evidence of things unheard, something transferred not only in the sound but in the ensemblic materiality of that world-encompassing gaze that sound only indicates. This something is not in the audio-visual experience of Baldwin or in the literary experience of his texts but in something that is really even before and in improvisation of Baldwin and of these formal projections of Baldwin, something upon which he improvises, something transferred to him from the way back and way before wounded kinship, forced and stolen labor, forced and stolen sexuality.[36]

Salvation, in the context of the civil rights era, is not about accepting the Christian order of the Southern Christian Leadership Council. Rather, national salvation arrives through pious address of the spiritual or psychological dangers that surround and inhabit us—white, black, and brown Americans. It is about accepting that "unheard," "wounded kinship" to American history. And, according to Baldwin, investing in the pious, illuminating power of blues-idiom improvisation is the route to salvation. Baldwin argues that once Americans learn to be pious, learn to make themselves up without recourse to the status quo or stereotype, they can form true community and fulfill America's democratic ideals.

By 1965 the rise in popularity of black nationalism, the aggressive, militant, and politically necessary ideas of Black Power and Black Art, crowded Baldwin out of his position as the primary independent public intellectual voice of the civil rights movement. Like it was for Baldwin, community formation was a chief concern of the Black Arts aesthetician LeRoi Jones/Amiri Baraka. However, Jones/Baraka wanted to revitalize Negro communities by theorizing a poetics of black essence. I argue, however, that Jones/Baraka's journey toward blackness was disrupted by his desire to merge poetics and jazz. In Movement IV I will analyze Jones/Baraka's transitional period, his turn from modernism to Black Art, paying special attention to his use of jazz in poetry and cultural criticism.

Improvising over the Changes

Improvisation as Intellectual and Aesthetic Practice in the Transitional Poems of LeRoi Jones/Amiri Baraka

In 1981 Ralph Ellison was invited to write letters of recommendation for a group of MacArthur "genius" grant nominees, including the likes of Cormac McCarthy, James Alan McPherson, and Amiri Baraka. After explaining his feelings about both McCarthy and McPherson, Ellison argues that Baraka is "more interested in ideology than in art, and thus I suspect he has little attraction for those whose interest lies in advancing the arts of the country."[1] Continuing with wit and dexterity, Ellison elucidates his intellectual dispute with Baraka, blanketing him with the same critical language that had stifled the poet since the mid-1970s:

> [During the sixties] I suggested that he might well win financial support—if he gave his energies to the creation of a vibrant experimental theater, but if so it would be art which would attract support and not his fascination with ideological posturing. Since then I have had no reason to change my opinion. For it seems that Baraka has gone through a series of ideological metamorphoses, in each instance of which, he has ended up as an ever more fantastic reincarnation of the Emperor Jones. In his most recent incarnation he has put away his African regalia and, he says, his anti-Semitism,

and has emerged as an exponent of Marxist literary theory. I am therefore surprised that he is being considered for what I'm sure he'd consider ill-gotten capitalist gains—Unless of course, like O'Neill's famous emperor he is searching for the wherewithal to fashion a silver bullet.

Ellison's characterization of Baraka as a modernist charlatan, a Marxist ideologue, and crucially, as an "on the wagon" anti-Semite, is the essentialized picture of Baraka that exists in the popular press and popular imagination. This image of Baraka as Marxist and recovering anti-Semite came back with some force during the furor over his 2001 poem "Somebody Blew Up America." While the quality and intelligence of that poem may be up for literary critical discussion, it is interesting that such a discussion never materialized in print media or on television. If the poem was meant to incite discourse, charge us to consider the world from a materialist political perspective, then it did just the opposite. In the media outlets where conversation should have been had, Baraka was castigated for being anti-Semitic and anti-American. What came back to the fore was the image of the racist black charlatan, a collective iteration in the mass media of that image, and the purposeful and distorted misreadings of the LeRoi Jones/Amiri Baraka oeuvre.

What all of this makes me think about is the general misunderstanding of black intellectuals or the tenets of black intellectual performance. What was missing from the talk around Jones/Baraka's oeuvre was an understanding of how to read his poems, his essays, his ideological changes, or how to reconcile the motivations for his changes and metamorphoses. Jones/Baraka's critical reception has become more about the collected weak misreadings than about the writing itself. In this movement I want to step back to Jones/Baraka's initial stage of transition in order to consider how jazz improvisation has informed his work and ideological changes as a poet and cultural critic, and how improvisation has become a theoretical practice integral to his work and to understanding his work.

I

LeRoi Jones/Amiri Baraka's "Tone Poem" is dedicated to Elvin Jones, one of the major drummers of jazz's post-bebop era, and

Bob Thompson, the avant-garde painter whose visual works symbolized the emerging black aesthetic in the early 1960s. This poem appears in Jones/Baraka's *Black Magic: Collected Poetry 1961–1967*. For many students of Jones/Baraka, the collection marks his full turn into the Black Arts Movement and a complete poetic statement of the black aesthetic.

Jones/Baraka builds the poem around an abstraction that mimics Elvin Jones's rhythmic techniques and the strange elegance of Thompson's powerful images—"An eagle hangs above them spinning. / Years and travelers / linger among the dead, no reports, gunshots white puffs / deciding the season and the mode of compromise."[2] Jones/Baraka's lyric also carries the weight of self-exposure.

> I leave it there, for them, full of hope, and hurt. All the poems
> are full of it. Shit and hope, and history. Read this line
> young colored or white and know I felt the twist of dividing
> memory. . . . (Jones/Baraka 1995, 131)

The speaker, "LeRoi," leaves the reader a mark of his shifting being in the "twist" of his divided psychology. As its title tells us, the poem is meant to be an extramusical narrative and lyrical illustration for Jones's pounding polysyllabic beats and Thompson's multicolored melting expressions. Though he claims late in the poem to have "no points, or theories," Jones/Baraka's "twist" is a turn away from history and hurt toward an abstract hope that lingers beyond the poem's "exit image," "the day growing old and sloppy through the window" (Jones/Baraka 1995, 131).

The point or theory that is behind Jones/Baraka's twist is his literary theorization of abstract expression and avant-garde jazz improvisation. Just as interesting, however, is the poet's call to both "young colored and white" readers to keep "the tone, and exit image" of the poem in mind. The call to this interracial audience sounds an ambiguous chord for a poet who claims in the introduction to his collection of essays *Home* (1965) that his writing presents him in the process of becoming psychologically "blacker." "Tone Poem" begs us to question our standard approach to Jones/Baraka—the readings that focus on him as the avatar of the black aesthetic, a radical militant and essentialist. How are we to understand Jones/Baraka's use of free jazz improvisation as a literary ideal combined with his theories of blackness and his calls to an (at least) interracial audience?

Tejumola Olaniyan argues that a useful way to understand the force of change that black writers have engineered in American cultural life is to note the way that poet/playwrights such as Derek Walcott, Ntozake Shange, and Amiri Baraka illustrate that "social relations have no essence, transhistorical or axiomatic, but are always paradigmatic, arbitrary, contextual—in short, historical. If society has an essence, then it is its permanent openness."[3] Olaniyan's idea suggests that the social relationships between individuals and the cultures they make, their relationships with the larger American cultural fabric, are not foundational, not essential, but arbitrary, and open.

Olaniyan explains that culture is made up of "diverse and mutually contradictory elements or parts," that its "composites of structures . . . are never immutable," and that those elements and the articulated identities born of that system do not "possess any natural, sacrosanct character. . . . Cultural identity could hence not be closed and positive but necessarily alterable: a conception of otherness in flux. The performative is the principle of a transgressive and transitional truth" (Olaniyan 1995, 35).

Jones/Baraka's poetry and jazz criticism reveal the processes of a cultural identification, the *articulations* of the self that are products of what Olaniyan calls an "agonistic process of arriving at the 'choice' [of self-identification] from the diverse and contradictory 'open set of options'"(Olaniyan 1995, 35). And in this process of choice and articulation the self is created. In the poems that express these dialectic movements, the swing between Anglo-Western and Afro-Western cultures and the swing between self-identity and the search for a useful black identity, Jones/Baraka's literary works make art out of his cosmopolitan sensibility.

Since the culture has no essential basis, neither do the identities that develop from engagements with it. Just as the culture is rootless and ever in flux, so too is the process of identification. In Jones/Baraka's case the best way to *articulate* these cultural and personal revolutions, how to imply these changes, is by turning jazz improvisation into a literary and cultural philosophy, into a way of stating poetically the "transgressive and transitional truth" of black identity. Jones/Baraka draws poetry and jazz improvisation together so that he can simultaneously exercise the culture's "diverse and mutually contradictory elements" while presenting a performance of the self in transition and flux. What Olaniyan is calling "articulatory practice" can also be called "improvisational practice."

Patrick Roney argues that critics who investigate the work of Jones / Baraka are forced to formulate an escape from his essentialism while trying to retrieve the poetry and explain its significance to postmodern claims of identity's constructedness.[4] According to Roney these critics exacerbate these faulty escapes from essentialism by developing bordered maps of Western culture that work to reify the West (Roney 2003, 412). Rather than searching for an out, Roney's examination of Jones / Baraka's poetics illustrates the mutual indebtedness of Western and African American cultures. That is, pieces like "Tone Poem" express Jones / Baraka's dialectic relation to both systems. But since those poems belong to both cultural systems but neither exclusively, they communicate a Negro attitude of "in-betweenness," a realization that African American identity resides in the "no-man's land" between the Anglo-American and African American cultural systems (Roney 2003, 406, 412).

Roney reads Jones / Baraka's theory of black identity as an extension of his movement between African American culture and Western culture, the poet's willingness to accept multiple cultural approaches at once. I want to suggest, however, that Jones / Baraka's poetics were born of a second, more subtle and provocative movement in the dialectic process. In that second shift Jones / Baraka moved between the hope to name the individual self while also searching for the essential basis of black group identity. These shifts are best represented in the poems from Jones / Baraka's transitional period, his turn from Beat modernism to black aesthetics. The transitional poems express the dialectic *swing* between Anglo-Western and Afro-Western cultures, between the construction of self-identity and the foundation of blackness. Though Jones / Baraka was on a quest to find the essence of African American identity, what the layering of jazz and poetry in his transitional poems revealed was blackness's foundation in improvisation. In other words the black self is, in fact, not foundational because the imperatives of improvisation actually force one to interrogate and subvert the search for essence.

Jones / Baraka's transitional work was in battle against a cultural system that denied his individuality and humanity as an African

American; that system was set up in manifold ways to render him invisible. Interestingly, hoping to express the cultural and personal changes afoot in postwar America, the poet had to choose from among the expressive forms of the very cultural system that refused him in order to produce his self-identifying articulations or even to produce new forms of articulation. But those lyrical attempts, nevertheless, force more change upon both Jones/Baraka and the culture. As Olaniyan explains, the complex structure of a culture's (or an individual's) identity is "always modified" as a result of engaging in an "articulatory practice."

The image of Jones/Baraka as a practicing improviser is rarely the prominent one. Actually, the picture of Jones/Baraka as a poet steeped in and wedded to blackness as essence has been promoted at the expense of the scribe who also penned the less aesthetically and ideologically constrained transitional poems. The result of the more prevalent readings—Black Arts Baraka—has been that Jones/Baraka is more often read as a political figure than as a literary figure whose work has fluctuated in kind and quality, certainly, but who has been, at bottom, part of a struggle to expose the complexities of African American culture and identity, and of American history.[5] In his transitional poems Jones/Baraka, like Langston Hughes, turns to jazz improvisation as a literary resource for articulating the human complexities of African American life.[6]

Brent Hayes Edwards suggests that critics must move beyond the tensions of the Black Arts Movement (BAM).[7] For instance, while Roney's "no-man's land" resembles Houston Baker's conception of the "black (w)hole" (both notions locate African American identity at a centralized "new order of [black] existence . . . [that] draws all events and objects into its horizon"),[8] Roney's image of liminality brings us one step away from Baker's "strategic essentialism," but the second step is to see that Jones/Baraka's attempts to find these "black (w)holes" were thwarted by his literary improvisations. Rather than reading Jones/Baraka's poetics as the simple knowledge of "blackness as essence," we see that his transitional poems *articulate* blackness as a process of *othering* the self. In Jones/Baraka's transitional poems the black self is presented as a product of spontaneous and "continual alteration."[9]

The poems describe Jones/Baraka's process of *othering* the self and illustrate the poet's cosmopolitan attitude.[10] Like John Dewey,

Jones/Baraka sees that "music is the highest of the arts, because it gives us not merely the external objectifications of Will but also sets before us for contemplation the very *processes* of Will."[11] Dewey sees that these processes of will expose the ways that experience in its variety shapes the self into a fluid, ever-shifting entity. Jones/Baraka's transitional poems present the *"processes* of Will" as the improvisational performance of identity and the rejection of essentialism.

What is at stake in reconsidering Jones/Baraka's transitional moment is that we can learn how Jones/Baraka folded his personal philosophical changes and political desires together into his literary aesthetic. The transitional poems communicate an influential theorization of jazz improvisation to an American audience that is, at least, biracial, if not multicultural. While my reading places Jones/Baraka within the complex picture of modern and postmodern American poetry, I maintain that the concept of *othering* the self also changes our relationship to Jones/Baraka's Black Arts poetry. Instead of seeing him primarily as the militant black essentialist and nationalist, we can read Jones/Baraka's multiple changes as part of a radical theorization of literary intellectual practice framed by a conception of improvisation as a metaphor for both intellectual work and African American identity. I think that Jones/Baraka's "continual alteration," his sameness, is what has made his theory of literary improvisation an influential element of contemporary criticism of African American culture from avant-garde jazz to hip-hop.

II

The best way to define Jones/Baraka's transitional interregnum is to alight on the work published between 1960 and 1967, specifically the poetry and music criticism from these years. In my thinking this period of transition is framed by the quintessential essays of Jones/Baraka's oeuvre, "Cuba Libre" (1960) and "The Changing Same" (written 1966, published 1967). "Cuba Libre" is Jones's memoir of his visit to postrevolutionary Cuba in 1960. The piece is a document of Jones's attraction to the militants and intellectuals of the new Communist regime in Havana. Although the full foment of Jones's Marxist leanings would not emerge until the mid-1970s, the essay is a record of Jones's initial attempt to situate the African American civil rights movement within an international context. Jones's search for new theories of political change is largely a product of his cosmopolitan modernist attitudes. While Jones's writing is a seminal tour de force expression of the burgeoning political radicalism that would become the Black Power Movement and the Black Arts Movement, he maintains a suspicion of essentialist political or philosophical theories.

Completely turned toward cultural Black Nationalism, Jones/Baraka's essay "The Changing Same" is also a tour de force theorization of black essentialism. Jones/Baraka mines the multiple styles and genres of black popular music to illustrate a unifying aesthetic of music making, and thus, black identity formation. Unlike the political ideologies that he was just forming in "Cuba Libre," Jones/Baraka has fully formed his aesthetic-cum-political sensibility in "The Changing Same."

For Jones/Baraka black music is held together by long-standing African sensibilities that survived the middle passage, slavery, and Reconstruction to form gospel, blues, ragtime, jazz, bebop, free jazz, soul, and rhythm and blues. Even as the music evolves into separate genres with differing performance ideals, Jones/Baraka finds that all the music is driven by improvisation. Jones/Baraka suggests that improvisation changes the music while maintaining itself as the core of African American aesthetics. Thus, at the core of African American identity—blackness—is a need to change and shift while remaining wedded to the foundational tenets of African cultural expression.

The poems and jazz criticism, not to mention the plays, fiction, and cultural criticism, that appear between these two essays are displays of Jones/Baraka's gradual, complex, and sometimes contradictory ideological and aesthetic shifts from Beat modernist to Black Arts Nationalist. The poems of Jones/Baraka's transitional period are provocative and compelling because many of them present antiessentialist conceptions of identity rather than a progression toward the theories of Black Nationalism. The same can be said about Jones/Baraka's jazz criticism. Even as he was trying to move toward a metaphysical theory of black music, Jones/Baraka found that the music resisted this essentialization.

III

Across his first three collections, *Preface to a Twenty Volume Suicide Note* [*Preface*] (1961), *The Dead Lecturer* (1964), and *Black Magic* (1969) we find the poet grappling with problems of identity, transition, and blackness by turning to the representative heroes of his personal history and eventually shedding them in favor of presenting the self as lyrical invention — the poet becomes the heroic interrogator of American ideals. As the titles of the collections suggest, Jones / Baraka's transitions are attempts to kill off the old selves in favor of newer, improvised selves. It is a progression, if you will, that moves toward a "blacker" American sensibility. As I will demonstrate, in these poems the poet claims that he and the culture are both on the verge of expiring.

Jones / Baraka's avatars of revival are the avenging cowboys and masked comic-book heroes invoked in poems such as "In Memory of Radio," "Look for You Yesterday, Here You Come Today," "Black Dada Nihilismus," and "Green Lantern's Solo." But what the poet realizes is that his calls to the Lone Ranger, Tom Mix, or the Red Lantern to save the land and the culture fail him because they are meant to ultimately protect the culture from his entrance to it. The poet's strident self-consciousness, his awareness of his own ambiguity and the culture's narrowness, is spoken over and again in the transitional poems. For instance, in some of the poems from *Preface,* such as "Look for You Yesterday, Here You Come Today," the speaker bemoans the banalities of his literary/cultural world by calling on his personal heroes.

It is a community more interested in describing "celibate parties / torn trousers: Great Poets dying / with their strophes on" (Jones / Baraka 1995, 17). And yet, the speaker, in the face of obviously distracting vagaries, is incapable of communicating "a simple straightforward / anger (Jones / Baraka 1995, 17). The speaker's anger is also a product of his uncomfortable realization that being alive is "so diffuse" and that awareness draws forward a jolt of painful truth: "nobody really gives a damn" (Jones / Baraka 1995, 17). The formal presentation of the poem, Jones / Baraka's inconsistent meter and stanza arrangement, also evokes the speaker's search for the proper mode to express his anger and describe a self against the "diffuse" and uncaring elements of his world. He is trying to do whatever he can to reverse a feeling that his "life / seems over & done with" (Jones/Baraka 1995, 19).

Cowboy heroes like Tom Mix, Dickie Dare, and the Lone Ranger are raised as shields against culture's decline; and superheroes such as Captain Midnight and Superman are called forth as reinforcements. However, the speaker is clear about his disillusionment, his sentimental hope for the heroes of his radio days to lift up the culture's wilting frame: these heroes meet unceremonious deaths— "Tom Mix dead in a Boston Nightclub"—or they are ultimately incomprehensible or inscrutable—"Where is my Captain Midnight decoder?? / I can't understand what Superman is saying!" (Jones/ Baraka 1995, 19). All of this wishing for heroic intervention is "a maudlin nostalgia / that comes on / like terrible thoughts about death" (Jones/Baraka 1995, 20). Ultimately, the poet is left with his own lyrical skills to protect himself or to revive the culture from its near death.

At the end of the poem, the speaker is left with his "silver bullets all gone" and his "black mask trampled in the dust" (Jones/Baraka 1995, 21). The lone cowboy riding to save the culture is finished as a useful model. And even Tonto has abandoned the speaker in favor of the comfort of the blues and Bessie Smith. What the poem does not explain is what kind of defibrillating instruments are available to the poet in order to speak his straightforward anger, to resuscitate the culture, once the heroes have been dispatched or demythologized. Bessie Smith is a great sign in this case.

As the poem speaks of the decline of the overarching heroes of American popular culture, Jones/Baraka follows Tonto out to the territory, so to speak, to find restoration in the blues and jazz. Unlike Baldwin and Ellison, who use Smith to access Southern Negro history and culture, Jones/Baraka's blues impulse propels what the speaker calls his "quest" for revival. The blues idiom is the prime impetus: the title comes from a common blues lyric and describes one of the poet's "charms."[12] The hope to articulate the blues feeling forces the poet to improvise, thus the search through "an avalanche of words" for the proper traditional Western sources—in this case, both Federico Garcia Lorca and Charles Baudelaire are invoked as possible poetic saviors.

One hint about the direction of Jones/Baraka's turning is in the epigraph to his poem "Hymn for Lanie Poo," Arthur Rimbaud's line, *Vous êtes de faux Nègres* (Jones/Baraka 1995, 6).[13] Against this fake Negroness, Jones/Baraka, like the modernists Ezra Pound and William Carlos Williams, is trying to find a way of making new poetic modes and remaking American culture but in this case by recycling the old parts of black American culture. This can only happen by entering the spaces between the old cultural systems and the new ones being improvised—between the old selves and new identities. Jones/Baraka's innovation is to turn this aesthetic concern into both a philosophical and political focus.

Turning away from *faux Nègres* and himself at once leaves the speaker in a liminal space between both the old culture and old self.[14] This is an improvisational space where the poet can merge political hopes and aesthetic ideals. Jones/Baraka's rejection and improvisation leads to new realities: a cultural critique with a political edge because the moral stand behind it is about creating a new American culture, a culture where change and improvisation are the privileged states of being. This is typified by transitional poems such as "The Bridge," named after Sonny Rollins's classic hard bop composition. There, the poet acknowledges that ". . . the changes are difficult, when / you hear them, & know they are all in you, the chords // of your disorder meddle with your would be disguises" (Jones/Baraka 1995, 31). This lyrical improvisation serves as self-invention. The voice acknowledges that recognizing the possibilities of self-naming is a product of speaking them, *articulating* them so that they can be known.

For Jones/Baraka the openness of culture (and its traditions) remains possible only when the structural incompleteness of the cultural fabric, its as yet unwoven threads, are exploited through renewal ad infinitum. This cultural openness creates the space for the antagonistic but cooperative transactions between the self and the culture. As Jones/Baraka illustrates in "The Bridge," the self becomes real through its internal discourse and in dialogue with both African American traditions and Western culture. The antagonism stems from the efforts of the individual to overcome the daunting influence that the culture has on the self in order to make personalized choices about the process of identification—stepping away from "would be disguises." The self is performed through interplay or in counterpoint to those disguises, like jazz musicians working the harmonic and rhythmic angles of a musical composition to respond to each other's ideas in order to improvise their internal compositions. It is useful to recall Michael Jarrett's explanation of the dialectic play between the musician's improvised ideas and the composed text with its parallels to Olaniyan's description of articulation: both critics suggest that the improvisation is an expression of a series of aesthetic choices.

IV

In his sociomusicological history *Blues People* (1963), Baraka explains African American musical tradition as the expression of African American experience. Even though "jazz and blues *are* Western musics, products of Afro-American culture," what makes those musics significant, Baraka writes, is that they belong to a people's history of oppression and marginality in the West and therefore they alter the way Western history is narrated once those musics are invoked as a frame of reference.[15] So, embedded in the musical styles, especially something like bebop, is a "distinct element of social protest, not only in the sense that it was music that seemed antagonistically non conformist, but also that the musicians who played it were loudly outspoken about who they thought they were" (Jones/Baraka 1963, 23).

It is worth remembering that bebop signifies a break between swing-era big bands and small combos, and late jazz — gospel-infused hard-bop and avant-garde free jazz — of the 1950s and 1960s. Bop is music independent of the jazz that preceded it. While the harmonics, speed, technical skills, and rhythmic dexterity needed to play bop extend the tradition of recordings and compositions of artists such as Jelly Roll Morton, Louis Armstrong, and Duke Ellington, it is the style of improvisation that marks the music's emergence and break from the preceding jazz aesthetic.

Bebop innovators like Thelonious Monk and Bud Powell proved, writes Jones/Baraka, "that so called 'changes,' i.e., the repeated occurrences of certain chords basic to the melodic and harmonic structure of a tune, are almost arbitrary. That is, [the chords] need not be *stated,* and that since certain chords infer certain improvisatory uses of them, why not improvise on what the chords infer rather than playing the inference itself"(Jones/Baraka 1963, 77).

While bebop refers to its own history, to the history of American music, it is always improvising away from its own generic composition, its structure as music. Jones/Baraka's analysis pulls together Olaniyan's reading of articulatory practice and Jarrett's illustration of the obligations of improvisation. Bebop's style of improvisation obliged musicians to compose intimate expressions of who they were, binding performance and identity together intimately.

In his classic essay "Jazz and the White Critic" (1963), Jones/Baraka argues that the general misunderstanding of jazz and bebop since the mid-1940s has shaped a critical status quo that hopes to make the music middlebrow, institutionalizes it under a rubric that denies any notions of cultural change or the vitality of African American culture as a shaping force. In other words, according to Baraka, white jazz critics ignore the music's evolution in order to ignore the ways in which the music has begun to express the philosophical, political, and cultural desires of African Americans. However, the best jazz criticism will illustrate that the music is as much the emotional expression of a culture as it is a technical style of music making.

Focused attention on emotional expression reveals Negro culture at work within Western history. Jones/Baraka argues that "Negro music, like the Negro himself, is strictly an American Phenomenon, and we have got to set up standards of judgment and aesthetic excellence that depend on our native knowledge and understanding of the underlying philosophies and local cultural references that produced blues and jazz in order to produce valid critical writing or commentary about it."[16] While this argument speaks a seemingly common sense critical notion, Jones/Baraka subtly demands that black cultural tools be brought to bear in the critique of black music—if white critics are to continue writing about jazz or any other black music (and surely Jones/Baraka knew that white criticism of "black" cultural production would continue), they must begin to learn about African American history and culture as well as incorporating those Negro cultural ideas into their critical vernaculars and theories.

Under Jones/Baraka's directive white critics would be forced to revise their conceptions of black life by refashioning their critical operating modes, by reconsidering, in fact, what about African American culture is "native" to American culture. A third and interesting valence of this idea arises when we think of Jones/Baraka's poetry during his transitional period. Jones/Baraka is also being self-reflexive in this critique; if improvisation becomes the name for identification, then self-realization, even with pious references to one's history, is always moving away from essence. For critics of his poems, rather than decontextualizing them from particular political and cultural histories, reading them in relation to the cultural systems that he was negotiating will force critics of American literature to expand their critical vernaculars as well as re-evaluate the American literary tradition in relation to African American cultural history.

V

In *The Dead Lecturer,* we find both a poet who realizes improvisation's power in "The Bridge" and one who is tormented by the revelations that spiritual focus creates in "An Agony. As Now"—"I am inside someone / who hates me" (Jones/Baraka 1963, 60). There are enough references to flesh and body in *The Dead Lecturer* to lead readers to interpret the collection as a turning away from old physical and spiritual forms in favor of developing new ones:

> It is a human love, I live inside. A bony skeleton
> you recognize as words or simple feeling.
> But it has no feeling. As the metal, is hot, it is not,
> given to love.
> It burns the thing
> Inside it. And that thing
> screams. (Jones/Baraka 1995, 61)

These articulations are also present in poems such as "Balboa, the Entertainer" and "Snake Eyes." These poems describe identity as poetic experience; identity is a process rather than a reification of static, stereotypical notions of blackness. "Let my poems be a graph / of me," Jones/Baraka proclaims in "Balboa, The Entertainer" (Jones/Baraka 1995, 54). The poet is asking us to see his articulations reshaping him. Thus, language becomes the poetic line "where flesh / drops off," where love dies and "does not / stretch to your body's / end," where, finally, "without / preface, / music trails" (Jones/Baraka 1995, 54–55). What is interesting here is the way that the end of the body, its death, is fleshy and epidermal not spiritual or physical as such—once the flesh drops off, music lies in the ready, new identities can be improvised.[17]

The skin only hides the chaotic action of self-identification—skin only holds it in place or masks the spiritual propensity for change. In the poem "Snake Eyes" the "old brown thing" is the forcefully shed skin of the body, dropped off in favor of a new linguistic beginning, a new music, and a new self. Baraka asks, "what is meat / to do, that is driven to its end / by words" (Jones/Baraka 1995, 109)?[18] The shedding of old skins and the masking of identity is what allows for the poetics of self-creation. For instance, masking as Rinehart allows Ralph Ellison's narrator in *Invisible Man* to see around corners and behind the meanings of things. Jones/Baraka's poems perform the drama of a similar realization. If Baraka's theory of identity has a foundation then it is in the ironic, ambivalent, blissfully protean essence. Shedding the skin of the Beat poet clears the bones and prepares the soul for the shape of a new visage. But attached to this exuberant realization is an equally ambivalent realization of the dialectic play between the self and the culture, the self and the community.

Take, for instance, "The Liar," also from *The Dead Lecturer,* in which the speaker articulates a self in transition while also illustrating the possibility of identification through self-naming.

> What I thought was Love
> in me, I find a thousand instances
> as fear. (Of the tree's shadow
> winding around the chair, a distant music
> of frozen birds rattling   5
> in the cold.
>   Where ever I go to claim
> my flesh, there are entrances
> of spirit. And even its comforts
> are hideous uses I strain   10
> to understand. (Jones/Baraka 1995, 113)

The speaker begins by calling attention to his own fears about the matter of self-realization. Love materializes as fear in line 3. By line 10 the speaker's acceptance of his spiritual self subverts the comforts of self-awareness. What is worth grasping in these early lines is the speaker's claim of his "flesh." If we are reading this as an expression of the historical moment, that claim has two valences: on one hand this claim is an oppositional act of self-assertion against a racist sociopolitical system. On the other hand, we can read this as the speaker's effort to claim his Negro body, an effort to push into blackness in search of its essence. The discomfort, the strain, and failure to understand the spiritual entrances reminds us of the dialectic play of articulation—movement between two cultural zones in an effort to name the self.

That Baraka's poem is part of an ongoing "articulatory practice" is amplified by the series of ideas beginning in line 11 that play the private "changes" of the soul publicly, antagonistically.

> Though I am a man
> who is loud
> of the birth
> of his ways. Publicly redefining   15
> each change in my soul, as if I had predicted
> them,
>   and profited, biblically, even tho
>   their chanting weight,
>   erased familiarity   20
>   from my face.
>   A question I think,
> an answer, whatever sits
> counting the minutes
> till you die. (Jones Baraka 1995, 113)   25

The self is literally in transition during the public redefinition and articulation of that self. Notice as well that the structure of the poem on the page is in the process of transition: it disintegrates as it flows down to the re-collected final thoughts. As the speaker changes, so does the form of the articulation; Jones/Baraka defamiliarizes the form of the poem. And when we reach the end of the lines we find ourselves confronted again with an ambiguous speaker.

> When they say, "It is Roi
> who is dead?" I wonder
> who will they mean? (Jones/Baraka 1995, 113)

Which Roi indeed—should we be concerned with the Newark schoolboy, the Howard flunky, the dishonorably discharged Air Force enlistee, the Beat bohemian, or the Village scribe? Rather than announce an essential Roi, Jones/Baraka's poem announces that skin does not count outside of its contextualization, that the chaos of self-realization, the improvisations of the soul do not end in a simple self. The self is altered, *othered* continuously.

We see "The Liar" is related to the avant-garde poetics of New American Poetry marked by the efficient innovations of Frank O'Hara, the formal deconstructions of Charles Olsen, Robert Creeley, and the Black Mountain school, and the angel-headed Whitmanisms of Allen Ginsberg's "Howl." Like these mid-twentieth-century American poets, Jones/Baraka replaces older standard forms—the refinement of high modernism—with an alternative, avant-garde, and revolutionary formal modernism. And yet, we rarely read of Jones/Baraka's influence on poets like Creeley and O'Hara, both of whom were edited by and published in Jones/Baraka's literary magazines *Floating Bear* and *Yugen*.[19] Understanding Jones/Baraka's theorization of improvisation also helps us understand better the innovations of postwar American poetry.

For example, when considering Jones/Baraka's redescriptive improvisations of black identity and the poetic tradition, Nathaniel Mackey calls Jones/Baraka's poems acts of "artistic othering."[20] As a way of overcoming his status as a social other, Mackey explains, Jones/Baraka invented forms and concepts that altered the American poetic tradition. Like a good modernist poet Jones/Baraka's best work stands as the union of critical activity with a personal poetics. The merger is what T. S. Eliot once called "creation in the labour of the artist" (Eliot 1975, 74). Jones/Baraka's transitional poems turn jazz's assault on essentialism into the surrealist practice of *deréglèment de sens*.[21] As Mackey describes Jones/Baraka's aesthetic, poetic improvisation becomes an act of creative criticism or critical artistry.[22]

The most significant proposition that emerges from artistic othering is that "the self" is presented as an action rather than as a static entity. This turn away from status as "the other" to othering-the-self is encapsulated in the word for jazz's bedrock rhythmic movement—"swing." Riffing on Baraka's ideas in *Blues People*, Brent Hayes Edwards explains that when *swing* becomes a noun, turning it into a genre rather than an expressive musical movement, it becomes stationary, immobile, it loses the "elusive and performative connotations of what is in its verb form a paradigmatic black cultural *action* or *process*."[23] Othering swings the self from noun to verb, from thing to action; Edwards calls this self in process a "verbal noun" (Edwards 1999, 590).

This is another moment where the poet's questioning (and questing) voice echoes the voice of Ellison's protagonist in *Invisible Man*. Both arise from the underground of American culture to speak through a bebop-infused improvisational structure. The questions at the end of "The Liar" point to Jones/Baraka's own disappearing act; they point to the poet's recognition of his own powers of invisibility, if you will. Paralleling Jones/Baraka's poem with Ellison's fiction also draws Jones's public articulation of private philosophical changes alongside of Ellison's ironic bluesy final statement: "who knows but that, on the lower frequencies, I speak for you."[24] But unlike Ellison's line or his political stance outside the public fray in the 1960s, Jones's poem (and all his poems of the transitional period) does not beg inference from the reader. Instead, the political gesture—the "public redefining" of black identity—is explicit. However, Jones/Baraka's transitional vision challenged the possibility of separating private philosophical changes and public political desires in the context of African American life well before that discussion had become a worn-out track in American criticism.

Jones/Baraka's poems ask, how do Negroes develop and maintain the private structures of individual identities and personal philosophies in a cultural system that works to eradicate those private sensibilities, that works quite well at dehumanizing and essentializing them and their cultural particulars? The Negro's act of publicly asserting her individuality or intellectual curiosity in the face of a historically racist social system is a political act. This is the significance of Jones/Baraka's poetics—he asserts his "will to change" as one part of the process of the transformative work of creating a new African American sensibility, a new American culture.

As we see in "Tone Poem," this process of verbalization is also at work in some of the poems contained in *Black Magic*. That collection contains "Black Art," the poem that ostensibly crystallized the lyrical aesthetic of the Black Arts Movement. In this poem Jones/Baraka, fully free of "Roi" (and finally turned into blackness), communicates both the desire for an essentialized world—"We want a black poem. And a / Black World"—and that the route to that ideal will be arranged by "Assassin poems, Poems that shoot / guns. Poems that wrestle cops into alleys" (Jones/Baraka 1995, 142). Undoubtedly, in his turn toward achieving this black world, the poet has also turned to essentialize every other racial, ethnic, and political group, albeit negatively.

Yet the poet of *Black Magic* can be read as one still in transition. Take the poem "Gatsby's Theory of Aesthetics." In F. Scott Fitzgerald's *The Great Gatsby*, Gatsby's aesthetic involves his remarkable ability to shed old skins, to mask and unmask himself, and to improvise new possibilities for himself. Jones/Baraka understands that theory rather well. In fact, Jones/Baraka wants to push that theory toward its lyrical and philosophical limits. I find the poet's reference to Fitzgerald both clever and mystifying. On one hand, Fitzgerald sets Gatsby's own masking against the novel's "jazz age" setting, Tom Buchannan's misnamed reference to Theodore Lothrop Stoddard's *The Rising Tide of Color against White World Supremacy* (1920), and the infamous image of Negroes masking as East Egg millionaires. On the other hand, Jones/Baraka's open borrowing suggests that he can perform outside of racially determined cultural circumstances.

Poetry's aim, Jones/Baraka writes, should be the exposition of "difficult meanings. Meanings not already catered to. Poetry / aims at reviving, say, a sense of meaning's possibility and ubiq- / uitousness. / Identification can be one term of that possibility" (Jones/Baraka 1995, 132). While Fitzgerald's final image of Gatsby in the novel explains the danger of unmediated self-invention, Jones/Baraka's notion of Jay Gatsby suggests that identity can be articulated through the linguistic exchange between the private self and the cultural network. The culture's openness is what gives rise to meaning's possibility and ubiquity. And in that exchange, the self also becomes open-ended and "othered." In Jones/Baraka's improvisation, the danger of self-invention is that it also others the culture through dialogue.

The best example of this self-othering comes in "Numbers, Letters," a poem that examines the ambiguity of the self still in process, still in action. Baraka wrote this poem sometime in 1964, the year he gave up his Jewish wife, his biethnic family, and left Greenwich Village for the blacker environs of Harlem. The series of questions that Baraka proposes in the opening stanza creates a crucial space for critique.

> If you're not home, where
> are you? Where'd you go? What
> were you doing when gone? When
> you come back, better make it good.
> What was you doing down there, freakin' off   5
> with white women, hangin' out
> with Queens, say it straight to be
> understood straight, put it flat and real
> in the street where the sun comes and the
> moon comes and the cold wind in winter   10
> waters you eyes. Say what you mean, dig
> it out put it down, and be strong
> about it.
> I cant say who I am
> unless you agree I'm real   15
> I cant be anything I'm not
> Except these words pretend
> to life not yet explained,
> so here's some feeling for you
> see how you like it, what it   20
> reveals, and that's Me. (Jones/Baraka 1995, 136)

Exactly who is the "you" being addressed here? Philip Brian Harper has written that in Baraka's Black Arts poems, this address of the second person encompasses the group of Negroes still uninitiated, unconvinced about the coming revolution of blackness.[25] However, notice that tonal change and perspective shift to first person in lines 14 and 15. That change forces a reevaluation of the opening stanza. Take note of the way that Baraka builds into those lines an antiphonal connection between the speaker and the audience. Baraka's opening stanza may be self-addressed—"Amiri, if Greenwich Village isn't home, where are you; darken your aesthetic so that it speaks a deep, strong blackness." But this paraphrase does not solve the mystery of the poem since lines 14 and 15 demand acknowledgment or agreement from both the speaker and his audience: "I can't say who I am / unless you agree I'm real."

The speaker's hope is for both self-actualization and acknowledgment. But notice the confusion that sets in for both of these

desires. The speaker cannot be anything "except these words pretend / to life not yet explained" in lines 16–18. However, the stanza
turns even further from firm ground when we see that while the
words function metaphorically—they imagine a future not yet
available—the feeling the language enables in line 21 is "Me," the
speaker. Very quickly though, we learn that whatever is real about
the voice, speaking alone doesn't reveal identity.

> Unless you agree I'm real
> that I can feel
> whatever beats hardest
> at our black souls   25
> I am real, and I can't say who
> I am. Ask me if I know, I'll say
> yes, I might say no. Still, ask.
> I'm Everett LeRoi Jones, 30 yrs old.
> A black nigger in the universe. A long breath singer,   30
> would be dancer, strong from years of fantasy
> and study. All this time then, for what's happening
> now. All that spilling of white ether, clocks in ghostheads
> lips drying and rewet, eyes opening and shut, mouths
>   churning.
> I am a meditative man, And when I say something it's   35
>   all of me
> saying, and all the things that make me, have formed me,
>   colored me
> this brilliant reddish night. I will say nothing that I feel is
> lie, or unproven by the same ghostclocks, by the same riders
> always move so fast with the word slung over their backs or
> in saddlebags, charging down Chinese roads. I carry   40
>   some words,
> some feeling, some life in me. My heart is large as my mind
> this is a messenger calling, over here, over here, open you
>   eyes
> and you ears and you souls; today is the history we must
>   learn
> to desire. There is no guilt in love. (Jones/Baraka 1995,
>   136–37)

While Jones/Baraka invites us to acknowledge him as the speaker
of these lines, he explains in lines 27 and 28 that he might not
know how to respond to our call. The call and response implicit

in Baraka's address of the second person makes this poem a blues poem like the ballads in Sterling Brown's *Southern Road* (1932). However, like the avant-garde jazz being developed out of a reevaluation of the jazz tradition, Jones/Baraka is exercising an avant-garde improvisation of old blues forms to mark the personal changes he's articulating in this poem. When Jones/Baraka exclaims, "I'm Everett LeRoi Jones," his "long breath" singing is an improvised riff on the performance styles of bluesmen like Jimmy Rushing and Big Joe Turner.[26] Baraka's ecstatic announcement communicates all the things that make him, form him, and color him.

Just as we are left wondering which Roi is dead in "The Liar," we must ask of "Numbers, Letters" who is the speaker who eventually calls us to a blackness made in his likeness? Is he or this blackness identifiable or knowable? Equally important to this idea is Ralph Ellison's insightful critique of blues singers. The blues singer's power, Ellison tells us, comes from her ability to illustrate through her song "some notion of our better selves."[27] If Jones/Baraka's poems tell us something about our better selves, then what is compelling about his transitional improvisations is that they speak to the open and complex possibilities of identifying as an African American rather than reifying any essentialist concepts of black identity. "This is a messenger calling," Jones/Baraka tells us; in the midst of the social and political revolution the poems are messages toward realizing our better selves.

When Jones/Baraka turned to jazz music as an artistic and critical resource he was searching for a way to escape boundaries between poetry and music, music criticism and philopolitical theories, literary and political statement. In the transitional poems Jones/Baraka expresses a notion of identity as artistic and improvisational. In *Art as Experience* Dewey explains that while works of art often spring from or start experiences that are enjoyable in themselves, the experiences do not become artful until the individual self is "organically" implicated in the very purpose of the art. Dewey writes that "it is in the purposes he entertains and acts upon that an individual most completely exhibits and realizes his intimate selfhood" (Dewey 1980, 276–77). What Jones/Baraka found in jazz improvisation was a way to articulate the self in battle with the culture, with history, and against the self. And like a soloist in the midst of a composition, the poetic voice within the transitional poems is drawing together both public and private cultural desires.

When jazz musicians improvise they are playing out their own private individual jazz educations, their own jazz histories against the musical context in which they are performing. This usually means that they are improvising within the universe of the composed song and in exchange with their fellow performers whose personal styles and improvisations explain their own trajectories of education and history. When a musician takes a solo she is communicating an aesthetic statement about her personal jazz history, her existential self, and making art. And, although the goals of the performance ensemble carry their own weight, the most important is always entertainment.

But I would argue that part of what makes modern jazz and modern improvisation entertaining is that in the midst of jazz group performance we hear the musicians present private philosophical ideas about the music, the culture, and the self in a public context. Considering jazz improvisation in light of Dewey's concept of artistic experience what we realize about improvisation is that the soloist's aesthetic expresses both the shell and the kernel of artistic expression: art as "enjoyable experience" and art as "intimate selfhood." Dewey explains further that "[I]n art as an experience actuality and the possibility of identity, the new and the old, objective material and personal response, the individual and the universal, surface and depth, sense and meaning, are integrated in an experience in which they are all transfigured from the significance that belongs to them when isolated in reflection. . . . The significance of art as experience is, therefore, incomparable for the adventure of philosophic thought" (Dewey 1980, 297). It is important to explain here that I am not claiming that every solo by every jazz musician equals a profound philosophical statement. Instead we should consider that improvisation (art) becomes experience when it is superb, excellent music making. Rather than see each improvisation of a particular artist as an individual aesthetic statement, we should hear them as being part of a larger, ongoing aesthetic process of stylization, self-identification. That is, Jones/ Baraka's transitional poems suggest ways of reimagining American identity as improvisational while also suggesting an alternate way of negotiating the poet's aesthetic and political changes.

Ultimately, rereading the transitional poems will help us place Jones/Baraka at a crucial axis: his poems exemplify an African American cultural attitude while also communicating a specifically American philosophical perspective.

Literary historian Cynthia Young writes that during the early 1960s Jones/Baraka wanted his literary work to be more than self-revelation, he wanted the work to assert that, "cultural production was central to the forging of oppositional identities."[28] Young argues further that at the heart of the work by radical black thinkers and revolutionary African American organizations during the 1960s was an antiessentialist conception of politics and identity. While people like Jones/Baraka were in the process of trying to develop new African American subjectivities they were not interested in fashioning "vehicles for a narrow identity politics" (Young 2001, 13). Instead, Young explains, at its inception radical intellectual work like Jones/Baraka's sought to link "local racial and ethnic oppression to global patterns of Western imperialism and economic exploitation. Often, this meant building coalitions across race, ethnicity, gender, generation and national lines. It meant crafting a new theoretical and political language and adapting the rhetoric and tactics of Third World anticolonial movements for First World" (Young 2001, 13). Jones/Baraka's key to revolution, to the opening up of new linguistic systems and the cross-pollination of theoretical practices, turned on gathering black Americans around the cultural markers of their "black past" and "black present." Jones/Baraka believed that by incorporating African American folk culture into critical and political theories, black people would have better access to the discourse of political revolution because they would already be literate in that cultural sign system.

This literacy is more striking when one considers that Jones/Baraka was interested in using revolution not only to forward a new African American ethos but in so doing to shift American life and culture along with black philosophical change. During this transitional period, when he was in search of a cultural form that would draw African America and their multiple cultural practices together, jazz improvisation stood out as the most powerful aesthetic and philosophical option for Jones/Baraka.

VI

Unfortunately, instead of maintaining his deep commitment to ambiguity and improvisation, in the late 1960s and 1970s Baraka's poetics turned full speed into the blackness of Black Art; the poet's nationalist ideology ultimately fostered an imprisonment within a rhetorical system that was essentialist, politically and philosophically. As Philip Brian Harper has explained this turn began to pose immediate difficulties for Baraka and other Black Arts writers because the desire for a concrete black cultural foundation rather than an acceptance of the myriad possibilities for performing blackness forced those artists to divide themselves further from the unconverted populace they hoped to turn toward black political solidarity.

Harper writes that "[BAM's] primary objective and continual challenge [was not the identification of] the external entity against which the black masses are distinguished—this is easy enough to do—but rather [the negotiation of] the division within the black population itself" (Harper 1993, 239). As Harper describes, the negotiations of Black Arts nationalist poets like Sonia Sanchez, June Jordan, and Baraka were not attempts to "overcome [the social and political division] but rather repeatedly to articulate it in the name of [achieving] black consciousness" (Harper 1993, 239). That hope for unification, while politically expedient at that historical moment, eventually proved to be philosophically and politically empty—that mixture of expediency and emptiness ultimately led to implosion of the BAM and, for Baraka, an eventual turn to the theories of Third World Marxism.

Regardless of this Marxist turn, Baraka continues to be read in relationship to the black essentialism and the untenable, reductive and racist positions he held during the heights of BAM. Even though Baraka has publicly repudiated those positions, he remains a fractious figure in American culture not because of his poetics but in spite of them. While Baraka has produced elegant and powerful poems since his reinvention as a Marxist, his national literary reputation has suffered largely because of his earlier efforts to articulate the criteria for achieving a unified black consciousness.

However, Baraka has spent a lot of time during the last twenty-five years describing his core personal philosophy, a critical attitude that privileges improvisational performance: "I have changed over the years because I have struggled to understand [the] world. . . . People who question change cannot really be trying to do this. How can you be in the world and your ideas over the years remain the same. Those who question change are intellectually lazy, or suffer from the passivity of the overstuffed or cryptically satisfied."[29] What remains exceptional about Jones/Baraka's literary and critical works is that even when he hasn't improvised well, his articulations and improvisations have continued to exhibit and promote a pragmatic vision that remains influential on the ways we interpret and conceptualize the intersection of black music and the philosophical concerns of African American life.

Coda

As a way of concluding, I want to offer this three-chorus solo emphasizing the ways in which jazz improvisation, as a mode of pragmatist philosophy in American culture, has helped writers elicit powerful social critiques.

Throughout *The Shadow and the Act* I've argued that Jones/Baraka, Baldwin, and Ellison redescribed, reimagined, and rethought the concept of Negro identity, the role of the black intellectual in American culture, and the relationship between African American experiences and the achievement of American democracy. All three writers derived analytical energy from the collision of blues idiom expressive forces and pragmatist philosophizing. During the political and social upheaval of the CRM, each writer argued individually that the best way to conceptualize the process of identification or the workings of democracy was by integrating jazz improvisation into the collection of tools that Americans used to describe and solve problems.

Of Ellison's additions to American cultural history the most significant ideas may well be his notions of the novel as a space for improvisation and as a symbolic democratic act. Shaping his literary aesthetic out of the jazz aesthetic, Ellison improvised on other literary novels in *Invisible Man* and improvised a new form of novel in *Juneteenth*. However, it seems clear that Ellison's inventions emerged from his sense that American cultural, social, and political practices demanded improvisation on both the intertextual and formal levels. In the first chorus of this final solo, I consider this Ellisonian theory at work in one of the major philopolitical texts in American culture, Martin Luther King's "Letter from Birmingham Jail."

151

I

In King's classically organized response to calls from Southern clergymen to cease SCLC protests, he provides the four basic tenets of the nonviolent campaign: collection of facts to determine whether injustices exist, negotiation, self-purification, and direct action.[1] This is a pragmatic method of engagement. The hub of the practice is negotiation because it insists upon dialogue and eventual consensus between parties on linguistic and symbolic meanings. The most interesting elements, however, are purification and direct action.

In the purification phase of the Birmingham involvement, SCLC workers and volunteers asked themselves repeatedly, "Are you able to accept blows without retaliating? Are you able to endure the ordeal of jail?" (King 2000, 67). Purification prepares the body for self-sacrifice but keeps it from becoming a sacrificial element in the rites of white opposition. Turning the questioning from an intragroup mantra to an outward challenge of the status quo inspires direct action. As King describes it, nonviolent direct action creates crisis, it fosters tension so as to force "a community which has constantly refused to negotiate" to confront the matter at hand.

The SCLC's "nonviolent direct action" is a form of democratic symbolic action. At the core of their direct action is the same kind of improvisation and linguistic "undoing/doing" that black intellectuals practiced during the CRM. Recalling Tim Parrish's conception of democratic doing and undoing we might see that "the Civil Rights movement is our most glorious example of this democratic undoing in the name of democratic doing" (Parrish 2001, 113). When King claimed that rabid segregationists distorted democracy by creating laws and ordinances that flouted Supreme Court edicts and denied Negroes the privileges of citizenship, his jailhouse note turned from being a plea for justice to a Pauline epistle urging his readers to act with "deliberate speed," to act disobediently but civilly, to enforce the desegregation rulings of 1954. King was encouraging revision and improvisation.

Flouting Birmingham ordinances against Negro assembly, King and the SCLC elaborate a concept of democratic undoing to create democratic doing: "In no sense do I advocate evading or defying the law, as would the rabid segregationist. That would lead to anarchy. One who breaks an unjust law must do so openly, lovingly, and with a willingness to accept the penalty. I submit that an individual who breaks a law that conscience tells him is unjust, and who willingly accepts the penalty of imprisonment in order to arouse the conscience of the community over its injustice, is in reality expressing the highest respect for law" (King 72). The ultimate point of King's directive was to illustrate that democracy could not be had by white Americans as long as it was corrupted in the suppression of Negroes. The democratic action advocated above rises out of King's linguistic understanding of our political principles. The possibilities for shifting the culture from segregated to diverse and open are already built into the culture's linguistic system.

In order to root out these possibilities the cultural worker must be an adept improviser. In a 1964 speech opening the Berlin jazz festival, King, remarking on the relationship between humanity and jazz, explains: "When life itself offers no order and meaning, the [jazz] musician creates an order and meaning from the sounds of the earth which flow through his instrument. It is no wonder that so much of the search for identity among American Negroes was championed by Jazz musicians. Long before the modern essayists and scholars wrote of racial identity as a problem for a multiracial world, musicians were returning to their roots to affirm that which was stirring within their souls."[2] Through his brief salutation, King invokes blues idiom performance as basic equipment for living and performing in the American sociopolitical context. In his letter from Birmingham, King names figures and events like Socrates, Jesus Christ, the Boston Tea Party, Thomas Jefferson, Reinhold Niebuhr, and, by implication, Mohandas Gandhi in order to place the SCLC's "creative protest" in both the philopolitical and spiritual tradition of these precedent setters and the blues idiom tradition which teaches him how to interpolate their signature licks and phrases into his own, individual, lyrical performance.

King's essay leans on old truths in the promotion of new ones. Surely, King's religious piety gives ballast to his epistle, but we can also read some sense of Burkean piety at work in his argument. Being secularly pious, as Baldwin's essays present so well, not only encourages us to reconsider our individual relationships to our experiences, it is an attitude that requires us to negotiate the connections between the self, history, and the social network. Baldwin argues over and again in his essays and fiction that the best method of navigating and narrating those connections is improvisation. However, Baldwin also explains in "Sonny's Blues" and "This Morning, This Evening, So Soon" that the path to self-identifying improvisational expression is treacherous. In fact, one of the key tropes emerging from Baldwin's oeuvre is that of the pugilistic improviser: the cultural producer willing to accept the mantle of essentialist narratives in order to negate them. Through his literary efforts Baldwin suggests that the prize for confronting and communicating one's painful experience in public is transcendent understanding. But the social group, the audience listening to the blues, also benefits because the performance will incite them to interrogate their own histories and the group's collective history. This process of artistic inspiration and pious narration, John Dewey tells us, is where community begins.

Baldwin's ultimate goal as an artist/intellectual was to bear witness for those Americans attempting to act, to perform, to represent physically the changes needed to realize American democracy. Just as Charlie Parker haunts Baldwin's lines in "Sonny's Blues," Baldwin haunts Don DeLillo's lines in the middle of his masterwork, *Underworld* (1997).

II

In *Underworld* DeLillo provides novelistic narrative shape to the multithreaded second half of the twentieth century, Cold War to new millennium.[3] One of the key figures in DeLillo's American cultural history is Charlie Parker. Bird reflects the opposing realities of black and white Americans even at the end of the century. In one instance, Nick Shay, DeLillo's main protagonist, argues with a black colleague about a photograph of Parker. The photograph in question is most likely Bob Parent's iconic shot of Parker's quintet taken at the Open Door jazz club in September 1953. While spending an evening roving around contemporary Los Angeles, visiting jazz and blues clubs, Shay and his colleague Simeon Biggs (Big Sims) circle through the urban night, urged on by bourbon-soaked music, conversing about work, marriage, race, and cultural ownership. At the center of their boozy repartee, Biggs and Shay argue about Parent's image of Parker in performance.

While they jab back and forth, trying to name the kind of shoes that Parker is wearing in the shot, the underlying battle is about who gets to own Parker's legend, whites or African Americans. The exchange between Nick and Simeon carries a Parkeresque eloquence—bluesy themes shift unexpectedly into lyrical lines that loop smoothly into repeated riffs that run together to become taut, emphatic statements. But Parker's music also contains a fistic energy. Once Parker enters their discourse, Shay notes a strident undertow in their conversation: "Out of nowhere I thought about how our faces changed, how I tried to spy out a sign in another man's eye that would tell me how worried I ought to be but at the same time how I avoided eye contact until I'd had a chance to gain a certain purchase on the situation and how we seemed to agree together, as the room whistled and groaned, that if we all carried the same face we would be free from any harm" (DeLillo 1997, 327). For Shay eye-to-eye contact, searched for yet avoided, signals an impending battle. Note the paradox in his final adjustment: if their faces were the same, the racial difference and history between them absent, harm could be avoided. The apparent agreement is an acknowledgment that harm cannot be circumvented.

Nick wants to forestall pain, but it surfaces when he and Biggs begin arguing about the population census and the true count of African American citizens. Thinking back to the 1940s and his childhood, Simeon explains that his mother would tell him to hide, to "stay down" when the census takers would come to his house.

"Thirty million people affected by your local blackout. But only twenty- five million, they're saying, black people in the whole huge country. . . . You're willing to accept this number."

"Twenty-five million. Yes, why not?"

"You don't think this number is way too low."

"Twenty-five million's not so low. It's twenty-five million. . . ."

'You don't think somebody's afraid that if the real number is reported, white people gonna go weak in the knees and black people gonna get all pumped up with, Hey we oughta be gettin' more of this and more of that and more of the other. . . . You don't think white people gonna be so depressed, so, I hate to say it, menaced by the true number."

"You think the census bureau is hiding ten million black people. . . ."

"Face the issue."

"What's the issue."

"We have a right to know how many of us there are."

"But you do know."

"We don't know. Because the number is too dangerous. How threatened do you feel by the real number? I'm talking to you. Think into your own heart."

"All right, I'm thinking."

"Tell me in your heart you don't think there's something genuine in what I'm saying."

"There's genuine paranoia. That's the only genuine anything I can see here." (DeLillo 1997, 335-336)

On one hand, in Shay's reading, Parker is distilled to his god-like parts in order to assemble an idol, a representation of coolness and a highly exoticized sign of manhood. Shay's fixation on Parker's very hip spectator shoes reifies the old claims about blackness strewn throughout American arts and letters. On the other hand, Simeon reads Parker as a chronicle of a complicated Negro history in which faces are masked or bodies are hidden in order to secretly circumvent the racial order or political status quo. Parker was "sacrificed" in order for bebop to become a platform for black masculine expression. For its audience, bebop marks the rise of the modern, postwar African American jazz as the province of "serious, politicized, and sometimes pathological black male creativity."[4]

But bebop is also a marker of Simeon's "enlightened paranoia;" it's a sensibility he cannot communicate clearly to Nick. The irony of the scene is not in DeLillo's emulation of the contrapuntal trading voiced in bebop performance but rather that Shay cannot connect Biggs's experiential claims to the way that the blues and jazz flesh out the rhythm of their exchange. When the night and the music end, Simeon refuses to offer either hug or handshake to Nick in favor of a hard head butt. Shay responds in kind and they knock each other several times with "monosyllabic" blows.

DeLillo's scene is an improvised riff on Baldwin's violence-driven contest over the nature of reality and masculinity. Like Baldwin, DeLillo sees jazz and violence intimately bound to narratives about urban American masculinity—DeLillo writes about Latino, white, and black New Yorkers in *Underworld*. DeLillo's novel spins around Parker, a cipher for the confluence of racial histories, cultural history, politics, and aesthetics in the second half of the "American century." This suggests that DeLillo is a product of a biracial cultural and intellectual tradition; Baldwin and Parker are his artistic forefathers. DeLillo's scene also feels particularly Baldwinian as it recalls the battle over reality between Vivaldo and Rufus in *Another Country*. Just as Baldwin's characters seem unable to reduce the gap between their experiences, the physical exchange between Biggs and Shay is an apt metaphor for what Biggs is unable to communicate to Shay about Parker, racial paranoia, or the verities of love and business. Luckily, the morning after their exchange, though bruised and hungover, Shay realizes from the swollen, bluish lump on his forehead that "pain is just another form of information."[5] Another way to say it is that the blues idiom encompasses both the narrative impetus for the pain and the aesthetic attitude for negotiating pain.

Like DeLillo's, LeRoi Jones/Amiri Baraka's aesthetic apprenticeship happened in 1950s New York City. Emerging from Beat culture and the jazz clubs and coffee houses of Greenwich Village and the Lower East Side, Jones/Baraka's poems display the attitudes and lyricism of high modernism. His modernist inclinations also fueled a taste for transitional modes, revolutionary manifestoes, and radical politics. As the liberation movement made deeper forays into the American consciousness, Jones/Baraka's plays, essays, and poems began to narrate his political concern for blues people and blues idiom music. The forms he invented to announce his and the culture's changes revealed the shapes of his literary theorization of blues idiom improvisation. Though his aesthetic ideals and political positions have often grated against the mainstream of American politics, his unique intellectual impression is clearly stamped on contemporary jazz studies and on the cultural and musicological study of the "post-soul" era. Even more, as this final solo burst suggests: Baraka remains an avatar of radical poetics and politics even into the twenty-first century. In Warren Beatty's film *Bulworth* and on The Roots' recording of *Phrenology* (2002) Baraka performs the role of secular priest or griot providing access to liminal zones of transition, improvisation, and swinging, lyrical power; these performances point toward the renewal of American life through investment in African American cultural practices.

III

In Beatty's *Bulworth,* senator Jay Bulworth imagines that if hip-hop aesthetics becomes the basis of American political discourse, more Americans, especially African Americans, will have access to the political mainstream. The consequences of hip-hop, according to Beatty's logic, are that a new interracial harmony will emerge and the new millennium will receive an injection of honest and righteous speech. In the film the avatar for this newness is Baraka. Playing a wandering street person/griot, Baraka speaks abstractions: "You gotta be a spirit. The spirit needs to sing. Don't be a ghost." Baraka lends gravitas to Beatty's vision; he is the literal representation of black radicalism. His lines are meant to crystallize the social protest at the base of hip-hop aesthetics. As well, constructing sampled music into significant sonic backdrops for hip-hop performance requires musical knowledge as rigorous as that required for intelligent jazz improvisation. More to the point, Baraka as radical, improvising poet is the precursor to hip-hop MCing, the art of storytelling and rhyme.

Near the end of The Roots' album *Phrenology* (2002) hip-hop meets 1960s avant-garde poetics when Baraka takes over MC duties from the band's main voice and lyricist, Black Thought. Rather than rhyming his lyrics, Baraka performs his poem "Something in the Way of Things (In Town)" buoyed by the machine-gun rhythm section of the band, Ahmir Thompson (drums), Kamal Gray (keyboards), and Hub Hubbard (bass). In a poem about the spirit of death and decay wafting through black urban experiences, Baraka argues that he "see[s] something in the way of our selves."[6] Much as he blends free improvised and abstract expressions in "Tone Poem," Baraka here layers strange images, like death "riding on top of the car peering through the windshield" and a Negro "squinting at us through the cage," with a smile "that ain't a smile but teeth flying against our necks," against the aural synthesis of several cultural practices from the American and African American traditions (The Roots 2002). Baraka, the writer nurtured in postwar bohemia and matured by Marxism, becomes the voice of a hip-hop band whose music channels jazz, funk, rock, and hip-hop fundamentals. The musical mixture is urbane, hip, street philosophical, and intellectual.

Though Baraka can see something, he can't call it by name. But the poet's inability to name the thing doesn't impede his performance with the band from describing the revitalizing force of hip-hop. Here, Baraka's lyrical expression in and through hip-hop "is *itself* a prolonged interaction of something issuing from [his experience] with objective conditions, a process in which [the poet, the musicians, and the music] acquire a form and order they did not at first possess."[7] In other words, Baraka's interaction with The Roots produces a new thing, an improvised art. Rather than iterating Black Nationalist rhetoric about narrowly defined black communities or the foundation of black consciousness, the recording ties inextricably "concrete historical and technological developments" in black music and literature that "unnerve and simultaneously revitalize American culture."[8]

That revitalization, like Jones/Baraka's notions of cultural revitalization and improvisation during his transitional period, is triggered through black musical narratives "which transmit, via a process of critique, the core values and sensibilities of the African American diaspora."[9] That continued process of critique helps to articulate the dialectical play between African American and Western culture, between the self and the search for blackness; both dialectics keep the music and its makers vital to our cultural churnings and self-realizations.

Acknowledgments

This book is a product of an excellent education. At various stages of my undergraduate and graduate interdisciplinary studies at Indiana University-Bloomington and the University of Virginia-Charlottesville, I was well tutored by David Baker, Rita Felski, Tom Foster, Susan Gubar, Eric Lott, Portia Maultsby, Carolyn Mitchell, Teju Olaniyan, Charles Perdue, Charles Rowell, Bill Wiggins, and Cary Wolfe.

While at UVA I was very lucky to study with the late Richard Rorty. Rorty illustrated, in thought and practice, how literary studies and pragmatism could produce serious cultural studies. I am also deeply indebted to John McCluskey, a master teacher and writer, who served as my dissertation director, helping me shape many of my notions about African American literature and jazz improvisation into a readable narrative. I remain his dutiful pupil.

Special thanks and high praise to Douglas Mitchell and the editorial team at the University of Chicago Press, who moved *The Shadow and the Act* from concept to complete text with care, confidence, and great patience. Thanks to the librarians in the Lilly Library at Indiana University and the Library of Congress, Manuscript Division, for allowing me easy access to special materials including the LeRoi Jones/Amiri Baraka Papers and the Ralph Ellison Papers.

Jenny Adams, Robert Upchurch, and Paul Menzer taught me how to be a scholar and writer; Jacqueline Foertsch, Stephanie Hawkins, Ian Finseth, Luis Velarde, and Nicole Smith have all had hands in making these pages stronger. All have been or are currently my colleagues at the University of North Texas. The university has aided my efforts to research, write, and complete this project by providing me two small but significant research grants.

I am grateful for the generosity of my friends who, in various ports around the United States and Europe, provided me always with good cheer and often with comfortable workspaces: in Paris, Elizabeth Adams; in London, Felicia Kanyinda; in Los Angeles, Dana Johnson, Mikette Miller, and Darius Holbert; in Philadelphia, the Maron family; in Baltimore, Michael, Amanda, and Brooks Rady; in New York City, Sarah Broom, Anique Halliday, Tres Miah, Keith Adkins, Somi Kakoma, and Alane Mason.

In Dallas, I am especially thankful for Merritt Tierce's friendship, intellectual partnership, and love. An indispensible editor and patron, she's made living in Dallas tolerable and this writing better than it could ever be. My cohort in Big D keeps me well fed gastronomically and intellectually: thanks to the Dallas Area Social History group, Chris Vognar, Anne Bothwell, Marta Harvell, David Mulcahy, Libby Russ, and the Herring-McCrossen family. These pages were edited in my adjunct offices, the Gachet Coffee Lounge and the Murray Street Coffee Shop. To the proprietors of the respective shops, the Beaumont sisters and Doug and Liz Davis, special thanks.

For their gracious and loving encouragement throughout my effort to finish this book, thanks to my extended family Isabelle Kalubi in Cincinnati, D. Winston Brown in Birmingham, and the Bokambas in Minneapolis and Champaign-Urbana. At every stage, from Washington DC to Paris, Kathleen Crowley has provided financial and emotional support, along with tough-minded critique. I could not have completed this book without her seventeen years of unconditional friendship and loving sisterhood.

Finally, exuberant thanks to my family, the Muyumbas, for enduring my distance away from them, for letting me back in when I come home, and loving me well in spite of my long absences.

An earlier version of Movement IV originally appeared as "Improvising over the Changes: Improvisation as Intellectual and Aesthetic Practice in the Transitional Poems of LeRoi Jones/Amiri Baraka," *College Literature* 34, no. 1 (2007): 23-51. Copyright 2007 Board of Trustees of West Chester University.

Notes

Introduction

1. Cornel West, *The American Evasion of Philosophy* (Madison, WI, University of Wisconsin Press, 1989), 36.

2. William James. *Writings 1902–1910*. New York: Library of America, 1987, 520.

3. Eddie S. Glaude Jr., *In A Shade of Blue* (Chicago: University of Chicago Press, 2007), 6–7.

4. Richard Rorty, *Objectivity, Relativism, and Truth* (New York: Cambridge University Press, 1991), 211.

5. I am indebted to several scholars of pragmatism. My definition has been culled from George Hutchinson's *The Harlem Renaissance in Black and White* (Cambridge, MA: Harvard University Press, 1997); William James's *Pragmatism* (in *Writings 1902–1910* [New York: Library of America, 1987]); Louis Menand's *The Metaphysical Club* (New York: Farrar Straus Giroux, 2001); Richard Rorty's *Philosophy and the Mirror of Nature* (Princeton, NJ: Princeton University Press, 1981), *Contingency, Irony, and Solidarity* (New York: Cambridge University Press, 1989), and *Philosophy and Social Hope* (New York: Penguin, 2000); and Cornel West's *The American Evasion of Philosophy* (Madison: University of Wisconsin Press, 1988).

6. Ross Posnock, *Color and Culture: Black Writers and the Making of the Modern Intellectual* (Cambridge, MA: Harvard University Press, 1999), 36.

7. See Posnock on Baldwin in *Color and Culture*, 224.

8. Michael Magee, *Emancipating Pragmatism: Emerson, Jazz, and Experimental Writing* (Tuscaloosa, AL: University of Alabama Press, 2004), 22.

9. Posnock, *Color and Culture*, 2, 21–23.

10. W. E. B. Du Bois, *Writings* (New York: Library of America, 1986), 364–65.

11. James, *Writings 1902–1910*, 508–9. One way to chart Du Bois's pragmatist turnings is to examine the multiple disciplines and styles he used to as a route to black liberation. As David Levering Lewis argues, Du Bois used, at the very least, propaganda, the novel, social science, history, criticism, and politics to reconstruct American life. We can see Du Bois's range even in his earliest works of American history (*The Suppression of the African Slave Trade* [see *Writings* (New York: Library of America, 1986)]), sociology (*The Philadelphia Negro* [Philadelphia: University of Pennsylvania Press, 1995]), and social critique (*The Souls of Black Folk* [see *Writings* (New York: Library of America, 1986)]).

12. Du Bois, *Writings*, 822. Interestingly, Du Bois spent the last sixty-six years of his life following the publication of these thoughts waiting for this practical possibility to finally arrive. Du Bois's essay appeared while he was teaching at Atlanta University and during the rise of what he named "white amusement"—lynching. As much as he could promote the ideal of "higher individualism," the social realities of American Negro life were still circumscribed by the hangman's line. The Sam Hose lynching would in fact force Du Bois to test his philosophical notions in a larger political arena. The lynching of Sam Hose, documented in Grace Hale's *Making Whiteness* (New York: Pantheon, 1998) and Leon Litwack's *Trouble in Mind* (New York: Knopf, 1998), forced Du Bois to turn away from academic work at Atlanta University and toward a certain kind of political truth—"propaganda." Du Bois describes as much in the chapter "Science and Empire" from *Dusk of Dawn* (see *Writings* [New York: Library of America, 1986]).

13. John Dewey, *Reconstruction in Philosophy* (Boston: Beacon Press, 1957), 192.

14. Rorty, *Philosophy and Social Hope*, 24.

15. In *Color and Culture* (1999) Posnock argues that in "Criteria of Negro Art" Du Bois "defamiliarizes" the use of "propaganda." In the opening pages of the essay, Posnock explains, Du Bois describes "the experience of beauty engendering moments of aesthetic bliss in the midst of daily life in philistine America. . . . He marries Beauty to Truth and Freedom, to 'facts of the world and the right action of men.' This enacts the Jamesian pragmatist's turn 'towards facts, towards action, and towards power'" (139, 141).

16. W. E. B. Du Bois, "Criteria of Negro Art," *Writings* (New York: Library of America, 1986), 1002.

17. Michael Soto, *The Modernist Nation: Generation, Renaissance, and Twentieth Century American Literature* (Tuscaloosa, AL: University of Alabama Press, 2004), 60. Soto's *The Modernist Nation* might be read

as a corollary to Ann Douglas's *Terrible Honesty* (New York: Farrar, Straus, Giroux, 1995). Douglas's description of this Emersonian rhetoric is drawn as a dramatic psychological battle. This genealogical theme becomes even more interesting when Douglas scripts her drama around key players like Sigmund Freud and his intellectual adversary, William James — family romance and the psychological self versus the stream of consciousness and philosophical "turning away". But rather than see this as a battle, we might consider American modernism as a combination of Freud's and James's perspectives. For instance, American artistic modernism might be read as a label placed on works by artists who exhibit or express Freudian themes about the psychological desire for metaphysical connection between the individual self and the memorial past while simultaneously "turning away" from that connection as the epistemological foundation of personal identity.

One productive way of reading U.S. literary modernism is as an effort to describe two different cultural desires simultaneously: 1) the desire to name the cultural generation born out of emancipation from feminine, sentimental Victorian England and 2) the desire to instigate America's renaissance as an expressly multiracial nation. The key to this process was a willfully constructed collective orphan ethos. "Orphans," writes Douglas, "by definition originate their own genealogy; they are disinherited, perhaps, but free" (Douglas 1995, 27). Disinherited but free, Americans had only the social community (and contract) to contextualize citizenship or achieve identity. Dewey offers a very similar reading in *The Reconstruction of Philosophy*. In the context of African American experiences, this composition of disinheritance, freedom (deferred), citizenship, and selfhood is poignant because it describes the failures of the American democratic experiment while also inspiring Negroes to experiment within the experiment, to improvise identity.

This liminality helps explain the development of the New Negro movement and the Harlem Renaissance. The use of terms like "generation" or "renaissance" as descriptive metaphors for literary groupings "endow[s] the literary artifacts falling within their rubrics with a socially significant aura; they teach us not just *what* to read, what counts as literature, but also *how* to read, why literature counts as literature" (Soto 2004, 7). Rhetorical narratives of self-creation and rebirth are quintessential elements of the American ethos because we desire such sensibilities.

The "New Negro" in Harlem was being invented through rebirth. The renaissance was an improvisation on the already existing Negro ethos. In order to destabilize the power of racial prejudice, intranational imperialistic practices, and social stigma associated with blackness, black cultural workers like Du Bois, Locke, and James Weldon Johnson knew that they had to balance radical pluralism with a clear understanding of the social implications of blackness.

Much like Emerson on American literature, Locke on African American artistry describes African Americans as political and cultural orphans who, in the process of recreating themselves, would create a whole, unified, and future-oriented Negro tradition (see Locke's introduction to the anthology *The New Negro* [New York: Atheneum, 1925]). Even before it had begun, the New Negro movement/Harlem Renaissance had to be identified — it had to be named before it could be. This agenda sets the Negro/Harlem Renaissance rhetoric apart from other American renaissances or generations. Writers like Langston Hughes, Claude McKay, and Zora Neale Hurston were, in various ways, writing "to re-create the past and to imagine the future of African American literature" (Soto 2004, 79). However, in order for the rebirth to become something other than the romance of Negroness, Locke argued that racial mythologies had to be evaded even while acknowledging the realities of being raced. Locke understood this argument well because he had conceptualized pragmatically an exit from racial essentialism.

18. Alain Locke, *Race Contacts and Interracial Relations* (Washington DC: Howard University Press, 1992), 88.

19. Nancy Fraser, "Another Pragmatism: Alain Locke, Critical 'Race' Theory, and the Politics of Culture," in *The Revival of Pragmatism*, ed. Morris Dickstein, 171 (Durham, NC: Duke University Press, 1998).

20. Locke, *The New Negro*, 15.

21. Walter Benn Michaels, *Our America* (Durham, NC: Duke University Press, 1995), 139.

22. Derek Nystrom and Kent Puckett, *Against Bosses, Against Oligarchies: A Conversation with Richard Rorty* (Charlottesville, VA: Prickly Pear Pamphlets, 1998), 24–25. However much one is troubled by Rorty's "liberal ethnocentrism," he does, at least, acknowledge that Western societies and philosophies have been defined primarily without recourse to the experiences of the non-white, non-European peoples dominated in order to establish what is "good" about Western ideals. Strangely, Rorty's forward-gazing hopefulness turns away from interrogating past or present human action and particularly avoids any analysis of the impediments to liberation imbedded in Western or American social practices. Rorty's narrative of human progress and pragmatist vocabulary does not take into account the material realities and *last things* that give rise to obstacles against hopefulness; there isn't a balance between pragmatist conceptions of truth, his postmodern bourgeois liberalism,

and a clear comprehension, for example, of the social and psychological implications of American racial history (see Eric Lott's "Boomer Liberalism: When the New Left Was Old," *Transition* 78 [1999]: 24–44). Lott's review of Rorty's *Achieving Our Country* (Cambridge, MA: Harvard University Press, 1998) contextualizes some of Rorty's missteps by interrogating the lineage of "Rortyites" who are eradicating the difficulties of American racial history from their analyses of American history and class politics.

23. We should read Shelby's work as part of an ongoing reconstruction of Western philosophies in order to produce narratives that redefine the terms and the practices to include the historical and social circumstances of African Americans. Several philosophers have begun such projects by reviving conceptions of blackness that highlight conflicts between the promises of American democratic life and the material history of black life in America. For Lucius Outlaw this has meant redefining the terms of Western philosophy by developing an insurgent theoretical analysis of both the historical and social circumstances of African Americans. Outlaw's project entails reviving an ideology of "blackness" that highlights the contradictions of the promise of American democratic life with the absurdities of Negro life in the New World. Mills has suggested as much except he has turned specifically to the cultural practices of New World Africans as a guide toward the definition of a philosophical practice derived from African American experience. All of this sounds quite appealing: Outlaw and Mills's ventures to revamp the applications of Western philosophical discourse are amenable to the liberal context of the academy. Except, as evidenced in the published exchange between Outlaw and another philosopher, Michael Roth, there is a grave resistance to the possibility of an "African American philosophy." The question of the existence of that philosophy is loaded with all the implications of late twentieth-century "culture wars." For further reading on the matter of African American experience and philosophy see Charles Mills's *Blackness Visible* (Ithaca, NY: Cornell University Press, 1998). Also see Lucius Outlaw's *On Race and Philosophy* (New York: Routledge, 1996). Finally, the exchange between Outlaw and Roth exposes the real resistance to the development of African American philosophy; see Lucius Outlaw and Michael D. Roth, "Is There a Distinctive African American Philosophy?" *Academic Questions* 10, no. 2 (Spring 1997): 29–46.

24. Tommie Shelby, *We Who Are Dark* (Cambridge, MA: Harvard University Press, 2005), 50–51. A philosopher like Kwame Anthony Appiah would caution Shelby in his attempt to fashion a philosophical perspective, even a thin one, from African American experience. A committed

cosmopolitan, Appiah argues that essentialists and ethnocentrists must travel slippery logical routes to make their claims about identity and philosophy (see Appiah's *Cosmopolitanism: Ethics in a World of Strangers* [New York: W. W. Norton, 2006] and *The Ethics of Identity* [Princeton, NJ: Princeton University Press, 2004]). Discussing the question of an "African philosophy," Appiah writes that "if the argument for an African philosophy is not to be racist, then some claim must be substantiated to the effect that there are important problems of morals or epistemology or ontology that are common in the situation of those on the African continent. And the source of that common problematic, if it cannot be racial, must lie in the African environment or in African history" (Kwame Anthony Appiah, *In My Father's House* [New York: Oxford University Press, 1992], 92). Even as it sounds a warning against biological fictions, Appiah's qualification suggests that critical close analysis of experiences, rituals, arts, and history will illuminate the common moral, political, philosophical, and psychological dilemmas of African Americans. But upon discovering these common problems, critics must also recognize and name those tools, often developed experimentally, that aid in coping with those social and existential impediments.

25. Mark Anthony Neal, *What the Music Said: Black Popular Music and Black Public Culture* (New York: Routledge, 1999), 1.

26. Houston Baker, *Blues, Ideology, and Afro American Literature* (Chicago: University of Chicago Press, 1984), 5.

27. Kenneth Burke, *The Philosophy of Literary Form* (Berkeley, CA: University of California Press, 1973), 61. Also in this volume see the chapter, "Literature as Equipment for Living," Burke's fuller explanation of literature's utility.

28. Albert Murray, *Omni Americans* (New York: De Capo Press, 1970), 55–66.

29. Ralph Ellison, *The Collected Essays of Ralph Ellison* (New York: Modern Library, 1995), 129.

30. John Dewey, *The Public and Its Problems* (New York: Henry Holt and Co., 1954), 151–52.

31. Mills, *Blackness Visible*, 13.

32. Paul F. Berliner, *Thinking in Jazz* (Chicago: University of Chicago Press, 1994), 486.

33. Ingrid Monson, *Saying Something* (Chicago: University of Chicago Press, 1996), 2. Monson's *Saying Something* is a theoretical analysis of improvisation as an African American vernacular language. Monson unfolds the ways improvisation functions not only as the jazz soloist's prime musical space but as the pulse of an interactive language for rhythm sections. Monson explains how improvised musical conversa-

tions, especially in jazz rhythm sections, articulate concerns of identity, politics, and culture in contemporary American culture.

34. See studies such as Jones/Baraka's *Blues People* (New York: Grove Press, 1963), Elieen Southern's *Readings in Black American Music* (New York: W. W. Norton, 1971), Paul Berliner's *The Soul of Mbira: Music and Traditions of the Shona People of Zimbabwe* (Chicago: University of Chicago Press: 1993), and Mellonee Burnim and Portia Maultsby's *African-American Music: An Introduction* (New York: Routledge, 2005).

35. Michael Jarrett, *Drifting on a Read: Jazz as a Model for Writing* (Albany, NY: SUNY Press, 1998), 61. This is the definition that Jarrett provides in his text. The particular version has been culled from the *Harvard Concise Dictionary of Music* (Cambridge, MA: Belknap Press, 1978). The italicized emphasis is Jarrett's.

36. Yusef Komunyakaa, *Thieves of Paradise* (Hanover, CT: Wesleyan University Press, 1998), 91.

Movement I

1. Ralph Ellison and Albert Murray, *Trading Twelves: The Selected Letters of Ralph Ellison and Albert Murray* (New York: Modern Library, 2000), 116–17.

2. Ellison, *The Collected Essays*, 259.

3. Ellison (1914–94), Baldwin (1924–87), and Jones/Baraka (1934–present) came of age along with the musicians who developed bebop into a specific tradition and developed multiple performance styles out of the music. Baldwin, two years younger than Charles Mingus and two years older than John Coltrane, was in Paris crafting his aesthetic when many boppers expatriated to France to escape the grips of American racism.

4. Hawkins, whose music served as a bridge between the theories of big band soloing and bebop improvisation, came to the fore with his 1939 recording of "Body and Soul." Hawkins's ability to narrate a story through his "uncomplicated and emotionally direct" improvised solos marks the success of the recording. "Body and Soul" displays Hawkins's play as "a continuous, carefully controlled crescendo of intensity on several fronts at once: a gradually thickening or hardening of timbre, a steady increase in volume, and a climb to melodic peak carefully withheld until very near the end" (Scott DeVeaux, *The Birth of Bebop* [Berkeley CA: University of California Press, 1996], 7).

5. Eric Porter, *What Is This Thing Called Jazz?* (Berkeley CA: University of California Press, 2002), 71.

6. Ralph Ellison, *Invisible Man* (New York: Vintage, 1995), 440.

7. Ellison and Murray, *Trading Twelves*, 193.

8. Magee, *Emancipating Pragmatism*, 18.

9. Kenneth Burke, *Language as Symbolic Action* (Berkeley, CA: University of California Press, 1966), 362.

10. Tim Parrish, *Walking Blues* (Amherst, MA: University of Massachusetts Press, 2001), 113.

11. Burke, *The Philosophy of Literary Form*, 40.

12. Think, for instance, of the google-eyed Rochester (Eddie Anderson) or the molasses-slow ineptitude of Stepin Fetchit (Lincoln Perry).

13. DeVeaux, *The Birth of Bebop*, 246–47.

14. Penny M. Von Eschen details this history in her fine study, *Satchmo Blows Up the World* (Cambridge, MA: Harvard University Press, 2004). See also Ingrid Monson's lucid history of jazz and the CRM, *Freedom Sounds* (New York: Oxford University Press, 2007) and Iain Anderson's excellent examination of political radicalism and jazz performance, *This Is Our Music* (Philadelphia: University of Pennsylvania Press, 2007).

15. James Baldwin, *Early Novels and Stories* (New York: The Library of America, 1998a), 846.

16. While Parker proclaimed himself the world's most famous heroin addict, the jazz world was littered with performers who squandered or nearly squandered their careers by finding solace in heroin: Sonny Rollins, Miles Davis, Fats Navarro, John Coltrane, Bud Powell, Dexter Gordon, to name a few. For Rollins, Davis, and Coltrane, kicking the habit allowed them to produce enduring and elastic influences over the aesthetic of jazz improvisation. In his own way each musician created music that illustrated the possibility of salvation through musical invention. Where Davis created and embodied the movie star hipness, disaffected cool (*Porgy and Bess* and *Sketches of Spain*), Rollins produced a macho lyrical style: muscular, brooding, playful, romantic, and sexual ("My Reverie" and "More Than You Know"). Coltrane, on the other hand, had a very public maturing process. The leaps in Coltrane's recorded performances from the late 1950s to his stellar work with the Classic Quartet in the early 1960s are great models for understanding the manner of growth that happens with Sonny in the Baldwin story.

17. Glaude, *In a Shade of Blue*, 16.

18. Kenneth Burke, *Permanence and Change* (Berkeley, CA: University of California Press, 1954), 71, 74.

19. Parker had a theoretical comprehension of classical music and composition that ran parallel to, but not counter to or unduly influential on, the Negro experimental music he invented along with Gillespie and Monk. It is important to note that in performance Parker could quote

freely from all musical concepts without disrupting the integrity of bebop's principles. See George E. Lewis's *A Power Stronger than Itself: The AACM and American Experimental Music* (Chicago: University of Chicago Press, 2008), 370–77.

20. Posnock, *Color and Culture*, 233.

21. Quoted in Scott Saul's *Freedom Is, Freedom Ain't: Jazz and the Making of the Sixties* (Cambridge, MA: Harvard University Press, 2005), 73. See also James Baldwin, *New York Times Book Review*, December 2, 1962.

22. John Dewey, *Art as Experience* (New York: Perigee Books, 1980), 273–74.

23. John Dewey, *The Public and Its Problems* (Athens, OH: Ohio University Press, 1954), 184.

24. Gary Giddins, *Visions of Jazz: The First Century* (New York: Oxford University Press, 1998), 261. The acceptance of Parker's innovations derived from bebop's cultural position as "the most demanding virtuoso music ever to take root in the American vernacular" and because bebop, a blues-based music, was elementally American roots music (Giddins 1998, 262).

25. Komuyakaa, *Thieves of Paradise*, 96.

26. LeRoi Jones/Amiri Baraka, *The Dutchman*, *The LeRoi Jones/Amiri Baraka Reader*, ed., William Harris (New York: Thunder's Mouth Press, 1999), 97.

27. Emerson, *Selections From Ralph Waldo Emerson*, 231.

28. For the recording of "Parker's Mood" referenced above, listen to *Bird/The Savoy Recordings [Master Takes]* (New York: Savoy Records, B00000E7QL, 1976) or *The Yardbird Suite: The Ultimate Charlie Parker* (Rhino Records, B0000033PW, 1997).

29. Richard Rorty, *Contingency, Irony, and Solidarity* (New York: Cambridge University Press, 1989), 53–54.

30. LeRoi Jones/Amiri Baraka, *The Fiction of LeRoi Jones/Amiri Baraka* (New York: Lawrence Hill Books, 2000), 185.

31. Ben Ratliff, *Coltrane: The Story of a Sound* (New York: Farrar Straus Giroux, 2007), 36.

32. John Gennari details this very battle in several chapters is his astute historical analysis of jazz criticism, *Blowin' Hot and Cool: Jazz and Its Critics* (Chicago: University of Chicago Press, 2006).

33. Ratliff, *Coltrane: The Story of a Sound*, xi. Ratliff's study provides an articulate explanation of the relationship between Monk and Coltrane. Monk's musical style, composing, improvising, and offhand way of conducting his groups inspired Coltrane to provide large swaths of solo space for his own bandmates in the classic Coltrane Quartet. Ratliff explains that "Monk was both more specific with answers to Coltrane

in questions about music and less direct in his style of bandleading" (Ratliff 2007, 38).

34. LeRoi Jones/Amiri Baraka, *Black Music* (New York: Apollo Editions, 1968), 61.

35. Brent Hayes Edwards, "The Seemingly Eclipsed Window of Form," in *The Jazz Cadence of American Culture,* ed. Robert O'Meally, 592 (New York: Columbia University Press, 1999).

36. John Dewey, *Art as Experience* (New York: Pedigree Books, 1980), 60.

37. Jones/Baraka, *Blues People,* xii.

Movement II

1. Ralph Ellison, *Invisible Man* (New York: Vintage 1995). Ellison explains that the voice of the narrator came to him from the underground of American culture. In fact, it might be said that the voice of the protagonist is a manifestation of Ellison's latent understanding of our violent and strange American racial history.

2. John Callahan, "The Historical Frequencies of Ralph Waldo Ellison," in *Chant of Saints,* ed. Michael S. Harper and Robert B. Stepto, 41 (Urbana, IL: University of Illinois Press, 1979).

3. C. Vann Woodward, *The Burden of Southern History* (Baton Rouge, LA: Louisiana State University Press, 1993), 193.

4. See Richard Rorty's late attempts to connect American liberal politics and social hope in *Achieving Our Country* and *Philosophy and Social Hope.*

5. Ellison, *The Collected Essays of Ralph Ellison,* 151–53. Ellison wanted *Invisible Man* to reproduce the mode of the nineteenth-century works of Stephen Crane, Herman Melville, and Mark Twain. Crane ("The Monster," *The Red Badge of Courage*), Melville ("Bartelby, the Scrivener," "Benito Cereno," *Moby Dick, Confidence Man*) and Twain (*Huckleberry Finn, Pudd'nhead Wilson*) confronted the problems of liberty and democracy by way of symbolic structures in which blackness functioned as the key to fulfilling the American political ideal. Given the social and political constraints placed on Negroes during the first half of the twentieth century, it seems difficult to imagine how Ellison could replicate that mood in terms of a young black male narrator. That difficulty must have been quite strenuous also given Ellison's awareness of the great literary obstacle he had to overcome, namely Richard Wright.

Ellison had to deal with not only the overwhelming presence of his mentor and friend, but also the towering stature of Wright's characters such as the underground man in "The Man Who Lived Underground," Bigger Thomas in *Native Son,* and the younger Wright himself as pictured in the memoir *Black Boy*. Ellison's out was to focus on the way in which Bigger Thomas projected an Anglo-invented stereotype of Negroness; he believed that Wright had accepted and extended the image of the tragic minstrel. In Ellison's estimation, unmasking Bigger would not reveal the complex, diverse, and multilayered experiences that Ellison had seen amongst American Negroes.

6. Ralph Ellison, *Flying Home and Other Stories* (New York: Random House, 1996), 152.

7. The story's title is borrowed from Lionel Hampton's signature composition, "Flying Home" (1939). The song was a staple of the swing era; Hampton's own big band and the Benny Goodman Sextet recorded the best versions of it. Benny Goodman's drawing power and musicianship brought him the title King of Swing during swing's greatest popularity in the 1930s. Goodman's small groups were significant for introducing integrated performance groups into the jazz world. Though there were few public spaces for integrated audiences at the time, Goodman's groups provided visible evidence of a different America emerging from and inspired by jazz. The Oklahoma City guitarist Charlie Christian performed in the Hampton and Goodman outfits and elevated the performance levels of both units. In choosing the title Ellison most likely had the Goodman band's recording in mind. Hampton and Christian both play on the sextet's 1941 recording of "Flying Home" with Christian spinning a solo blending southwestern blues riffs, swing time, and bebop melodies into an incomparable improvisational style. Ellison and Christian had been childhood friends in Oklahoma City. He must have been impressed by Christian's ability to leap "directly from regional obscurity to a position of high visibility" in the jazz world (DeVeaux 1996, 220). Even more, Ellison probably noted the way that Christian, whether in performances with the Goodman or Hampton bands or in jam session venues like Minton's, created a cosmopolitan art style for Oklahoma territorial materials.

8. Beth Eddy, *The Rites of Identity: The Religious Naturalism and Cultural Criticism of Kenneth Burke and Ralph Ellison* (Princeton, NJ: Princeton University Press, 2003), 140.

9. The blues, like Federico Garcia Lorca's concept of duende, comes when it smells blood or imminent death. Ellison draws a connection between the blues and duende in his essay "Flamenco," in *The Collected Essays of Ralph Ellison*. For other essays that draw relationships between duende and the blues see Yusef Komunyakaa's "The Forces that Move," in *Blue Notes* (Ann Arbor: University of Michigan Press, 2000) and Nathaniel Mackey's "Cante Moro," in *Sound States,* ed. Adalaide Morris (Chapel Hill, NC: University of North Carolina Press, 1997).

10. See Ellison's "The Little Man at Chehaw Station," in *The Collected Essays of Ralph Ellison*, 489-519.

11. In *Pragmatism*, James suggests that even as we develop new truths out of our experiences, we also maintain some continuity with "older truths." New ideas are adopted as true ones largely because they preserve "the older stock of truths with a minimum of modification, stretching them just enough to make them admit the novelty, but conceiving that in ways as familiar as the case leaves possible" (James, *Writings 1902-1910*, 513). We might read this insight as support for Ellison's deep valuation of jazz as a cultural and theoretical resource. Paul Allen Anderson argues, for instance, that Ellison's preference for southwestern territory bands stems from his William James–like desire for continuity with traditional African American rituals. Jazz dance bands maintain relationships with their audiences by reminding them of traditional musical themes and styles while improvising recognizably new musical "truths" about the art form and the cultural tradition (Paul Allen Anderson, "Ralph Ellison on Lyricism and Swing," *American Literary History* 17, no.2 [2005], 296).

12. Kenneth W. Warren, *So Black and Blue: Ralph Ellison and the Occasion of Criticism* (Chicago: University of Chicago Press, 2003), 41.

13. Tejumola Olaniyan, *Scars of Conquest, Masks of Resistance* (New York: Oxford University Press, 1995), 4.

14. This is from Eddy's discussion of Burke's theory of piety: "This is piety; this is also Burke's version of the Emersonian art of poetry. Poets are in the business of making new language out of old through the use of metaphors and other symbols. They breathe new life into language by disclosing connections we may have categorically overlooked in our habitual use. '[I]f we are all poets,' Burke writes, 'and all poets are pious, we may expect to find great areas of piety, even at a ball game. Indeed, all life has been likened to the writing of a poem, though some people write their poems on paper, and others carve theirs out of jugular veins'" (Eddy 2003, 30).

15. We might also follow Christopher Hanlon's idea of calling this kind of moment eloquence. Hanlon argues Ellison's connection to the jazz tradition is an outlet by means of which the artist may distinguish him- or herself as an "individual": "jazz concocts an equilibrium between the artist's sense of indebtedness and belonging, on the one hand, and this same artist's impulse to distinguish his or her own voice within that of the collectivity, on the other." To maintain that equilibrium and write artfully is eloquence. Christopher Hanlon, "Eloquence and *Invisible Man*," *College Literature* 32, no. 4 (2005): 86-87.

16. Grace Hale, *Making Whiteness* (New York: Pantheon, 1998), 203.

17. However, we know from the slave narratives written by black women that this mythology had always been at work: white male slave owners placed white women high in the social hierarchy, setting them on metaphorical pedestals while using black female bodies to "satisfy" their desires for sexual and economic domination.

18. Robin Wiegman, "The Anatomy of Lynching," in *American Sexual Politics,* ed. John Fout and Maura Shaw Tantillo (Chicago: University of Chicago Press, 1993), 223.

19. In these moments where justice, (dis)engendered "blackness," and citizenship collide, Ellison highlights the flammable contradictions of American democracy. The lynching bee is loaded with all the sociopolitical and sexual difficulties of race and gender and in Ellison's early stories these moments marked the repetition of the racism of post-Reconstruction Southern life.

20. While Wright found "Richard Wright's Blues" a profound and intelligent critique of *Black Boy,* he found Ellison's blues theorization puzzling. Wright explained to Ellison that he saw the blues working only "slightly" in *Black Boy.* See Lawrence Jackson's *Ralph Ellison: Emergence of Genius* (New York: John Wiley & Sons, 2002), 314.

21. Adam Gussow, "'Fingering the Jagged Grain': Ellison's Wright and the Southern Blues Violences," *boundary 2* 30, no.2 (2003): 142.

22. Richard Wright, *Black Boy* (New York: Harper Collins, 1995), 264.

23. William Faulkner, *Absalom, Absalom!* (New York: Vintage, 1936, 1995). Faulkner intimates this idea by presenting Sutpen's miscegenated line. It is not so much the gnashing of teeth, the smacking skins, thrusts or blows of violent embrace that set Ms. Coldfield ajar as it is the imagined sight of "the two Sutpen faces . . . once on Judith and once on the negro girl beside her—looking down through the square entrance to the loft" (Faulkner 1995, 22). There in the frame of the loft entrance, in the frame of Coldfield's memory is the manifestation of the violence—here sex and lynching and prizefighting meet. Of course Shreve McCannon, a Canadian, is the only one who can read the narrative with any clarity and without any crippling self-hatred.

> You've got one nigger left [Jim Bond (Bon), grandson of Charles Bon, great-grandson of Thomas Sutpen]. One nigger Sutpen left. . . . I think in time the Jim Bonds are going to conquer the western hemisphere. Of course it won't quite be in our time and of course as they spread toward the poles they will bleach out again like the rabbits and birds do, so they won't show up so sharp against the snow. But it will still be Jim Bond;

and so in a few thousand years, I who regard you will also have sprung from the loins of African kings. Now I want you to tell me just one thing more. Why do you hate the South? (Faulkner 303)

McCannon's question is the wrong one, for it is not the South that Quentin hates; he hates himself. In Quentin's reasoning the curse of the South is violent and suicidal.

24. Faulkner, *Absalom, Absalom!*, 20–21.

25. Alfred Kazin, *On Native Grounds* (New York: Harcourt Brace, 1985), 466.

26. After stumbling upon an advertisement for a contemporary minstrel show (a "Tom" show—so named for the infamous blackface interpretations of Harriet Beecher Stowe's famous novel) the author realized that the historical past of the U.S. is always "part of the living present." The poster worked on the author to awaken his latent comprehension of the moral evasions at the core of American cultural practices, particularly the evasive masking that converts America's "deepest experience of tragedy" into "blackface farce" (Ellison 1995b, xvi).

27. Thomas Schaub, "Ellison's Masks and the Novel of Reality," in *New Essays on Invisible Man,* ed. Robert O'Meally (New York: Cambridge University Press, 1988), 128.

28. Eric Lott, *Love and Theft* (New York: Oxford University Press, 1994), 24–29.

29. The power of most of Ellison's essays comes from his overwhelming mastery for explicating the "remarkable kind" of innate ironies within American cultural forms and norms. See Stanley Edgar Hyman's "The Folk Tradition," *Partisan Review* 25, no. 2 (1958): 197–211.

30. Baker, *Modernism and the Harlem Renaissance,* 15–36.

31. Lawrence Jackson, "Ralph Ellison, Sharpies, Rinehart, and Politics in *Invisible Man.*" *Massachusetts Review* 40, no. 1 (1999): 81.

32. Lewis Erenberg, *Swingin' the Dream: Big Band Jazz and the Rebirth of American Culture* (Chicago: University of Chicago Press, 1998), 103.

33. Jarrett, *Drifting on a Read,* 90.

34. Here I refer to the Jimmy Rushing/Count Basie Orchestra recording of "Harvard Blues" found on the disc.

35. Russell, as the leading Southerner in the Senate during the 1950s, authored the *Southern Manifesto.* The document was meant to rebuff the Supreme Court's decision to strike down the separate but equal clause that girded Jim Crow laws and segregation in the Southland.

36. Ellison and Murray, *Trading Twelves,* 175.

37. Barry Shank, "Bliss, or Blackface Sentiment," *boundary 2* 30, no. 2 (Summer 2003): 64.

38. Burke, *The Philosophy of Literary Form*, 41.

39. Ellison published the following stories between the 1960s and 1990s in lieu of his completed second novel: "And Hickman Arrives," *The Noble Savage* 1 (1960); "The Roof, the Steeple and the People," *Quarterly Review of Literature* 10, no. 3 (1959–60); "It All Breaks Out," *Partisan Review* 30, no. 1 (Spring 1963); "Juneteenth," *Quarterly Review of Literature* 13, no. 3-4 (1965); "A Song of Innocence," *Iowa Review* 1, no. 2 (Spring 1970); "Night-Talk," *Quarterly Review of Literature* 16 (1972); "Backwacking: A Plea to the Senator," *Massachusetts Review* 18, no. 3 (Autumn 1977); "Cadillac Flambé," *Callaloo* 18, no. 2 (Spring 1995).

40. See Vijay Iyer's "Exploding the Narrative in Jazz Improvisation," in *Uptown Conversation: The New Jazz Studies,* ed. Robert G. O'Meally, Brent Hayes Edwards, and Farah Jasmine Griffin (New York: Columbia University Press, 2004), 401.

41. John K. Young, *Black Writers, White Publishers: Marketplace Politics in Twentieth-Century African American Literature* (Jackson, MS: University Press of Mississippi, 2006), 175.

42. Ralph Ellison, *Juneteenth* (New York: Vintage, 1999), 128.

43. John Dewey, *Art as Experience* (New York: Perigee Books 1980), 279.

Movement III

1. While addressing Baldwin's homosexuality seems a logical move, I have purposely avoided addressing it in my analysis of his essay. Though it is probably possible to *do* a queer reading of boxing, Baldwin did not. Gerald Early's critique of "The Fight" suggests that Baldwin refused to invoke his sexuality as a theoretical lense. Early believes that boxing appalled Baldwin to the extent that he wouldn't read a homoerotic power into the match. See Early's essay "James Baldwin's Neglected Essay: Prizefighting, the White Intellectual, and the Racial Symbols of American Culture," in *Tuxedo Junction* (Ecco Press: Hopewell, NJ, 1989), 183–207. It is also worth noting, as Rosemary Bray does, that Baldwin's focus in his fiction is almost totally male oriented, especially in the early novels and stories. However, Bray suggests that this had nothing to do with Baldwin's homosexuality but rather that Baldwin's implicit cultural critique has everything to do with the myths associated with American masculinity. Rosemary Bray, "An Eloquent, Pitiless Prophet," *American Scholar* 67, no. 2 (Spring 1998): 162–65.

2. Gerald Early (in his essay "The Unquiet Kingdom of Providence," in *The Culture of Bruising* [Ecco Press: Hopewell, NJ, 1994]) and David Remnick (in *King of the World* [Vintage: New York, 1999]) have both

written excellent contextual summaries of the social subtexts of the 1962 and 1963 Liston/Patterson bouts. At the height of the CRM black prizefighters, especially those in the heavyweight division, embodied the conundrums of American domestic possibilities.

In the early 1960s Patterson, Liston, and Cassius Clay/Muhammad Ali gave face to three possible representations of Negro integration into mainstream American life. Patterson, the former juvenile delinquent, became the "reformed," good Negro and Catholic convert. Because of his sensitive, respectable (philistine and non-threatening), and intro-spective demeanor (his nickname was "*Freud* Patterson") Patterson was the poster boy for the liberal political establishment. Liston was the Bad Nigger, the barely reformed Mafia thug whose visage recalled Jack Johnson minus the visceral threat of miscegenation.

The threat from Liston was a remorseless, murderous militancy—a synonym for what many white Americans felt vibrating below the surface of the CRM itself. Clay/Ali would come to represent a trickster combination of his boxing nemeses. Think of the name change, the "free jazz" boxing style, his conversion to the ultraradical and ultra-conservative Nation of Islam: Clay/Ali was a frightening prospect even to liberal white Americans. Clay/Ali with his street corner lyricism and hyped-up masculinity brought the "dozens" to American living rooms and signified the revolutionary possibility of liberated black masculin-ity. The U.S. sporting public saw the heavyweight championship as the national marker of masculinity. Without the prospect of a "white hope," the meaning of American masculinity was about to change radically. The genuine prospect of a militant or thuggish black champion shook the philosophical structure of white identity and thus, status quo American identity was perilously at risk.

3. James Baldwin, "The Fight," in Gerald Early's *Tuxedo Junction* (Hopewell, NJ: Ecco Press, 1989), 329.

4. For Baldwin's battles again his "parental figures" see his essays such as "Notes of a Native Son," "Everybody's Protest Novel," "Many Thousands Gone," "Faulkner and Desegregation," and "Alas, Poor Richard."

5. Robert Reid-Pharr, *Once You Go Black: Choice, Desire, and the Black American Intellectual* (New York: NYU Press, 2007), 104.

6. See LeRoi Jones's "The Dempsey-Liston Fight," in *Home* (Hopewell, NJ: Ecco Press, 1965, 1995) and Eldridge Cleaver's "Lazarus, Come Forth," in *Soul on Ice* (New York: Dell, 1991).

7. See Movement II for Ellison's definition of antagonistic cooperation.

8. For instance, in an early essay, "Equal in Paris," Baldwin notes

the tragicomedy of his naked self-awareness. After having his "trumped-up" charges dismissed in a French court and suffering the humiliation of having the French officials laugh at his social impotence, Baldwin explains that "this laughter is the laughter of those who consider themselves to be at a safe remove from all the wretched, for whom the pain of the living is not real. . . . It was borne in on me that this laughter is universal and never can be stilled" (Baldwin 1998b, 116). Baldwin's "blackness," his foreignness, his otherness, is humiliating. This humiliation displaces him even further than his exile from America because he is reminded of his alienation from himself, the utter homelessness of his body.

9. Early, *The Culture of Bruising*, 32, 39. Early's work on black intellectual responses to popular culture helps us to think about black intellectuals as individual performers rather than as one static enterprise or unit.

10. Arnold Rampersad, "The Legacy of Black Intellectuals," *Raritan* 18, no. 4 (1999): 116–58. According to Rampersad, this oscillation between demystification and essentializing is tied up in the definitions of "black intellectual." Rampersad explains that in at least three ways the term "black intellectual" is considered oxymoronic. The first sense develops out of the long history of scientific mythology: "blacks are not and cannot be sufficiently cerebral to merit the term 'intellectual.'" A subtle rereading of this first idea creates the second sense in which the word "black" denies the intellectual status of the individual "by announcing what is in effect an extreme act of cultural self isolation"; for one to embrace his or her "blackness" is a chauvinistic act that belies intellectual seriousness (Rampersad 1999, 116).

The third sense of the term emerges from within the black cultural nationalist tradition. There, "intellectual" is "a term of opprobrium," a title that renders one unfit for defending "the interests of a people as despised and persecuted as blacks have been in America" (Rampersad 1999, 116). Attached to Rampersad's short list of oxymorons are two corollary problems. The first problem arrives when we consider that the term "black intellectual" has become a label that essentializes individual critics and intellectuals under the tent of an agreed-upon set of interests and theoretical approaches. A second absolute crops up when the body of the African American intellectual comes to represent the supposed ideas and inclinations of all black people rather than her own critical perspectives.

Rampersad's description of the problems attached to the term "black intellectual" reveals the nature of the coercion involved in this intellectual prizefight. Not only is the game rigged, so are the terms of the battle. The way to turn away from the oxymoronic valences and problematic implications of the term is to recontextualize "black intellectual" in order to produce definitions that derive from the performances, the critical practices of particular intellectuals. If we redescribe the history of black intellectual work with a new vocabulary, a new set of metaphors (such as the prizefighter), then we can better contextualize and name the critical styles of individual intellectuals. We can free ourselves from essentializing those black critics while exposing the flaws and benefits of their performances.

11. Tejumola Olaniyan, *Scars of Conquest, Masks of Resistance* (New York: Oxford University Press, 1995), 4.

12. James Baldwin, *Collected Essays* (New York: Library of America, 1998), 100.

13. Carlo Rotella, "Cut Time," *American Scholar* 69, no. 2 (Spring 2000): 65.

14. Norman Mailer, "The White Negro," in *The Time of Our Time* (New York: Random House, 1998), 210–11. It is worth noting that even with the imprecision of Mailer's measurements of "the Negro's" temperature during the 1950s, the author was well aware of the social maelstrom and controversy that his concepts were springing from at the time. In expressing that awareness Mailer does expose the "milque toast" quality of 1950s white liberalism. It is quite interesting that Mailer can have such an insightful awareness of American racial complexities and yet maintain the most essentialist conceptualizations of African Americans. For a more precise indictment of intellectual irresponsibility during the post–World War II era and civil rights movement see Carol Polsgrove's useful intellectual history *Divided Minds* (W. W. Norton, 2000).

15. While Davis's pimping helped support his heroin habit in the late 1940s and early 1950s, Mingus's "pimping" was a metaphor for his relationship to his music and the music industry. For further reading on this subject see Eric Porter's *What Is This Thing Called Jazz?* (2002), Scott Saul's *Freedom Is, Freedom Ain't* (Cambridge, MA: Harvard University Press, 2003), and David Yaffe's *Fascinating Rhythm* (Princeton, NJ: Princeton University Press, 2006); all three scholars spend significant time deconstructing Mingus's metaphorical pimping. Mingus's disgust for the large music corporations, their limiting of artistic expression and the stranglehold they had on distributors, made him "pimp" his music and himself in order to maintain his own artistic independence while marking the commercial network with his avant-garde leanings.

16. Charles Mingus, *Beneath the Underdog: His World as Composed by Mingus* (New York: Vintage, 1991), 353.

17. Early, *Tuxedo Junction*, 308.

18. Manuel Martinez, *Countering the Counterculture* (Madison: University of Wisconsin Press, 2003), 91.

19. John Eakin, "The Referential Aesthetic of Autobiography," *Studies in the Literary Imagination* 23, no. 2 (Fall 1990): 129–45. Also see Eakin's *How Our Lives Become Stories: Making Selves* (Ithaca, NY: Cornell University Press, 1999).

20. These two essays are collected in *Notes of a Native Son* (in Baldwin 1998b). Baldwin's first essay collection is a complex mixture of ambivalence and alienation; it is the intellectual autobiography of an American Negro writing in Europe and thinking of nowhere else but home. Both of these essays are dramatically pugilistic. Baldwin wrote them intent on debunking directly or circuitously the symbolic meanings of Richard Wright's *Native Son*. In his study of expatriate Beats and black American writers, *Exiled in Paris,* James Campbell suggests that Wright took these essays as personal affronts, as fistic challenges, if you will. In fact, Campbell reports that Wright tried to diffuse these attacks by pointing out in personal letters to others that Baldwin was a homosexual and thus a suspect black man (James Campbell, *Exiled in Paris,* [New York: Scribner, 1996], 32, 112–15). Baldwin draws us into a battle royal that includes whites, Wright, and Bigger Thomas. It is a battle where the stakes are about masculinity and Negro identity.

21. Lawrie Balfour, *The Evidence of Things Not Said* (Ithaca, NY: Cornell University Press, 2001), 138.

22. Dewey, *The Public and its Problems,* 148.

23. James Baldwin, *Early Novels and Stories* (New York: Library of America, 1998a), 862.

24. Charles Mingus, *Mingus Ah Um* (New York: Columbia Records, CK 65512, 1959). The personnel on the album includes John Handy on alto sax, clarinet, and tenor sax, Booker Ervin on tenor sax, Shafi Hadi on tenor sax and alto sax, Walter Dennis on trombone, Jimmy Knepper on trombone, Horace Parlan on piano, Charles Mingus on bass and piano, Dannie Richmond on drums. My critique is influenced by both Scott Saul's *Freedom Is, Freedom Ain't,* 193–205, and Eric Porter's *What Is this Thing Called Jazz?,* 124–48. Saul and Porter evaluate the recording of "Fables of Faubus" that Mingus produced for the album *Charles Mingus Presents Charles Mingus* (New York: Candid Records, B00004Z3R3, 1960).

25. See, for instance, the compilation edited by Robert O'Meally, *The Jazz Singers 1919–1994* (Washington DC: Smithsonian Collection, B0000060IW, 1998). Across one hundred different recordings presented on this five-disc set, female artists are the overwhelming representatives of the jazz vocal tradition.

26. James Baldwin, "The Fire Next Time," in *Collected Essays,* 311.

27. Barbara Judson and Andrew Shin, "Beneath the Black Aesthetic: James Baldwin's Primer of Black American Masculinity," *African American Review* 32, no. 2 (Summer 1998): 247–62.

28. The interpretive angles for viewing Baldwin's work are manifold, especially when we regard his work within various queer theoretical frameworks. However, Judson and Shin are developing a Baldwinian framework for examining that author as well as others. Robert Reid-Pharr offers a stellar reading of Baldwin's queer theories in "Tearing the Goat's Flesh: Homosexuality, Abjection and the Production of a Late Twentieth-Century Black Masculinity," *Studies in the Novel* 28, no. 3 (1996): 372–94.

29. In 1956, while still firmly committed to life in Paris, Baldwin was awarded significant grants from the National Institute of Arts and Letters and *Partisan Review.* He used the funds to secure his living circumstances while he advanced work on the short story "Sonny's Blues" and began working on the manuscript that became *Another Country.* In return for these monies Baldwin placed both "Sonny's Blues" and the essay "Faulkner and Desegregation" in *Partisan Review.*

30. Though Baldwin acknowledges in the preface to *Notes of a Native Son,* "Autobiographical Notes," that he holds William Faulkner in the highest regard, his impression must have been charged by Faulkner's Nobel award in 1948. Faulkner went from being read as a Southern regionalist by the likes of Lionel Trilling and Alfred Kazin to receiving real critical attention from both the American and international literary establishments during the 1950s.

31. See Baldwin's "East River, Downtown: Postscript to a Letter from Harlem" (Baldwin 1998b, 180–86).

32. For an excellent example of this kind of reinvention listen to Charlie Parker's exuberant revisions of George Gershwin's "Embraceable You." During a 1947 recording session for Dial Records, Parker produced two versions of the song. On the first take Parker slides away from the song's basic arrangement to improvise a radical new composition built from his imaginative response to Gershwin's notational structure. In his essay "Charlie Parker (Flying Home)," Gary Giddins presents a detailed critique of Parker's recording. Giddins focuses especially on Parker's ability to invent radical musical ideas while also maintaining distinct connections to the traditions of jazz instrumental performance. See Giddins, *Visions of Jazz.*

33. Richard Rorty, *Philosophy and Social Hope* (New York: Penguin Books, 1999), 20.

34. Keith Byerman, "Words and Music: Narrative Ambiguity in 'Sonny's Blues,'" *Studies in Short Fiction* 19, no. 4 (1983): 367–72.

35. King James Bible, Isaiah 51:17, 22. As Byerman explains, Yahweh takes the cup of trembling away, thereby forgiving the Israelites their transgressions. However, Yahweh gave the cup of suffering to Israel to begin with. "If the cup is given," Byerman explains, "then Sonny will continue to suffer and feel guilt; if the cup is taken away, then Sonny returns to a state of grace" (Byerman 1983, 271).

36. Fred Moten, *In the Break: The Aesthetics of Black Radical Tradition* (Minneapolis: University of Minnesota Press, 2003), 192.

Movement IV

1. Ralph Ellison, "The Ralph Ellison Papers," Library of Congress Manuscripts, box 106, "MacArthur Grants" folder.

2. LeRoi Jones/Amiri Baraka, *Transbluesency* (New York: Marsilio, 1995), 131.

3. Olaniyan, *Scars of Conquest, Masks of Resistance,* 35.

4. Patrick Roney, "The Paradox of Experience: Black Art and Black Idiom in the Work of Amiri Baraka," *African American Review* 37, nos. 2–3 (2003): 407–29. Roney details usefully Houston Baker's argument that the Black Arts Movement ultimately succumbed to its roots in essentialist metaphysical thought. In this case, an investment in Blackness as a foundation to African American cultural practices—a way of returning to origins in Africa—backfired because it replicated the racist system that it meant to displace in the first place. Roney draws specific attention to the work of William Harris and Kimberly Benston as examples of the critical gymnastics involved in these escape and retrieval missions.

In both Harris's study of Jones/Baraka, *The Poetry and Poetics of Amiri Baraka* (Columbia, MO: University of Missouri Press, 1985), and Benston's essay "Late Coltrane: A Re-membering of Orpheus" (in *Imamu Amiri Baraka* [Englewood Cliffs, NJ: Prentice-Hall, Inc.,1978]), jazz improvisation is read as a theory for overcoming the metaphysical traps built into the black aesthetic. However, Roney points out correctly that both critics actually read Jones/Baraka's use of improvisation as an access port into a particular black idiom, toward a specific "black" origin that is post-Western or outside of Western aesthetics and philosophy. Roney's ultimate critique suggests that even in light of Jones/Baraka's turn to nationalist and Marxist ideologies what we are supposed to "get" is that the poet presents black identity as "rootless."

5. Even though two significant studies of Baraka have been pub-

lished since 1999, notice that the critiques of Baraka that drove the 2002 imbroglio surrounding his New Jersey poet laureate post and his poem "Somebody Blew Up America" were fueled by voices who had very little ability to thoroughly critique the changes in Baraka's political career, let alone contextualize "Somebody Blew Up America" within the varied body of his poetry. Justin Driver illustrated in his review of Watts's *Amiri Baraka* (2001) that Baraka's politics have eroded the possibility of examining his poetry without being overcome by poor misreadings. See Driver's "Pillar of Ire," *New Republic,* April 29, 2004: 33–37. As well, see the anonymously written "Notebook," *New Republic,* October 14, 2002: 8. For further contextualization of and response to Baraka and "Somebody Blew Up America" see the following articles: William Harris and Aldon Lynn Neilsen, "Somebody Blew Off Baraka," *African American Review* 37, nos. 2–3 (2003): 183–87; Richard L. Cravatts, "Campus Diversity and the Failure of Good Intentions," http://www.intellectualconservative.com/article2197.html; Robert Fleming, "Trouble Man," *Black Issues Book Review* 5, no. 2 (2003): 22–27 and Michael Kelly, "What Now," *Atlantic Monthly* (December 2003): 25, 28.

6. See Meta DuEwa Jones's "Listening to What the Ear Demands: Langston Hughes and His Critics," *Callaloo* 25, no. 4 (2002): 1145–76. As well, scholars have begun to reevaluate Jones/Baraka as an improvising poet. See both William J. Harris's "'How You Sound??': Amiri Baraka Writes Free Jazz" and Travis Jackson's "'Always New and Centuries Old': Jazz, Poetry and Tradition as Creative Adaptation" in *Uptown Conversation: The New Jazz Studies,* ed. Robert G. O'Meally, Brent Hayes Edwards, and Farah Jasmine Griffin (New York: Columbia University Press, 2004). See also Jones's "Politics, Process and (Jazz) Performance: Amiri Baraka's 'It's Nation Time,'" *African American Review* 37, nos. 2–3 (2003).

7. Brent Hayes Edwards, "Introduction to Jazz Poetics: A Special Issue," *Callaloo* 25, no. 1 (2002): 6.

8. Houston Baker, *Blues, Ideology, and Afro-American Literature* (Chicago: University of Chicago Press, 1987), 154–55.

9. Meta DuEwa Jones, "Politics, Process and (Jazz) Performance," 247. See also Craig Werner's *Playing the Changes: From Afro-Modernism to the Jazz Impulse* (Champagne: University of Illinois Press, 1995). Drawing from the African American vernacular culture, American poetic tradition, and the jazz tradition, Jones/Baraka's aesthetic is already centerless, "rootless."

But, as Werner has written, the limits of the blues matrix are exposed by jazz improvisation's "synthetic multiculturalism." While black musicians have been the signature innovators of jazz and jazz improvisation, the musical elements they draw together to create the performance palette have not come from exclusively Negro contexts. Musicologists such as Paul Berliner and Ingrid Monson have studied the ethnically and racially diverse arts communities that jazz artists live and work in. Those performance milieus, while steadily fed by African American cultural history and tradition, are always informed by multiple cultural concepts. Werner's concept of "synthetic multiculturalism" helps explain why, as Brent Edwards writes, students of jazz poetics are working to erect new critical models rather than fix jazz and/or African American writing as referents of "what black people 'simply know'" (Edwards 2002, 6).

10. Ross Posnock, *Color and Culture*, 44–45.

11. John Dewey, *Art as Experience*, 296.

12. For an example listen to the Jimmy Rushing/Count Basie Orchestra recording "Sent For You Yesterday," *Mr. Five By Five* (East Sussex, England: Pavilion Records LTD, TPZ 1019, 1995).

13. See Arthur Rimbaud's poem "Mauvais Sang" from *Une Saison en Enfer.* The edition used as reference is *Rimbaud Complete,* ed. Wyatt Mason (New York: Modern Library, 2002), 196–201.

14. See Jiton Sharmayne Davidson's "Sometimes Funny, but Most Times Deadly Serious: Amiri Baraka as Satirist" *African American Review* 37, nos. 2–3 (2003): 399–406 and Ben Lee's "LeRoi Jones/Amiri Baraka and the Limits of Open Form" *African American Review* 37, nos. 2–3 (2003): 371–87. Both Davidson and Lee explore the way that Jones/Baraka's aesthetic is born and most effectively performed in the liminal zones between cultural systems and practices.

15. Jones/Baraka, *Blues People*, 70.

16. Jones/Baraka, *Black Music*, 20.

17. The death that Jones/Baraka suggests in this context strikes me as wholly different from the suicidal impulses of some of his postwar contemporaries, confessional poets like Anne Sexton, Sylvia Plath, or Robert Lowell. While Lowell's poems sometimes emerged from his Brahmin, Bostonian liberalism and Plath is most often read as a paragon of righteous feminist poetics, Jones/Baraka's poems admit a psychological awareness, a confessional sensibility that expressed the complexities of African American freedom.

18. The implied answer to the poet's interrogative connects keenly to the protagonist's proclamation at the end of Ralph Ellison's *Invisible Man*. Ellison's narrator explains that he is "shaking off the old skin" in favor of a new sensibility, he is donning a new mask that disguises his chaotic, malleable self (Ellison, *Invisible Man* [New York: Vintage, 1995], 580–81).

19. The impulse is to see the move from old to avant-garde as a

move from white, European forms to black diasporic ones. However, Jones/Baraka is heavily indebted to European surrealists and their ideological stance against Western rationality. So, even as he is trying to create a particularly black sound—poetry devoid of white influence, Jones/Baraka cannot expunge his sources from his improvisations. See Daniel Won-gu Kim's article "In The Tradition: Amiri Jones/Baraka, Black Liberation and Avant-Garde Praxis in the U.S." *African American Review* 37, nos. 2–3 (Summer 2003): 345–64. See also Michael Magee's essay "Tribes of New York: Frank O'Hara, Amiri Baraka, and the Poetics of the Five Spot," *Contemporary Literature* 42, no. 4 (Winter 2001): 694–727. Magee's article is one of the few places to see Jones/Baraka contextualized as an influence of New American poetry. Magee uses O'Hara's poetry to describe an aesthetic practice that ties jazz improvisation to pragmatist philosophical ideas.

20. Nathaniel Mackey, "Other: From Noun to Verb," in *The Jazz Cadence of American Culture,* ed. Robert O'Meally (New York: Columbia University Press, 1999), 513. Mackey's essay describes the confluence of jazz and poetry as an illustration of the "other" in the process of identification. Mackey's title is meant to recall Jones/Baraka's chapter in *Blues People,* "Swing: from Verb to Noun." That chapter describes the appropriation of black musical styles, forms, and ideas by white musicians and entrepreneurs. See Jones/Baraka's *Blues People,* chapter 10. Because of his analysis of the commodification of jazz and black dance music within the context of American social history Jones/Baraka's seminal effort continues to influence the still-evolving reevaluation of African American musical and cultural history. To understand Jones/Baraka's continued influence and importance to jazz studies see, for instance, Scott DeVeaux's *The Birth of Bebop* and Eric Porter's *What Is This Thing Called Jazz?*.

21. Nathaniel Mackey, "The Changing Same: Black Music and the Poetry of Amiri Baraka," in *Imamu Amiri Baraka (LeRoi Jones),* ed. Kimberley Benston (Englewood Cliffs, NJ: Prentice-Hall, Inc., 1978), 124.

22. We should read the poems of Jones/Baraka's transitional period as part of a larger ironic critical project in the same way that we read for the contingencies between Eliot's poetic oeuvre and his criticism. This strikes me as the core of Jones/Baraka's efforts during his transitional phase: developing critical analyses in the act of poetic creation whether that creation is focused for individual expression (that of the literary artist/jazz critic) or group performance (think for instance of Jones/Baraka's plays *Dutchman* and *The Slave*). As with Eliot's search for a new moral order in *The Waste Land,* Jones/Baraka's transitional

efforts are the poetics of action and the hope for cultural revival. Like Eliot, Jones/Baraka wants a figure to navigate the ruined land and revive its reproductive power, the land's power to propel the self and the culture toward revolution, change. As we know though, at the end of *The Waste Land* Eliot's questing knight cannot find any language that can restore order to the culture or revive the landscape. Jones/Baraka's only recourse is to create a model for himself to follow: the poet as spiritual force or critical improviser becomes the representative figure in the ruined land. So, in exuberant modernist fashion, both poets become questing savants—they become the new heroes—and search for Gods, hoping to establish new moral codes. This may not be that different from Eliot's recourse to a new God, a new religion, Anglo-Catholicism, and a new self.

23. Edwards, "The Seemingly Eclipsed Window of Form," 590.

24. Ellison, *Invisible Man,* 581.

25. Philip Brian Harper, "Nationalism and Social Division in Black Arts Poetry of the 1960s," *Critical Inquiry* (Winter 1993): 234–55. Harper suggests that poems of the Black Arts Movement don't really promote a particular agenda in terms of their calls to arms. Harper explains that "while Black Arts poetry very likely does depend for its effects on the division of its audience along racial lines, it also achieves its maximum impact in a context in which it is understood as being *heard* directly by whites and *overheard* by blacks" (Harper 1993, 247).

26. Rushing is particularly emblematic as a reference to Jones/Baraka's work. Rushing toured with big dance orchestras, singing the blues in front of bands like the Oklahoma City Blue Devils and Count Basie's Kansas City–based outfit. As Ellison notes in the introduction to *Shadow and Act,* Rushing was known for his ability to bellow songs over the top of the horn players without the aid of microphones.

27. Ellison, *The Collected Essays of Ralph Ellison,* 250.

28. Cynthia Young, "Havana Up In Harlem: Le Roi Jones, Harold Curse, and the Making of a Cultural Revolution," *Science & Society* 65, no. 1 (Spring 2001): 12.

29. See Jones/Baraka's interview with Robert Fleming, "Trouble Man," 25.

Coda

1. Martin Luther King, Jr., *Why We Can't Wait* (New York: Signet, 2000), 66.

2. Martin Luther King, Jr., "Humanity and the Importance of Jazz,"

HR-57: Center for the Preservation of Jazz and Blues, available at http://www.hr57.org/mlkonjazz.html.

3. DeLillo sets the theme of *Underworld* by opening the work with a fictional account of the real 1951 playoff game between Willie Mays's New York Giants and Jackie Robinson's Brooklyn Dodgers. This prologue creates a palimpsest of the game, which ended with Bobby Thompson's "Shot Heard Round The World," the story of the Martins, a black family trying to escape their Harlem tenement, and the Soviet Union's successful test of an atomic weapon.

4. Porter, *What Is This Thing Called Jazz?*, 79.

5. Don DeLillo, *Underworld* (New York: Scribner, 1997), 338.

6. The Roots, *Phrenology* (Los Angeles: Geffen Records, 2002), my transcription.

7. John Dewey, *Art As Experience* (New York: Perigee Books, 1980), 64.

8. Tricia Rose, *Black Noise: Rap Music and Black Culture in Contemporary America* (Hanover, NH: Wesleyan University Press, 1994), 185.

9. Mark Anthony Neal, *What the Music Said* (New York: Routledge, 1999), 172.

Reference List

Anderson, Iain. 2007. *This Is Our Music*. Philadelphia: University of Pennsylvania Press.

Anderson, Paul Allen. 2005. Ralph Ellison on Lyricism and Swing. *American Literary History* 17, no. 2.

Appiah, Kwame Anthony. 2006. *Cosmopolitanism: Ethics in a World of Strangers*. New York: W. W. Norton.

———. 2004. *The Ethics of Identity*. Princeton, NJ: Princeton University Press.

———. 1992. *In My Father's House*. New York: Oxford University Press.

Baker, Houston. 1987. *Blues, Ideology, and Afro-American Literature*. Chicago: University of Chicago Press.

———. 1989. *Modernism and the Harlem Renaissance*. Chicago: University of Chicago Press.

Baldwin, James. 1998. *Collected Essays*. New York: Library of America.

———. 1989. The Fight. In Gerald Early, *Tuxedo Junction*. Hopewell, NJ: Ecco.

———. 1962. *New York Times Book Review*. December 2.

Balfour, Lawrie. 2001. *The Evidence of Things Not Said*. Ithaca, NY: Cornell University Press.

Benston, Kimberly, ed. 1978. *Imamu Amiri Baraka*. Englewood Cliffs, NJ: Prentice-Hall, Inc.

Berliner, Paul F. 1994. *Thinking in Jazz*. Chicago: University of Chicago Press.

———. 1993. *The Soul of Mbira: Music and Traditions of the Shona People of Zimbabwe*. Chicago: University of Chicago Press.

Bray, Rosemary. 1998. An Eloquent, Pitiless Prophet. *American Scholar* 67, no. 2 (Spring).

Burnim, Mellonee, and Portia Maultsby. 2005. *African-American Music: An Introduction*. New York: Routledge.

Burke, Kenneth. 1973. *The Philosophy of Literary Form*. Berkeley CA: University of California Press.

———. 1966. *Language as Symbolic Action*. Berkeley, CA: University of California Press.

———. 1954. *Permanence and Change*. Berkeley, CA: University of California Press.

Byerman, Keith. 1983. Words and Music: Narrative Ambiguity in "Sonny's Blues," *Studies in Short Fiction* 19, no. 4.

Callahan, John. 1979. The Historical Frequencies of Ralph Waldo Ellison. In *Chant of Saints*, ed. Michael S. Harper and Robert B. Stepto. Urbana, IL: University of Illinois Press.

Campbell, James. 1996. *Exiled in Paris: Richard Wright, James Baldwin, Samuel Beckett, and Others on the Left Bank*. New York: Scribner.

Cleaver, Eldridge. 1991. *Soul on Ice*. New York: Dell.

Cravatts, Richard L. Campus Diversity and the Failure of Good Intentions, http://www.intellectualconservative.com/article2197.html.

Davidson, Jiton Sharmayne. 2003. Sometimes Funny, but Most Times Deadly Serious: Amiri Baraka as Satirist. *African American Review* 37, nos. 2–3.

DeLillo, Don. 1997. *Underworld*. New York: Scribner.

DeVeaux, Scott. *The Birth of Bebop*. 1996. Berkeley, CA: University of California Press.

Dewey, John. 1980. *Art as Experience*. New York: Pedigree Books.

———. 1957. *Reconstruction in Philosophy*. Boston: Beacon Press.

———. 1954. *The Public and Its Problems*. New York: Henry Holt and Co.

Douglas, Ann. 1995. *Terrible Honesty*. New York: Farrar, Straus, Giroux.

Driver, Justin. 2004. Pillar of Ire. *New Republic*, April 29.

Du Bois, W. E. B. 1996. Criteria of Negro Art. In *The Crisis Reader*. New York: Modern Library.

———. 1986. *Writings*. New York: Library of America.

Eakin, John. 1999. *How Our Lives Become Stories: Making Selves*. Ithaca, NY: Cornell University Press.

———. 1990. The Referential Aesthetic of Autobiography. *Studies in the Literary Imagination* 23, no. 2 (Fall).

Early, Gerald. 1994. *The Culture of Bruising*. Hopewell, NJ: Ecco Press.

———. 1989. *Tuxedo Junction*. Hopewell, NJ: Ecco Press.

Eddy, Beth. 2003. *The Rites of Identity: The Religious Naturalism and Cultural Criticism of Kenneth Burke and Ralph Ellison*. Princeton, NJ: Princeton University Press.

Edwards, Brent Hayes. 2002. Introduction to Jazz Poetics: A Special Issue. *Callaloo* 25, no. 1.

———. 1999. The Seemingly Eclipsed Window of Form. In *The Jazz*

Cadence of American Culture, ed. Robert O'Meally. New York: Columbia University Press.

Eliot, T. S. 2002. *The Waste Land.* New York: Modern Library.

Ellison, Ralph. 1996. *Flying Home and Other Stories.* New York: Random House.

———. 1995. Cadillac Flambé. *Callaloo* 18, no. 2.

———. 1995a. *The Collected Essays of Ralph Ellison.* New York: Modern Library.

———. 1995b. *Invisible Man.* New York: Vintage.

———. 1995c. *Shadow and Act.* New York: Vintage.

———. 1977. Backwacking: A Plea to the Senator. *Massachusetts Review* 18, no. 3.

———. 1972. Night-Talk. *Quarterly Review of Literature* 16.

———. 1970. A Song of Innocence. *Iowa Review* 1, no. 2

———. 1965. Juneteenth. *Quarterly Review of Literature* 13, nos. 3–4.

———. 1963. It All Breaks Out. *Partisan Review* 30, no. 1.

———. 1960. And Hickman Arrives. *The Noble Savage* 1 no. 1.

———. 1959–60. The Roof, the Steeple and the People. *Quarterly Review of Literature* 10, no. 3.

———. N.d. The Ralph Ellison Papers. Library of Congress, manuscripts, box 106, "MacArthur Grants" folder.

Ellison, Ralph, and Albert Murray. 2000. *Trading Twelves: The Selected Letters of Ralph Ellison and Albert Murray.* New York: Modern Library.

Emerson, Ralph Waldo. 1960. *Selections From Ralph Waldo Emerson.* Boston, MA: Houghton Mifflin.

Erenberg, Lewis. 1998. *Swingin' the Dream: Big Band Jazz and the Rebirth of American Culture.* Chicago: University of Chicago Press.

Faulkner, William. 1936/1995. *Absalom, Absalom.* New York: Vintage.

Fleming, Robert. 2003. Trouble Man. *Black Issues Book Review* 5, no. 2.

Fraser, Nancy. 1998. Another Pragmatism: Alain Locke, Critical "Race" Theory, and the Politics of Culture. In *The Revival of Pragmatism,* ed. Morris Dickstein. Durham, NC: Duke University Press.

Gennari, John. 2006. *Blowin' Hot and Cool: Jazz and Its Critics.* Chicago: University of Chicago Press.

Giddins, Gary. 1998. *Visions of Jazz: The First Century.* New York: Oxford University Press.

Glaude, Eddie S., Jr. 2007. *In a Shade of Blue.* Chicago: University of Chicago Press.

Gussow, Adam. 2003. "Fingering the Jagged Grain": Ellison's Wright and the Southern Blues Violences. *boundary 2* 30, no. 2.

Hale, Grace Elizabeth. 1998. *Making Whiteness.* New York: Pantheon.

Hanlon, Christopher. 2005. Eloquence and *Invisible Man*. *College Literature* 32, no. 4.

Harper, Philip Brian. 1993. Nationalism and Social Division in Black Arts Poetry of the 1960s. *Critical Inquiry* (Winter).

Harris, William, and Aldon Lynn Neilsen. 2003. Somebody Blew Off Baraka. *African American Review* 37, nos. 2–3.

Harris, William J. 2004. "'How You Sound??': Amiri Baraka Writes Free Jazz. In *Uptown Conversation: The New Jazz Studies*, ed. Robert G. O'Meally, Brent Hayes Edwards, and Farah Jasmine Griffin. New York, Columbia University Press.

———. 1985. *The Poetry and Poetics of Amiri Baraka*. Columbia, MO: University of Missouri Press.

Hutchinson, George. 1997. *The Harlem Renaissance in Black and White*. Cambridge, MA: Harvard University Press.

Hyman, Stanley Edgar. 1958. The Folk Tradition. *Partisan Review* 25, no. 2.

Iyer, Vijay. 2004. "Exploding the Narrative in Jazz Improvisation." In *Uptown Conversation: The New Jazz Studies*, ed., Robert G. O'Meally, Brent Hayes Edwards, and Farah Jasmine Griffin. New York: Columbia University Press.

Jackson, Lawrence. 2002. *Ralph Ellison: Emergence of Genius*. New York: John Wiley & Sons

———. 1999. Ralph Ellison, Sharpies, Rinehart, and Politics in Invisible Man. Massachusetts Review 40, no. 1.

Jackson, Travis. 2004. "Always New and Centuries Old": Jazz, Poetry and Tradition as Creative Adaptation." In *Uptown Conversation: The New Jazz Studies*, ed. Robert O'Meally, Brent Hayes Edwards, and Farah Jasmine Griffin. New York: Columbia University Press.

James, William. 1987. *Writings 1902–1910*. New York: Library of America.

Jarrett, Michael. 1998. *Drifting on a Read: Jazz as a Model for Writing*. Albany, NY: SUNY Press.

Jones, Le Roi/Amiri Baraka. 2000. *The Fiction of Le Roi Jones/Amiri Baraka*. New York: Lawrence Hill Books.

———. 1999. *The Le Roi Jones/Amiri Baraka Reader*, ed. William Harris. New York: Thunder's Mouth Press.

———. 1995. *Transbluesency*. New York: Marsilio.

———. 1968. *Black Music*. New York: Apollo Editions.

———. 1965/1995. *Home*. Hopewell, NJ: Ecco Press.

———. 1963. *Blues People*. New York: Grove Press.

Jones, Meta DuEwa. 2003. Politics, Process and (Jazz) Performance:

Amiri Baraka's "It's Nation Time" *African American Review* 37, nos. 2–3.

———. 2002. Listening to What the Ear Demands: Langston Hughes and His Critics. *Callaloo* 25, no. 4.

Judson, Barbara, and Andrew Shin. 2003. Beneath the Black Aesthetic: James Baldwin's Primer of Black American Masculinity. *African American Review* 32, no. 2 (Summer).

Kazin, Alfred. 1942/1985. *On Native Grounds*. New York: Harcourt Brace.

Kelly, Michael. 2003. What Now. *Atlantic Monthly*. December.

Kim, Daniel Won-gu. 2003. In The Tradition: Amiri Jones/Baraka, Black Liberation and Avant-Garde Praxis in the U.S. *African American Review* 37, nos. 2–3 (Summer).

King James Bible, Isaiah 51:17, 22.

King, Martin Luther, Jr. 1963. *Why We Can't Wait*. New York: Signet.

Komunyakaa, Yusef. 2000. *Blue Notes*. Ann Arbor: University of Michigan Press.

———. 1998. *Thieves of Paradise*. Hanover, CT: Wesleyan University Press.

Lee, Ben. LeRoi Jones/Amiri Baraka and the Limits of Open Form. 2003. *African American Review* 37, nos. 2–3.

Lewis, George E. 2008. *A Power Stronger than Itself: The AACM and American Experimental Music*. Chicago: University of Chicago Press.

Litwack, Leon. 1998. *Trouble in Mind*. New York: Knopf.

Locke, Alain. 1992. *Race Contacts and Interracial Relations*. Washington DC: Howard University Press.

———. 1925. *The New Negro*. New York: Atheneum.

Lott, Eric. 1999. Boomer Liberalism: When the New Left Was Old. *Transition* 78.

———. 1994. *Love and Theft*. New York: Oxford University Press.

Mackey, Nathaniel. 1999. Other: From Noun to Verb. In *The Jazz Cadence of American Culture*, ed. Robert O'Meally. New York: Columbia University Press.

———. 1997. Cante Moro. In *Sound States*, ed. Adalaide Morris. Chapel Hill, NC: University of North Carolina Press.

———. 1978. The Changing Same: Black Music and the Poetry of Amiri Baraka. In *Imamu Amiri Baraka (LeRoi Jones)*, ed. Kimberly Benston. Englewood Cliffs, NJ: Prentice-Hall, Inc.

Magee, Michael. 2004. *Emancipating Pragmatism: Emerson, Jazz, and Experimental Writing*. Tuscaloosa, AL: University of Alabama Press.

———. 2001. Tribes of New York: Frank O'Hara, Amiri Baraka, and the Poetics of the Five Spot. *Contemporary Literature* 42, no. 4 (Winter).

Mailer, Norman. 1998. *The Time of Our Time*. New York: Random House.

Martin, Henry, and Keith Waters. 2005. *Jazz: The First 100 Years*. New York: Shirmer.

Martinez, Manuel. 2003. *Countering the Counterculture*. Madison, WI: University of Wisconsin Press.

Menand, Louis. 2001. *The Metaphysical Club*. New York: Farrar Straus Giroux.

Michaels, Walter Benn. 1995. *Our America*. Durham, NC: Duke University Press.

Mills, Charles. 1998. *Blackness Visible*. Ithaca, NY: Cornell University Press.

Mingus, Charles. 1960. *Charles Mingus Presents Charles Mingus*. New York: Candid Records, B00004Z3R3.

———. 1959. *Mingus Ah Um*. New York: Columbia Records, CK 65512.

Monson, Ingrid. 1996. *Saying Something*. Chicago: University of Chicago Press.

Moten, Fred. 2003. *In the Break: The Aesthetics of the Black Radical Tradition*. University of Minnesota Press.

Murray, Albert. 1997. *The Blue Devils of Nada*. New York: Vintage.

———. 1970. *Omni Americans*. New York: De Capo Press.

Neal, Mark Anthony. 1999. What the Music Said: Black Popular Music and Black Public Culture. New York: Routledge.

New Republic. 2002. Notebook, October 14.

Nystorm, Derek, and Kent Puckett. 1998. *Against Bosses, Against Oligarchies: A Conversation with Richard Rorty*. Charlottesville, VA: Prickly Pear Pamphlets.

Olaniyan, Tejumola. 1995. *Scars of Conquest, Masks of Resistance* New York: Oxford University Press.

O'Meally, Robert. 1998. *The Jazz Singers 1919–1994*. Washington DC: Smithsonian Collection, B0000060IW.

———. 1980. *The Craft of Ralph Ellison*. Cambridge, MA: Harvard University Press.

Outlaw, Lucius. 1996. *On Race and Philosophy*. New York: Routledge.

Outlaw, Lucius, and Michael D. Roth. 1997. Is There a Distinctive African American Philosophy? *Academic Questions* 10, no. 2 (Spring).

Parker, Charlie. 1997. *The Yardbird Suite: The Ultimate Charlie Parker*. New York: Rhino Records, B0000033PW.

———. 1976. *Bird/ The Savoy Recordings [Master Takes]*. New York: Savoy Records, B00000E7QL.

Parrish, Tim. 2001. *Walking Blues*. Amherst, MA: University of Massachusetts Press.

Polsgrove, Carol. 2000. *Divided Minds*. New York: W. W. Norton.

Poirier, Richard. 1992. *Poetry and Pragmatism.* Cambridge, MA: Harvard University Press.

Porter, Eric. 2002. *What Is This Thing Called Jazz?* Berkeley, CA: University of California Press.

Posnock, Ross. 1999. *Color and Culture: Black Writers and the Making of the Modern Intellectual.* Cambridge, MA: Harvard University Press.

Rampersad, Arnold. 1999. The Legacy of Black Intellectuals. *Raritan* 18, no. 4.

Ratliff, Ben. 2007. *Coltrane: The Story of a Sound.* New York: Farrar Strauss Giroux.

Reid-Pharr, Robert. 2007. *Once You Go Black: Choice, Desire, and the Black American* Intellectual. New York: NYU Press.

———. 1996. Tearing the Goat's Flesh: Homosexuality, Abjection and the Production of a Late Twentieth-Century Black Masculinity. *Studies in the Novel* 28, no. 3.

Remnick, David. 1999. *King of the World.* Vintage: New York.

Rimbaud, Arthur. 2002. Mauvais Sang. In *Rimbaud Complete,* ed. Wyatt Mason. New York: Modern Library.

Roney, Patrick. 2003. The Paradox of Experience: Black Art and Black Idiom in the Work of Amiri Baraka. *African American Review* 37, nos. 2–3.

The Roots. 2002. *Phrenology.* Los Angeles: Geffen Records.

Rorty, Richard. 1999. *Philosophy and Social Hope.* New York: Penguin.

———. 1998. *Achieving Our Country.* Cambridge, MA: Harvard University Press.

———. 1991. *Objectivity, Relativism, and Truth.* New York: Cambridge University Press.

———. 1989. *Contingency, Irony, and Solidarity.* New York: Cambridge University Press.

———. 1981. *Philosophy and the Mirror of Nature.* Princeton, NJ: Princeton University Press.

Rose, Tricia. 1994. *Black Noise: Rap Music and Black Culture in Contemporary America.* Hanover, NH: Wesleyan University Press.

Rotella, Carlo. Cut Time. 2000. *American Scholar* 69, no. 2 (Spring).

Saul, Scott. 2003. *Freedom Is, Freedom Ain't.* Cambridge, MA: Harvard University Press.

Schaub, Thomas. 1988. Ellison's Masks and the Novel of Reality. In *New Essays on Invisible Man,* ed. Robert O'Meally. New York: Cambridge University Press.

Shelby, Tommie. 2005. *We Who Are Dark.* Cambridge, MA: Harvard University Press.

Soto, Michael. 2004. *The Modernist Nation: Generation, Renaissance, and*

Twentieth Century American Literature. Tuscaloosa, AL: University of Alabama Press.

Southern, Elieen. 1971. *Readings in Black American Music*. New York: W. W. Norton.

Stevens, Wallace. 1990. Thirteen Ways of Looking at a Blackbird. In *The Collected Poems of Wallace Stevens*. New York: Vintage.

Von Eschen, Penny. 2004. *Satchmo Blows Up the World*. Cambridge, MA: Harvard University Press.

Warren, Kenneth W. 2003. *So Black and Blue: Ralph Ellison and the Occasion of Criticism*. Chicago: University of Chicago Press.

West, Cornel. 1989. *The American Evasion of Philosophy*. Madison, WI, University of Wisconsin Press.

Werner, Craig. 1995. *Playing the Changes: From Afro-Modernism to the Jazz Impulse* Champagne: University of Illinois Press.

Wiegman, Robin. 1993. The Anatomy of Lynching. In *American Sexual Politics,* ed. John Fout and Maura Shaw Tantillo. Chicago: University of Chicago Press.

Woodward, C. Vann. 1993. *The Burden of Southern History.* Baton Rouge, LA: Louisiana State University Press.

Wright, Richard. 1995. *Black Boy.* New York: Harper Collins.

Yaffe, David. 2006. *Fascinating Rhythm.* Princeton, NJ: Princeton University Press.

Young, Cynthia. 2001. Havana Up In Harlem: Le Roi Jones, Harold Curse, and the Making of a Cultural Revolution. *Science & Society* 65, no. 1 (Spring).

Young, John K. 2006. *Black Writers, White Publishers: Marketplace Politics in Twentieth-Century African American Literature.* Jackson, MS: University Press of Mississippi.

Index

abolitionism, 71

abstract expressionism, 127-28

African American identity: bebop as symbol of discourse on, 36-40; choices in, 92; Jones/Baraka's transitional work in, 129-31, 132; Parker as model for narrative about, 24-25, 27, 41-42; prizefighting and black masculinity in context of, 89-93, 177-78n2; protagonist's search for, 49-50; revising terms of, 95-97, 141-46; tragicomic confrontation of, 51-55

African American intellectuals: Black Public Sphere and, 12-13; crisis of, 68; as individual performers, 179n9; jazz and pragmatist possibilities for, 6, 18; misreadings of, 125-26; political and cultural battles of, 92-94; Posnock's view of, 4-5; problematics of term, 179-80n10; radical attitude of, 106-7; recontextualization of, 95-97. See also intellectual work

African American men: audience ownership of, 110-12; celebrating sensual black body of, 112-13, 123; democracy as violence played out on bodies of, 58-65; literal and figurative emasculation of, 117-18; Mailer's view of, 98-99; sexuality of, 60-64, 68-70, 98-103. See also improvisational masculine identity theory (Baldwin); lynchings; masculinity

African Americans: coping and survival tools of, 12; implications of white ignorance about, 122; minstrel performances of, 72-73; philosophy based on experience of, 167-68n24, 167n23; realities and complexities of, 12-13, 24-25, 118; slave narratives of female, 175n17

African American writers: as critics and artists simultaneously, 58; expatriate experiences of, 23-24, 95-96; force of change wrought by, 128-29; humanistic goal of, 70-71; in Posnock's pragmatism, 4-5. See also specific writers

Akst, Harry, 119

Ali, Muhammad (Cassius Clay), 177-78n2

197

America: definitions of, 82, 83–84; delusions of, 117–18; fostering new version of, 76, 87–88; founding documents of, 5–6. *See also* citizenship; democracy

American culture: African American writers' impact on, 128–29; bebop as form of resistance to, 27; capitalist ethos of, 96; cowboys and heroes of, 133–34; improvisation as imperative of, 17; jazz ambassadors of, 20, 25–26, 34–35, 40, 41; jazz and bebop in context of, 25–26; jazz and blues as frame of reference for, 136–38; liminal space between old self and, 135–36, 185n14; mythologizing in escape from, 31–32, 41; relational development of, 8–9. *See also* consumerism; ethnocentrism

American underworld: beboppers and sharpies in, 75–76; DeLillo's narrative of, 154–57; Ellison's understanding of, 172n1; as inspiration for remaking society, 30–31; Parker as guide through, 24–25, 41–42, 154–57; Parker in marginal social space of, 29

"Am I Blue?" (song), 119

Anderson, Eddie, 170n12

Anderson, Iain, 20

Anderson, Paul Allen, 174n11

antagonistic cooperation: as accepting humiliations, 94, 178–79n8; blues triggered by, 56–58; boxing and battle royals as versions of, 60–63, 95; concept of, 56

anti-Semitism, 125–26

Appiah, Kwame Anthony, 167–68n24

Armstrong, Louis "Satchmo": Ellison's invocation of, 59–60; as model for using vernacular, 33; musical context of, 136; Parker juxtaposed to, 32, 36, 39

artistic practices and aesthetics: advocacy and recognition of, 8; cosmopolitan nationalism and, 5; expansion/invocation and innovation/maintenance in, 77–79, 82–83; improvisation as central to, 17, 102–3; masculinity tempered by Romanticism in, 38; music as central to, 132; Parker's music as inventing discourse for, 33–34, 43, 44–45; play in, 87–88; public and private mingled in, 146–48; public space for, 12–13; reinvention imperative in, 119–20; secondary racial consciousness in, 9–10, 12, 13, 17, 46–47; tools for critique of, 137–38. *See also* blues idiom aesthetics; improvisational masculine identity theory (Baldwin); literary improvisation theory (Ellison); poetics of black essence (Jones/Baraka)

audiences: autobiographer's inclusion of, 104–6; bebop misheard by, 41; communal circumstances of, 16–17; in Ellison's critique of Parker, 31; gospel tune's implications for, 112, 122; language of jazz for, 18–19; Parker as thrice-alienated by, 29; potency of black male performer for, 110-11. *See also* masking

Baker, Houston, 73, 130, 183n4
Baldwin, James: autobiographical style of, 104-6; background of, 90, 93, 94, 96; bebop development and, 25-26, 169n3; on blues idiom, 13-14, 112-13; civil rights concerns of, 35-36, 93, 107-8, 116-17; critical experimentation of, 20-21; on Faulkner, 91, 116-17, 182nn29-30; funding support for, 182n29; heteronormative narratives disrupted by, 112-15; homosexuality of, 38-39, 177n1, 181n20; on jazz moment, 121-22; on Mailer's essay, 91-92, 100-103, 104, 113, 118, 122; on Mingus, 108; pragmatism of, 4-5, 39-40; in queer theoretical framework, 182n28; radical intellectual attitude of, 106-7; South visited by, 117-18; as symbol of Negro complexity, 24-25; works: *Another Country,* 157, 182n29; "The Black Boy Looks at the White Boy," 93, 101-4; "The Discovery of What It Means to Be an American," 93, 100-101, 107; "East River, Downtown," 105-7; "Equal in Paris," 94, 178-79n8; "Everybody's Protest Novel," 104-5; "Faulkner and Desegregation," 116-17, 182n29; "The Fight," 89-93; *The Fire Next Time,* 112-13; *Go Tell It on the Mountain,* 90; "Many Thousands Gone," 93, 104-5; *Nobody Knows My Name,* 39, 105; "Nobody Knows My Name," 117-18; *No Name in the Street,* 39; *Notes of a Native Son,* 39, 105, 181n20, 182n30; "A Question of Identity," 93, 95. *See also* improvisational masculine identity theory (Baldwin); "Sonny's Blues" (Baldwin); "This Morning, This Evening So Soon" (Baldwin)
BAM. *See* Black Arts Movement (BAM)
Baraka, Amiri. *See* Jones/Baraka, LeRoi (Amiri)
baseball playoffs, 188n3
Basie, William "Count," 77, 108, 187n26
battle royals: Ellison's version of, 60-63; Faulkner's, Wright's, and Ellison's compared, 66-68; self-identification and ironies of democracy in, 69-70. *See also* boxing/prizefighting; cutting sessions (battle royals)
Baudelaire, Charles, 134
Beats. *See* bebop; hipster-bebop culture
Beatty, Warren, 157, 158
bebop: aesthetics and politics merged in, 42-45; in Baldwin's "Sonny's Blues," 35-40; Coltrane's expansion of, 45-47; as cultural frame of reference, 136-38; development of, 25-26, 169n3; Ellison's critique of, 28-34; in Mailer's analysis and Baldwin's response, 98-103; mainstream co-opting of, 34-35; as marker, 156; Parker's innovations in, 25-26, 27, 41-42, 171n24;

bebop (*continued*)
    reconciliation processes aestheticized in, 107-8; revolutionary impetus in, 32-33; simultaneous, multiple sensibilities in, 41-42. *See also* hipster-bebop culture
Bechet, Sidney, 46
Benston, Kimberly, 183n4
Berliner, Paul: on African and African American traditions, 19; on jazz improvisation, 17-18, 38; on multicultural milieus of jazz, 184-85n9; on thinking in jazz, 21
Birmingham (Ala.): nonviolent direct action in, 152-53
Black Arts Movement (BAM): essentialist argument in, 183n4; evaluating poetry of, 187n25; global coalition building and, 148; Jones/Baraka linked to, 127, 130, 132, 142-46; nationalist ideology of, 149-50
black intellectual: use of term, 4. *See also* African American intellectuals
Black Mountain school, 141
black nationalism: emergence of, 124; "intellectual" in, 179-80n10; Jones/Baraka's engagement with, 132. *See also* Black Arts Movement (BAM)
blackness: alternate representations of, 89-93, 177-78n2; as always present, 59; Baldwin's deconstruction of, 104-6; as central to white American ethos, 70-76; commodification of, 32, 170n12; cosmopoli-

tan type of, 24-25; Crane and Twain on, 172-73n5; definitions of, 5-6; destigmatization of, 11-12; displacements due to, 94, 178-79n8; improvisation as synonym for, 42; "intellectual" and, 179-80n10; narrative constructs of, 9-11; philosophy based on experience of, 167-68n24, 167n23; protagonist's attempt to transcend, 51-55; radical pluralism and, 164-66n17. *See also* poetics of black essence (Jones/Baraka)
Black Power, 132. *See also* black nationalism
Black Public Sphere, 12-13
Blue Devils Orchestra, 77, 187n26
blues: antagonistic cooperation as triggering, 56-58; Baldwin's borrowings from lyrics of, 104; as cultural frame of reference, 136-38; definitions of, 1, 14-17, 51, 65; duende and, 173n9; expressiveness of, 65, 69-70; Jones/Baraka's engagement with, 13-14, 157; limits of, 184-85n9; salvation linked to, 118-23; sensuality and irony in, 112-13; as universal language, 39-40. *See also* bebop; jazz; swing
blues idiom aesthetics: African American intellectuals' use of, 5; Baldwin on, 13-14, 112-13; Baldwin's emergence and salvation in, 39-40, 107-11, 115-16, 118-23; as central American artistic idiom,

15-16; Ellison's engagement of, 13-14; emergence of, 12-13; protagonist's search for self told in, 49-51; quest for revival in, 134-36

blues idiom pragmatism: antagonistic cooperation as triggering, 56-58; conception of, 1, 13-21; in liminal spaces of tragicomedy, 54-56; modes of social critique in, 151-59; public and private selves acknowledged in, 50-51

blues shout, 47

"Body and Soul" (song), 169n4

boxing/prizefighting: African American intellectuals and, 92-94; alternate representations of, 177-78n2; Baldwin's autobiographical approach and, 105; improvisation in, 103, 114-15, 154; intraracial violence fostered by whites, 66-67; masculinity as focus of, 89-93, 177-78n2; revising meanings of, 89, 95, 97; as version of antagonistic cooperation, 60-63. *See also* battle royals

Bray, Rosemary, 177n1

Brown, Sterling, 146

Brown v. Board of Education (1954), 27, 80, 107

Buchannan, Tom, 143

Bulworth (film), 157, 158

Burke, Kenneth: on dialectics of comfort/discomfort, 15-16; Ellison's relationship with, 27-28; on language as symbolic action, 30, 32; mentioned, 58; on piety, 37-38,

82, 83, 95, 174n14; on revising meanings, 96-97; on rituals, gods, and men, 14, 32

Byerman, Keith, 121, 183n35

Callahan, John, 49-50, 85

call and response, 108, 145-46

Campbell, James, 181n20

capitalist ethos, 96

Charles, Ray, 39

Charlotte (N.C.): desegregation in, 93

Christian, Charlie, 78, 173n7

citizenship: asserted via music, 43-44, 47; Baldwin's ambivalence about, 93; male genitalia as symbols of, 64-65; reality at issue in, 94; revising terms of, 97; social community necessary to, 92, 106-7, 120-21, 164-66n17; whiteness as defining, 61-64. *See also* democracy; political and social equality

civil rights movement (CRM): Baldwin's engagement in, 36, 93, 107-8, 116-17; bebop as language for transformation in, 42-43; blues idiom pragmatism in context of, 15-16, 151; bus boycott in, 23, 27, 34, 81, 93; Ellison's engagement in, 79-84; international context articulated for, 132; nonviolence tenets in, 152-53; Parisian perspective on, 113-14; prizefighting and black masculinity in context of, 89-93, 177-78n2; salvation in context of, 123

Clarke, Grant, 119

field of possibility, 29–30; founding documents of, 5–6; impediment to realizing, 7, 106, 122; jazz ambassadors of, 20, 25–26, 34–35, 40, 41; jazz improvisation as transforming violence into, 42–43; nonviolent direct action as symbolic in, 152–53; novels as symbolic act in, 34–35, 151; responsibility for, 51, 83–84; revising terms of, 97; self-identification juxtaposed to ironies of, 69–70; southern racism as corruption of, 27, 80; tools for achieving, 12, 76; used in doing and undoing, 31, 32; as violence played out on black male bodies, 58–65; vocabulary for, 3–4, 159–60, 166–67n22. *See also* citizenship; political and social equality

Dennis, Walter, 181n24

DeVeaux, Scott, 27, 169n4

Dewey, John: on art as experience, 47, 146, 147; on citizenship and community, 16, 92, 106–7, 120–21, 164–66n17; on democracy and communication, 40; Ellison compared with, 29–30; on joining old and new, 46; on linguistic utility, 20; on music, 130–31; on play in art, 87–88; pragmatism of, 2–3, 4, 7

difference: limiting stigmatization of, 11–12; narratives of, 10–11; as seat of power vs. choice of self-invention, 103. *See also* identity

Dionysus, 31–32

direct action, nonviolent, 152–53

discourse: for artistic practices, 43; bebop as symbol of, 36–40; for humans, 59; improvisation as building, 35; for liberal democracy, 3–4; revising terms of, 96–97; as violence imposed upon bodies, 58, 94

Dostoevsky, Fyodor, 65

double consciousness: Baldwin's awareness of, 102; Du Bois's description of, 6, 7; Parker's music in, 42–43; as radical political theory, 13; simultaneous, multiple sensibilities in, 41–42

Douglas, Ann, 164–66n17

Driver, Justin, 183–84n5

drug use, 29, 31, 36, 40, 41, 170n16

Du Bois, W. E. B.: on blackness and radical pluralism, 164–66n17; cultural agenda of, 8, 9; Ellison's revision of, 51; on lynching, 164n12; multiple disciplines utilized by, 164n11; on political and racial solidarity, 6–7, 12, 17; in Posnock's pragmatism, 4; propaganda contextualized by, 8, 164n15. *See also* double consciousness

duende concept, 173n9

Early, Gerald, 177–78n2, 177n1, 179n9

Eddy, Beth, 86, 95, 174n14

Edwards, Brent Hayes, 46, 141–42, 184–85n9

Eisenhower, Dwight D., 25, 34, 41

Eliot, T. S., 141, 186–87n22

Ellington, Edward Kennedy "Duke," 99, 108, 136

Ellison, Ralph: African American psychological theory of, 54–55, 83–84; on American founding documents, 5–6; background of, 77–78; Baldwin compared with, 107, 118; Baldwin on, 35; on bebop and Parker, 24–25, 28–33, 75–76; bebop development and, 25–26, 42, 169n3; on blues and duende, 173n9; blues defined by, 15–17, 51, 65; blues idiom engagement of, 13–14; on blues singers, 146; circle of, 27–28, 173n7; civil rights concerns of, 5, 49–50, 79–84; critical experimentation of, 20–21; ironic historicism of, 50, 176n29; on jazz moment, 57, 174n15; jazz preferences of, 76–79, 174n11; on Jones/Baraka, 125–26; on Negroes as "vanishing tribe," 23; on past as always present, 176n26; pragmatism of, 27–28; Rome Prize for, 79; on Rushing, 78, 187n26; on Wright, 65–68, 70; Wright on, 175n20; works: list of stories, 177n39; "The Birthmark," 64; "Cadillac Flambé," 84; "Change the Joke and Slip the Yoke," 71–72; "Flamenco," 173n9; "Golden Age, Time Past," 32; "On Bird, Bird-Watching, and Jazz," 28–29; "Party Down at the Square," 64–65; "Richard Wright's Blues," 65, 175n20; "Society, Morality, and the Novel," 82; "Tell It Like It Is," 83–84; "Twentieth Century Fiction and the Black Mask of Humanity," 59; "The World and the Jug," 82–83. *See also* "Flying Home" (Ellison); *Invisible Man* (Ellison); *Juneteenth* (Ellison); literary improvisation theory (Ellison)

"Embraceable You" (song), 182n32

Emerson, Ralph Waldo: on American culture, 8–9, 121; individual difference emphasized, 11; poetics of, 42–44; "quest for certainty" refused, 1–2

Ervin, Booker, 181n24

essentialism: alternative to, 129–31; in Black Arts Movement, 183n4; demystification vs., 179–80n10; improvisation as resistance to, 100–103; Jones/Baraka's theorization of, 132, 149–50; of Mailer's essay, 98–100; perils of, 167–68n24; rejection of, 5

ethnocentrism: perils of, 167–68n24; vocabulary for, 3–4, 166–67n22; Western liberal, 3–4, 11, 50, 166–67n22

"Fables of Faubus" (song), 108, 181n24

Faubus, Orval, 80, 107–8

Faulkner, William: Baldwin on, 91, 116–17, 182nn29–30; Ellison's allusion to, 85; on self-hatred, 175–76n23; Wright juxtaposed to, 67–68

Fitzgerald, F. Scott, 143

Five Spot (Manhattan), 45

Floating Bear (periodical), 141

"Flying Home" (Ellison): *Juneteenth* compared with, 82;

masculine violence and tragi-comedy themes of, 51–55; title of, 173n7

"Flying Home" (song), 173n7

Freud, Sigmund, 83, 164–66n17

Garcia Lorca, Federico, 134

Gennari, John, 171n32

Gershwin, George, 182n32

Giddins, Gary, 171n24, 182n32

Gillespie, Dizzy: as ambassador of democracy, 34–35, 40, 41; bebop development and, 26; "sharpie" style of, 75

Ginsberg, Allen, 98, 141

Glaude, Eddie S., Jr., 37

Goodman, Benny, 173n7

Gordon, Dexter, 45, 170n16

Gray, Kamal, 158

"Great Getting Up in the Morning" (song), 111–12

Great Migration, 109

Greenwich Village: Beat pose in, 98–99; Bird mythologized in, 41–42; Jones/Baraka and, 143–44, 157

Gussow, Adam, 65, 69–70

Hadi, Shafi, 181n24

Hale, Grace, 61–62

Hammerstein, Oscar, 45, 46

Hampton, Lionel, 173n7

Handy, John, 181n24

Hanlon, Christopher, 174n15

Harlem: Jones/Baraka and, 143–44

Harlem Renaissance, 9, 76, 164–66n17

Harper, Philip Brian, 144, 149, 187n25

Harris, William, 183n4

"Harvard Blues" (song), 79

Hawkins, Coleman, 26, 169n4

Hegel, G. W. F., 2

hip-hop and improvisation, 158–59

hipster-bebop culture: Mailer vs. Baldwin on, 98–103; misinterpreted masks of, 32–33; possibilities in, 28; as radical politics of margin, 75–76

Holiday, Billie, 111

Hose, Sam, 164n12

House Un-American Activities Committee, 80

Hubbard, Hub, 158

Hughes, Langston, 130, 164–66n17

humans and humanity: affirmation of, 9–10; ambiguities of existence, 70–71; discourse for, 59; implications of white ignorance about, 118, 122; jazz's relationship with, 153; mask as veiling, 72–73; notion of progress and, 10–11, 166–67n22; recognition of, 16–17, 55, 56, 63–64. See also rituals

Hume, David, 2

Hurston, Zora Neale, 164–66n17

Hyman, Stanley Edgar, 71–72

identity: as ethnic or cultural, 10, 11–12, 57; expansion/invocation and innovation/maintenance in, 77–79; improvisation as, 104–7; individual, 11, 27–28, 35, 57; manhood and democracy in, 92; masking of, 70–76, 87–88; other's construction of, 101–2; reimagining of, 37–39; universalist vs. racial, 4–5; whiteness as

identity (*continued*)
"American," 61–65. *See also* African American identity; cultural identity; improvisational masculine identity theory (Baldwin); racial identity

improvisation: in accepting then defeating status quo, 95–97; blackness as synonym of, 42; in boxing/prizefighting, 103, 114–15, 154; choices in, 128–29, 130, 136; as critical experimentation, 20; definition and centrality of, 17–18, 102–3; as discourse building, 35; as doing and undoing, 31, 32; as identity, 104–7; of identity and visibility, 56–60; in masking and minstrelsy, 70–76, 87–88; as metaphor for intellectual work, 131; of multicolored truths, 44; in public and private selves, 17–18, 38; as resistance to essentialism, 100–103; Romantic notions of, 99; salvation accessed via, 40; secondary racial consciousness linked to, 46–47; simultaneous, multiple sensibilities in, 41–42, 108. *See also* blues idiom pragmatism; improvisational masculine identity theory (Baldwin); jazz improvisation; literary improvisation theory (Ellison); poetics of black essence (Jones/Baraka)

improvisational masculine identity theory (Baldwin): conception of, 92; cosmopolitan nationalism and blackness in concerns of, 5; DeLillo's riff on, 156–57; democracy

reimagined in, 91–92, 103–7; escape and emancipation possibilities in, 107–12, 121–24; familial past and, 115–16, 118; function of, 121–23; masculinity recontextualized in, 92–97; role of improvisation in, 35, 38, 153–54; salvation and blues linked in, 118–23

institutions: African American, 13, 77, 81; dehumanization embedded in, 59–65

instrumentalism, 2–3

intellectual work: freedom in, 27–28, 35; global coalition building as, 148; improvisation as metaphor for, 131; public attitudes toward, 95–96. *See also* African American intellectuals

interracial encounters: desire and hatred mixed in, 61–65; in groups of jazz musicians, 173n7; in liminal space of ocean voyage, 110. *See also* audiences; white racial violence

Invisible Man (Ellison): black male sexuality and castration in, 60–64, 68–70; coercion and seduction in, 94; confrontation, improvisation, and visibility in, 55–60, 68; democracy vs. social realities in, 49–50; hipsters as symbols of possibility in, 28; improvisations on others' works in, 58–60, 67, 69–70, 151; *Juneteenth* compared with, 85, 86; literary models for, 172–73n5; masking and minstrelsy in, 70–76, 111, 139, 185n18; as pragmatist cultural critique, 34, 50–51; self-identification

and ironies of democracy
in, 69–70, 79, 142; source of
narrator's voice, 172n1; trickster figure in, 72
ironic historicism concept, 50
Israel: reference to, 122, 183n35
Iyer, Vijay, 86, 120

Jackson, Lawrence, 74, 75
Jackson, Mahalia, 111–12
James, Henry, 39
James, William: on consequences,
7; as Freud's adversary, 164–
66n17; on improvisation, 57;
on old and new truths, 174n11;
pragmatism of, 2, 4, 15
jam sessions, 26, 103–7
Jarrett, Michael: on dialectic play,
136, 137; on naming, 79; on
obbligato, 19, 169n35
jazz: Baldwin's reclaiming of,
101–3; as cultural frame of reference, 136–38; as existential
and commercial, 110–11; as experience (not entertainment),
77–78; humanity's relationship with, 153; mainstream
co-opting of, 34–35; masculine
ethos tempered by feminine
in, 38, 99–100; moment of,
57, 121–22, 174n15; as music of
democracy, 41; performance
of, 99, 109–11, 115–16, 119–20,
184–85n9. See also bebop;
blues; hipster-bebop culture;
swing
jazz criticism: by artist/critic, 58;
experimentation in, 20–21;
historical analysis of, 171n32;
misreadings in, 45–46, 137;
music and political action
linked in, 45–47; race in,

31–32; tools for, 137–38. See
also Baldwin, James; Ellison,
Ralph; Jones/Baraka, LeRoi
(Amiri); specific musicians
jazz improvisation: as demonstration of cosmopolitan blackness, 24–25; effects of listening
to, 37–38; expansion/invoca-
tion and innovation/main-
tenance in, 77–79, 82–83;
as metaphor, 103; musical
concepts underlying, 19–20,
46–47; as name for piety, 119;
paradox of, 33; political action
merged with, 45–47; as private
self heard in public, 147–48;
synthetic multiculturalism of,
184–85n9; as transforming violence into democracy, 42–43;
as vernacular language, 17–19,
168–69n33; as way of life,
17–18, 38, 39–40
jazz musicians: as ambassadors
of democracy, 20, 25–26,
34–35, 40, 41; black masculinity and, 109–11; conversations
among, 17–18; familial past of,
115–16; feminine sensibilities
of, 38, 99–100; identity formation process in group of, 57;
integrated groups of, 173n7; as
pimps or hustlers, 99, 180n15;
self-reinvention and redemption of, 119–20; southwestern
territory bands of, 76–79,
174n11; as storytellers, 86; as
symbol of Beat generation aesthetics, 98–99; synthetic multicultural milieus of, 184–85n9.
See also audiences; masking;
specific musicians
Jazz Workshop, 108, 181n24

Johnson, James Weldon, 164–66n17
Jones, Elvin, 126–27
Jones, Meta DuEwa, 184n6, 184–85n9
Jones/Baraka, LeRoi (Amiri): bebop development and, 25–26, 169n3; blues idiom engagement of, 13–14, 157; coalition building by, 148; on Coltrane, 45–47; DeLillo compared with, 157; Ellison's characterization of, 125–26; hip-hop vocabulary of, 158–59; on Liston, 92; literary magazines of, 141; Marxism of, 126, 131–32, 149; nationalist ideology of, 149–50; on Parker, language, and bebop, 24–25, 42–45; personal changes of, 23–24; on poetry's aim, 143; politics and controversy over (2002), 183–84n5; surrealism as influence on, 141, 185–86n19; transitional poems of, 129–36, 138, 146–48, 186–87n22; works: "An Agony. As Now," 138; "Balboa, The Entertainer," 138; "Black Art," 142–43; *Black Magic*, 127, 133, 142–43; *Blues People*, 136, 141, 186n20; "The Bridge," 135, 138; "The Changing Same," 131–32; "Cuba Libre," 131–32; *The Dead Lecturer*, 133, 138–39; *The Dutchman*, 42–44; "Gatsby's Theory of Aesthetics," 143; *Home*, 127; "Hymn for Lanie Poo," 135; "Jazz and the White Critic," 137; "The Liar," 139–42, 146; "Look for You Yesterday, Here You Come Today," 133–34;

"Numbers, Letters," 143–46; *Preface to a Twenty Volume Suicide Note*, 133; "Screamers," 44–45, 46–47; "Snake Eyes," 138, 139; "Somebody Blew Up America," 126, 183–84n5; "Something in the Way of Things (In Town)", 158; "Tone Poem," 126–28, 129, 142, 158. *See also* poetics of black essence (Jones/Baraka)
jook joints, 13
Jordan, June, 149
Joyce, James, 65, 85
Judson, Barbara, 113, 182n28
Juneteenth (Ellison): improvisations in, 84–88; as new form of novel, 151; as pragmatist cultural critique, 34; ritual and innovation in, 84; summary of, 81–82

Kennedy, Adrienne, 4
Kim, David Won-gu, 185–86n19
King, Martin Luther, Jr., 151, 152–54
Knepper, Jimmy, 181n24
Komunyakaa, Yusef, 21, 41

language and language systems: bebop as, 26; critical experimentation in, 20–21; democratic vocabulary and, 3–4, 159–60, 166–67n22; in doing and undoing, 31, 32; emancipating effects of, 42–45; of hip-hop, 158–59; jazz as, 17–19, 168–69n33; limits of, compared with music, 121–22; in narratives of pragmatism, 5–6, 10–11; Negro universal or Negro classical, 44–45; possibilities of, 15; revising meanings in, 96–97; as symbolic action, 30, 32; universal blues as, 39–40

Lee, Ben, 185n14

Lincoln, Abraham, 83–84

Liston, Sonny, 89–93, 177–78n2

literary improvisation theory (Ellison): confrontation and visibility in, 55–60, 68; cosmopolitan nationalism and blackness in, 5; devices used in, 84–88; dream analysis and memoir in, 83–84; introduction of, 51; jazz models of, 78–79; in King's "Letter," 151, 152–54; masking in, 70–76, 87–88, 139; novel as democratic act in, 34–35, 151; others' works in, 58–60, 67, 69–70, 151; racial violence and democracy in, 49–50

literary theory and tradition: blues, vernacular, and pragmatism linked to, 15–16; cultural desires described in, 164–66n17; cultural production and oppositional identities in, 148; improvisation in, 57–58; New American poetry and, 141, 185–86n19; trickster figure in, 72; Wright placed in, 65. See also Harlem Renaissance; improvisational masculine identity theory (Baldwin); literary improvisation theory (Ellison); poetics of black essence (Jones/Baraka); novels

Little Rock (Ark.) Central High School, 80, 93, 107–8

lived experience: blues as equipment for, 14–16; complexities

of, 101; experimentalism in, 2–3; jazz as, 77–78; music vs. realities of, 27; as public and private, 8; as "self-evolving circle," 1

Locke, Alain I.: African American cultural agenda of, 8; on African Americans as orphans, 164–66n17; on destigmatization, 11; in Posnock's pragmatism, 4; on secondary racial consciousness, 9–10, 12, 17

Locke, John, 2

Lorca, Federico Garcia, 173n9

Lott, Eric, 71, 166–67n22

Lowell, Robert, 185n17

Lumumba, Patrice, 105

lynchings: attempt to turn into intraracial murder, 66–67; castration as recalling effects of, 69–70; as defining whiteness, 63–65; Du Bois on, 164n12; as legally protected disenfranchisement and eradication, 64–65; masking and minstrelsy interwoven with, 70; power of white racial identity solidified in, 61–62; South as shrouded by, 117–18

Mackey, Nathaniel, 141, 186n20

Magee, Michael, 5, 185–86n19

Mailer, Norman: Baldwin's response to, 91–92, 100–103, 104, 113, 118, 122; on the Negro, 98–100, 180n14

manhood: recontextualization of, 92, 95–97. See also masculinity

Marxism, 126, 131–32, 149

masculinity: accepting cage of, in order to transcend, 114–15; alternate representations of,

masculinity (*continued*)
89–93, 177–78n2; Baldwin's
definition of, 112–13, 123; in
Baldwin's fiction, complexities
of, 109–11; bebop as symbol of
discourse on, 36–40; Ellison's
models of, 78–79; intellectual-
ism as contradiction of, 95–96;
Mailer's analysis of, 98–103;
male genitalia as symbols of,
64–65; narrative space for
analysis of, 104–7; private ironies and public hopes juxtaposed to, 51–55. *See also* African
American men; manhood
masking: Ellison's improvisations
with, 70–76, 87–88, 139; escaping and observing of, 111–12;
of Gatsby, 143; of performer
for audience, 32–33, 170n12; as
self-creation, 139, 185n18
Maultsby, Portia, 19
Mays, Willie, 188n3
McCarthy, Cormac, 125
McCarthy, Joseph, 80
McGee, Howard, 26
McKay, Claude, 164–66n17
McPherson, James Alan, 125
Melville, Herman, 172–73n5
memory: jazz performance as
means of accessing, 115–16;
recovery of suppressed, 95;
responsibility for, 83–84
Michaels, Walter Benn, 10,
11–12, 57
Mills, Charles, 167n23
Mingus, Charles: Baldwin juxtaposed to, 118–19; Baldwin
on, 108; musical context of,
169n3; "pimping" of, 99–100,
180n15; recordings: "Fables of
Faubus," 108, 181n24

Mingus Ah Um (album), 108,
181n24
minstrelsy: advertisement for
show, 176n26; Ellison's improvisations with, 70–76. *See
also* masking
miscegenation: blackface performances as negotiating, 70–76;
desire and hatred mixed in
fears of, 61–65; white supremacy undercut by, 67–68
modernism: cultural desires
described in, 164–66n17;
cultural pluralism in, 10, 11;
Jones / Baraka in context of,
157–59; poets as new heroes
in, 186–87n22
Monk, Thelonious: bebop
development and, 26, 136;
Coltrane's relationship with,
45, 171–72n33; as influence,
40; "sharpie" style of, 75
Monson, Ingrid: on cultural
identity, 18, 57, 168–69n33; on
jazz ambassadors, 20; on jazz
milieus, 184–85n9
Montgomery (Ala.) bus boycott,
23, 27, 34, 81, 93
Moore, George, 65
Morton, Ferdinand "Jelly Roll,"
99, 136
Moten, Fred, 123
Murray, Albert: on blues and
improvisation, 1; blues defined
by, 1, 14–15, 17; Ellison's correspondence with, 23, 28, 80–81
music and music theory: bridge
between big band soloing and
bebop improvisation, 169n4;
cultural perspective of, 18; as
highest of arts, 131; language
compared with, 121–22; spon-

taneous, disciplined creation
and obbligato concepts in,
19–20; as universal (idea), 110.
See also bebop; blues; jazz;
swing
"My Favorite Things" (song),
45, 46

naming: of African American
realities, 12–13; inability of,
158–59; of objects, 30, 32; of
self, 79, 107, 139–41
National Institute of Arts and Letters, 182n29
Navarro, Fats, 170n16
Neal, Mark Anthony, 12–13
Nehru, Pandit Motilal, 65
New American poetry, 141,
185–86n19
New Negro movement, 9, 76,
164–66n17
New Orleans, Storyville district,
99
novels: as democratic act, 34–35,
151; development of form,
57–58; expansion/invocation
and innovation/maintenance
in, 82–83; psychological questions in function of, 84; as
social/cultural critique tool,
86–88. *See also specific authors
and novels*
Nystorm, Derek, 166–67n22

obbligato: definition of, 19,
169n35
O'Hara, Frank, 141, 185–86n19
Oklahoma City: Blue Devils
Orchestra of, 77, 187n26; as
southwestern jazz crucible,
76–79
Olaniyan, Tejumola: on articula-

tory practices, 128–29, 130,
136, 137; on discourse, 58, 94
"The Old Ship of Zion" (song),
119
Olsen, Charles, 141
O'Meally, Robert, 181n25
Outlaw, Lucius, 167n23

Page, Oran Thaddeus "Hot Lips,"
77
Parent, Bob, 154
Paris (France): Baldwin and
Mailer's meeting in, 101;
Baldwin's experience of, 93,
96, 182n29; Baldwin's fiction
on, 110, 113–14
Parker, Charlie "Bird": Armstrong juxtaposed to, 32, 36,
39; Baldwin compared with,
107; bebop development and,
25–26, 27, 41–42, 171n24; drug
addiction and death of, 27,
29, 31, 36, 40, 41; Ellison's
critique of, 24–25, 28–33,
75–76; emancipating poetics
of, 42–45; as guide and as sign
of Negro complexity, 24–25,
27, 41–42; as model for using vernacular, 33–34; music
knowledge of, 170–71n19; mythologizing of, 31–32, 41–42; as
shadow in DeLillo's underworld, 154–57; as shadow
in "Sonny's Blues," 35–40,
154; recordings: "Embraceable You," 182n32; "Parker's
Mood," 43
"Parker's Mood" (song), 43
Parlan, Horace, 181n24
Parrish, Tim, 31, 152
Partisan Review (periodical),
182n29

Patterson, Floyd, 89–93, 177–78n2
Patterson/Liston fight, 89–93, 177–78n2
Perry, Lincoln, 170n12
philosophy: absolutism vs. radical empiricism in, 6; African American experience as basis for, 167n23, 167–68n24; avoidance of power relations in, 3–4; search for truth in, 2. *See also* pragmatism
Phrenology (recording), 157, 158
piety (secular): art of poetry and, 174n14; concept of, 37–38, 40, 95; imprudence toward or refusal of, 82, 83–84; in nonviolent direct action, 153–54; salvation and blues linked in, 118–23
pimping as metaphor, 99, 180n15
Plath, Sylvia, 185n17
pluralism: of blues, 14; cultural, as oxymoron, 10, 11; radical, 164–66n17
poetics of black essence (Jones/Baraka): abstraction and improvisation of, 127–28; articulations of self and culture in, 128–29; bebop and emotional expression in, 136–38; cosmopolitan nationalism and blackness in, 5; essentialist turn in, 149–50; experimentation in, 20–21; flesh and body in, 138–48, 185n17; hip-hop and improvisation in, 158–59; improvisational performance still privileged in, 149–50; in larger critical context, 186–87n22; othering, transitions, and improvisation in, 141–46; othering of self and articulating blackness in, 130–31; public and private mixed in, 146–48; as rootless, 130, 184–85n9; self as lyrical invention in, 133–36, 138; self-naming potential of, 139–41; swing between cultures and self-identity in, 129–31
poets: as pious, 174n14; as sayers, 43–44
political action: crisis of black intellectuals and, 68; Du Bois's call for solidarity in, 6–7; jazz and improvisation merged with, 45–47; music as symbolic, 44–45; nonviolent direct, 152–53; secondary racial consciousness in, 9–10. *See also* symbolic action
political and social equality: Baldwin's engagement with, 35, 93; bebop as integral to, 36; Ellison's engagement with, 79–84; global coalition building for, 148; Liston/Patterson as two positions on, 91–93; recognition of humanity in, 63–64; role of essay form in hope for, 104–7. *See also* citizenship; democracy
politics: bebop at center of, 25–34; hip-hop vocabulary in, 158; implications of boxing match for, 89–93, 177–78n2. *See also* cold war
Porter, Eric, 99, 180n15, 181n24
Posnock, Ross, 4–5, 38–39, 164n15
Pound, Ezra, 135
Powell, Bud, 136, 170n16
pragmatism: African American writing central to, 4–5;

Roney, Patrick, 129, 130, 183n4

Roots, The, 157, 158–59

Rorty, Richard: on human progress, 10–11, 166–67n22; on "inherited narratives," 91; on ironist philosopher, 50; on poeticized culture, 44; on pragmatism, 3–4; on societal changes, 97

Roth, Michael D., 167n23

Rousseau, Jean-Jacques, 65

Rushing, Jimmy, 78, 79, 146, 187n26

Russell, Richard, 80, 176n35

salvation: Baldwin's blues and, 39–40, 107–11, 115–16, 118–23; in CRM context, 123–24; improvisation and illumination as access to, 40; in Isaiah, 183n35

Sanchez, Sonia, 149

Saul, Scott, 39, 180n15, 181n24

Schaub, Thomas, 70–71

SCLC (Southern Christian Leadership Council), 123–24, 152–53

Scottsboro Boys, 117

secondary racial consciousness: concept of, 9–10; improvisation linked to, 46–47; as radical political theory, 13; "thin" notion of identity merged with, 12, 17

secular piety. *See* piety (secular)

sensuality: definition of, 112–13

Sexton, Anne, 185n17

Shange, Ntozake, 128

Shank, Barry, 81

Shelby, Tommie, 12, 17, 167n23

Shin, Andrew, 113, 182n28

Smith, Bessie, 107, 134

social framework: analysis of status quo of, 105–7; antiessentialist possibilities below surface of, 100–101; disrupting heteronormative narratives of, 112–15; pimping as evasion of, 99–100. *See also* identity; political and social equality

social race: Locke's notion of, 9

social responsibility: for democracy, 51, 83–84; invisible acting out of, 76

"Sonny's Blues" (Baldwin): blues and salvation linked in, 118–20, 121–23; Creole's performance in, 108; familial past accessed via jazz in, 115–16, 118; improvisational escape passages in, 107, 109, 154; improvisational masculine identity in, 92; Parker's shadow in, 35–40, 154; writing of, 182n29

Soto, Michael, 164–66n17

Southern Christian Leadership Council (SCLC), 123–24, 152–53

Stoddard, Theodore Lothrop, 143

Stowe, Harriet Beecher, 91

"Strange Fruit" (song), 111

Strayhorn, Billy, 108

surrealism, 141, 185–86n19

Swift, Jonathan, 59

swing: as alternative to status quo, 60; balancing past and future as, 164–66n17; from being other to othering the self, 141–42; "Flying Home" as staple of, 173n7; Jones/Baraka's transitional poems as, 129–31; whites' appropriation of, 186n20 symbolic action: Ellison's belief in, 27–28, 85–87; language as, 30, 32; models for, 33–34; music as, 44–45; of white youths, 30–31

Taylor, Cecil, 45
"This Morning, This Evening So Soon" (Baldwin): heteronormative narratives disrupted in, 113–15; histories underlying, 118; improvisational escape passages in, 109–12, 154; improvisational masculine identity in, 92
Thompson, Ahmir, 158
Thompson, Bob, 127
Thompson, Bobby, 188n3
Till, Emmett, 117
Time magazine, 80
"Trinkle, Tinkle" (song), 45
Turner, Big Joe, 146
Tuskegee Airmen, 52
Tuskegee Institute, 81
Twain, Mark (Samuel Clemens), 172–73n5

United Nations: "riots" outside, 105
U.S. Congress, House Un-American Activities Committee, 80
U.S. Constitution, 5–6
U.S. Supreme Court, 27, 80, 107, 176n35

vernacular practices: bebop as revolutionary impetus in, 32–33; blues, pragmatism, and literary theory linked to, 15–16; ethnicity and race in, 5; jazz as language of, 17–19,

168–69n33; Parker's improvisations of, 31
Von Eschen, Penny M., 20, 34

Walcott, Derek, 128
Washington, Booker T., 61, 73
Weigman, Robin, 64
Werner, Craig, 184–85n9
West, Cornel, 1
"When Will I Ever Get to Be a Man?" (song), 112
whiteness: Baldwin's deconstruction of, 104–7; blackface performances as complicating, 70–76; definitions of, 6; Faulkner as representative of, 116–17; lynching as defining, 63–65
white racial violence: democratic ideals vs., 49–50; Faulkner in context of, 116–17; Faulkner's and Wright's versions juxtaposed, 67–68; against integration, 80–81, 83–84, 107–8, 114; one murder as symbol for all, 115–16; private ironies and public hopes juxtaposed to, 51–55. *See also* lynchings
whites: black female slave narratives on, 175n17; democratic symbolic action of youth, 30–31; gospel tune's implications for, 112, 122; ideal womanhood among, 61–63; implications of ignorance about African Americans, 118, 122; Parker mythologized by, 31–32
white supremacy: democratic project correlated with, 59–65; history hidden by illusions of, 117–18; lynching as solidifying

white supremacy (*continued*)
    ethos of, 61–62; miscegenation
    and uncertainties undercut-
    ting, 67–68; musical parody
    of, 108, 181n24
Whitman, Walt, 141
Williams, Bert, 72
Williams, William Carlos, 135
Woodward, C. Vann, 50, 83
Wright, Richard: Baldwin's
    difference with, 91, 181n20;
    battle royal of, 60; on citizen-
ship battles, 94; on Ellison,
175n20; Ellison's perspective
on, 65–68, 70; status of, 65,
172–73n5; works: *Black Boy*,
60, 172–73n5, 175n20; *Native
Son*, 172–73n5

Yaffe, David, 119, 180n15
Young, Cynthia, 148
Young, John K., 85
Young, Lester, 45, 77
Yugen (periodical), 141